CHILDREN AND YOUTH
Social Problems and Social Policy

CHILDREN AND YOUTH
Social Problems and Social Policy

Advisory Editor
ROBERT H. BREMNER

Editorial Board
Sanford N. Katz
Rachel B. Marks
William M. Schmidt

THE DEPENDENT CHILD

HENRY W. THURSTON

ARNO PRESS
A New York Times Company
New York — 1974

HV
713
.T5
1974

Reprint Edition 1974 by Arno Press Inc.

Copyright © 1930, Columbia University Press
Reprinted by permission of Columbia
  University Press

Reprinted from a copy in
  The Newark Public Library

CHILDREN AND SOCIETY
Social Problems and Social Policy
ISBN for complete set: 0-405-05940-X
See last pages of this volume for titles.

Manufactured in the United States of America

Library of Congress Cataloging in Publication Data

Thurston, Henry Winfred, 1861-1946.
  The dependent child.

  (Children and youth: social problems and social
policy)
  Reprint of the ed. published by Columbia University
Press, New York, in series: New York School of Social
Work. Publications.
  Bibliography: p.
  1. Child welfare--United States. 2. Child welfare
--Great Britain. 3. Orphans and orphan-asylums--United
States. I. Title. II. Series. III. Series: Co-
lumbia University. School of Social Work. Publications.
[DNLM: 1. HV713 T545d 1930a]
HV713.T5 1974   362.7'1   74-1709
ISBN 0-405-05986-8

THE DEPENDENT CHILD

THE DEPENDENT CHILD

A STORY OF CHANGING AIMS AND METHODS IN
THE CARE OF DEPENDENT CHILDREN

BY

HENRY W. THURSTON

THE NEW YORK SCHOOL
OF
SOCIAL WORK

PUBLISHED FOR
THE NEW YORK SCHOOL OF SOCIAL WORK
BY
COLUMBIA UNIVERSITY PRESS
NEW YORK

1930

Copyright 1930
COLUMBIA UNIVERSITY PRESS

Published October, 1930

Printed in the United States of America
by the COMMONWEALTH PRESS, Worcester, Mass.

To my fellow students everywhere
who are trying to understand
what life means to a dependent child

ACKNOWLEDGMENTS

As one more "dependent child" is about to leave the shelter of its own home to try its fortune in the great outside world, the writer wishes to make grateful acknowledgment to all persons who have already helped to make the way of the adventurer pleasant and successful.

First there are many students, secretaries, friends, and even strangers who have written biographies, letters and observations or have given access to original studies and surveys, to cherished annual reports, to private office records, and to other sources of valuable material, some of it unpublished.

Among those who have thus helped, the writer is glad to mention two persons by name: Mrs. Martin Van Buren Van Arsdale, who gave intimate details of the origin and first years of the work of her pioneer husband in the West; and Charles Loring Brace, who gave freedom of access to all the files of the New York Children's Aid Society from 1853. Also to those authors who have given courteous consent to quote from recent books, the writer would express due appreciation. These writers and their books are: Ida R. Parker, *Fit and Proper;* Robert W. Kelso, *History of Public Poor Relief in Massachusetts;* Sidney and Beatrice Webb, "English Local Government," *Poor Law History,* Part II, "The Last Hundred Years"; Mrs. Bertrand Russell, *The Right To Be Happy;* and Healy, Bronner, Baylor, and Murphy, *Reconstructing Behavior in Youth.* Special appreciation is also felt for permission to quote from unpublished surveys and studies by the Child Welfare League of America; by the Bureau of Jewish Social Research, of New York; and by the New England Home for Little Wanderers, of Boston.

Again, younger readers should be told what their elders already know, that Homer Folks in his pioneer book *Care of Destitute, Neglected and Delinquent Children,* charted the road which all later writers have had to follow. This road the present writer has never lost from sight, notwithstanding his frequent loitering, straying and gossiping by the way.

Still further, although he has not quoted them in the text, the writer would name two active sources of information and inspiration that will grow in value and that the reader should study for himself.

First, the nation-wide but individualized program for the care of dependent children of ex-service men already adopted and put into operation by the American Legion, with headquarters at Indianapolis.

Second, the reports (as yet unpublished) of the unprecedentedly authoritative and extensive studies of child dependency and neglect that have been in the making all the year by sub-committees of The Third White House Conference on Child Health and Protection, which is to be held in Washington, November next.

Finally, to all those intimates who at all stages of planning, writing and revision have helped, I am particularly indebted. These persons include my wife, Charlotte S. Thurston; and Georgia G. Ralph, Ethel Taylor and Philip Klein of the New York School of Social Work.

HENRY W. THURSTON

Montclair, New Jersey
September 8, 1930

PREFACE

The words of this book have slowly been brought together into successive chapters as a result of the coöperative efforts of students and teacher to understand what each community, and especially what child welfare workers and students of social work, ought to try to do for and with dependent children. In trying to show as clearly as possible things as they were the writer has not intended to find fault. He believes that each change in the development of agencies, institutions, and methods for the care of dependent children was, at the time it was made, based upon a sympathetic recognition of actual conditions and so, though not always scientific in use of resources, was a real step forward. He also believes that no step, past or present, has brought us to the journey's end. It is hoped that these chapters taken as a whole may add something to the clarity of the reader's time perspective. They suggest the asking over and over again of Whitman's question:

"What is the present after all but a growth out of the past?"

and also frequently illustrate the truth of Lowell's couplet:

"New occasions teach new duties;
Time makes ancient good uncouth."

It is believed that past aims and methods in the care of dependent children can be most clearly understood by quoting at some length the words of those who first described these aims and used these methods. Likewise it is assumed that to help the reader to understand how various methods actually worked out in the lives of dependent children autobiographical statements and descriptions by contemporary observers are of great value. In general, the words and passages italicized have been chosen by the present writer.

To us of the present who face the question of our own duty and opportunity for the care of dependent children, Chapter VII develops a clue for us to follow. Something of the reach and social complexity of the problem is suggested by this question of forty years ago, and still unanswered:

The child problem is an integral part of this whole vital and urgent social question. . . . Who shall say how far the number of the wretched might be reduced if, first, every friendless and exposed child should be given such protection and opportunity as an informed and determined community has the power to afford: and if, secondly, the causes that lie back of the juvenile exposure should be sought out, and their due recognition secured in *education,* in *industry,* in the *home,* in the *church,* in *our courts of justice,* in *state* and *municipal government,* in *public opinion,*—in a word, in *all the fundamental institutions of society?*[1]

The quest for an answer is still not an easy one, for success depends not only upon a mastery of the teachings of the other sciences, but of mental hygiene which is shedding new light upon both the importance and difficulty of understanding the real needs of the child as an individual personality. Also, the successful social worker of the future must more and more clearly see and help to straighten out all phases of the industrial and other forms of social entanglement in which the individual dependent child is enmeshed. The time is ripening for such an advance as the world has never yet seen in the discovery and development of personality, happiness and capacity for social achievement, not only in the dependent child but in every child. If we can gradually raise the level of our standards of care for dependent children, the standards of positive welfare of all children in families just above that level will also be raised.

May all readers who long for a life of chivalrous adventure accept the challenge of the ever-present opportunity to buckle on the armor as champions of childhood, and enter the lists against all comers.

---

[1] Birtwell, Charles W. See Chapter VII, pp. 161-201.

CONTENTS

INTRODUCTION	xiii
I. LOOKING BACKWARD AND FORWARD FROM THE DAYS OF QUEEN ELIZABETH	1
I. The Care of Dependent Children under Slavery and Feudalism	
II. First Substitutes for Feudal Care	
II. INDENTURE AS A FORWARD STEP IN CHILD CARE	10
III. THE ALMSHOUSE DOOR OPENED WIDER IN 1824	19
IV. REALITIES OF CHILD LIFE IN THE MIXED ALMSHOUSE	27
V. ORPHAN ASYLUMS AS A STEP FORWARD IN CHILD CARE	39
I. Origins, Early Methods and Philosophies of Selected Institutions	
II. Orphan Asylums as They Seemed to Inmates and Neighbors	
VI. THE FORM OF INDENTURE REJECTED: DEVELOPMENT OF THE FREE FOSTER FAMILY HOME MOVEMENT	92
I. Emigration from Eastern Cities to Villages and Farms	
II. Origin and Development of State Children's Home Societies	
VII. SYMPATHY AND SENTIMENT BEGIN TO INVOKE THE AID OF SCIENCE: "WHAT DOES THE CHILD REALLY NEED?"	161
VIII. SURVIVALS OF OUTWORN ATTITUDES AND METHODS IN PRESENT-DAY INSTITUTIONS AND AGENCIES	202
IX. TRENDS IN ENGLAND SINCE 1834	243
X. TRANSITIONS TOWARD BETTER ATTITUDES AND METHODS	258
BIBLIOGRAPHY	325
INDEX	331

INTRODUCTION

> Tell men what they knew before;
> Paint the prospect from their door.
> Emerson

The reader of this book is advised at the outset to think over some of the children whose parental and home relationships he knows. The greater the variety of relationships between children and their parents and homes of which the reader can think, the better his understanding of the dependent child will be. Possibly he may know children on four different levels of such relationships.

Having in mind certain actual children, how would you describe the level of home care on which, probably, the majority of these children live? They are, I assume, fed and clothed and sheltered at the expense of their parents. If they are sick the parents pay for the doctor and the nurse. Father and mother provide the dolls, toys, bicycles, automobiles, radio, movies, theaters and other means of having a good time that are offered by many American homes. If the children are scouts, or members of fraternities, sororities, and other clubs, Dad's pocketbook usually furnishes the money for dues and all the incidental expenses. Father also pays (at least indirectly in rents, extra prices for goods, etc.) his share of the taxes with which the public schools, the libraries and parks, the roads and bridges, the police, street cleaning and health departments are kept up. Should the children go to a private school, to college or to a summer camp, father and mother foot the bills. If this is the general level upon which most of the children live whom you have in mind, do the words *independent* or *self-supporting* describe fairly well their type of home? If so, we shall hereafter use the expression *independent home level* for this group of children. In these days of behavior clinics, mental hygiene specialists, parent-teacher associations, child study groups, and parental education, we shall not claim that parents on this level receive no outside help for which they do not pay in the support, discipline, and education of their children. On the whole, however, and in comparison with lower levels of economic relationship between home and child, the care of children on this level is independent or self-supporting.

But every reader also knows children of other homes, for some of whose needs the parents at times cannot fully pay. On the independent home level, when a mother of one or more children is to be delivered of another child, a grandmother or aunt or other relative may be available to care for the older children while mother goes to the hospital; if not, a nurse or companion or housekeeper is hired to come in so that the home care of the children may not be interrupted until mother can come back again. In poorer families, if a relative or neighbor is not available, father often has no money to pay for the extra help. Mother even has to go to a free ward in a hospital. As for the care of the children while mother is away, either the services of a Red Cross or public health nurse, or some other form of social care not wholly paid for by father may keep the family going until mother comes back from the hospital or, if this is not feasible, father must stay home from his work, and not only lose his wages but run the risk of losing his job, thus making the whole family dependent.

In the same way, when father or mother, or one of the children, contracts tuberculosis, or any other long illness, or if some industrial accident has killed or disabled the father, the scant resources of many a self-respecting family are soon exhausted, so that there is need of some supplementary help in order to care for the children. Sometimes the school attendance or the discipline of the children is more than parents can look after by themselves, so that outside help is needed. Dr. Southard, in his book *The Kingdom of Evils,* pictures even the independent home as in constant danger of attack by one or another of five enemies: sickness, incompetence, the wrong-doing of its members, entanglements in legal and social regulations, and poverty. The reader has only to think of the frequency of strikes, lockouts, explosions, mine disasters, floods, hurricanes, epidemics; of crime, misdemeanor, insanity, and mental deficiency, to realize how ceaselessly and remorselessly children on the independent home level are being pushed down, at least temporarily, to the lower level of the home that needs unpaid-for help from the outside. Among the social means, both public and private, of helping such families, the reader will at least have heard of various relief societies, mothers' pensions, public health nurses, truant or school attendance officers, probation officers, visiting teachers, child labor laws, hospitals, behavior clinics, etc. Children requiring such supplementary aids as these may be said to live on a *supplemented home level*. As a rule the children who live on this level still stay in their own homes and are subject to the legal custody and guardianship of their parents.

The forces of evil attacking the home are sometimes so strong and persistent that, at least temporarily, the children cannot stay in it. Children from such a home are on a lower level of actual care-relationship to parents than those in the supplemented home. We may call this third type the *temporary substitute for the home* level. For these children, whether all in one place or separately in different places, some other home than their own must be found. In most of these families also, as with the children in supplemented homes, the legal guardianship still remains with the parents or parent.

There is only one other lower level than this—namely that of the *permanent substitute for the home*. In cases upon this level both parents may be dead, or both so hopelessly incapable of caring for their children that it is thought the home can never be restored. Frequently, however, children are pushed down to this level for lack of wise and persistent effort to restore the natural home, the substitute for which need have been only temporary. On this fourth level, the actual custody and often the legal guardianship of the child is with some one else than the parent.

The children whose care this book will discuss are all found on levels two, three, or four. Therefore our attention will be centered not upon the children who live in independent homes, but upon those who in some degree must be dependent for their welfare upon others in the community than their own parents.

A Professional Vocabulary

Social workers in speaking and writing about the care of dependent children are in the habit of using many words and phrases which may not be fully understood by one who sees or hears them for the first time. This book will try to show enough of the actual processes of child care with which these words and phrases are associated to make their meaning clear:

Almshouse	Adoption
Workhouse	Farming out
Poorhouse	Widow's pension
Indenture	Children's Home Society
Orphan asylum	Children's Aid Society
Placing out	After care
Free home	County home
Boarding home	County agent
Receiving home	State public school
Group homes	Supervision
Scattered homes	Foster mother
Congregate institution	Standards of child care, etc.
Cottage institution	

The reader will find this book to have interest and meaning to the degree that he continues to think, as he reads, of actual children on each of the levels of dependency described. He may profitably ask himself some of the following questions: How did these children get where they are? How did people come to think that the care they were giving them was just the right kind of care? What did the children themselves think of the care they were getting? Was it the best possible care for these particular children at the time? If not, how could it have been better? How could the people who gave the care have been led to see that something better might be devised? Would the story of the historical development of child care throw light upon such questions? Is our present practice growing satisfactorily out of the experiences of the past, and will the future evolve satisfactorily out of the present? How many people are interested in having these questions answered rightly? How may more people become so interested? Do any children near me get inadequate care now? If so, what can I do about it? Would I like to have the child I love best cared for in the same way as dependent children in my state and in my county and town are now cared for?

Chapter I

LOOKING BACKWARD AND FORWARD FROM THE DAYS OF QUEEN ELIZABETH

I. The Care of Dependent Children under Slavery and Feudalism

The ancient line between slavery and feudalism is sometimes hard for us to define. While some who read this book may claim that their ancestors never were slaves, there will be few indeed who can claim that their ancestors never lived under the feudal order. Moreover, in this country and in our own lifetime we have had experience with children brought up as slaves. The care of dependent negro children is one of the major problems of child care in the United States which is yet to be solved. It is partly, at least, because of the background of slavery that the solution of the problem is still in its first stages as compared with the progress made in caring for the white child who is dependent.

The Dependent Child under Slavery

The basic fact about the care of children under slavery, whether in the United States, or among our remote white ancestors, is that children and parents alike were the property of some owner, much as horses and cows and dogs are today. The young of horses and cows and dogs receive such care from their mothers as the owner of both mother and young thinks it advantageous to himself as owner to have given. The mothers and fathers of slave children were likewise permitted or encouraged to take such care of their children as the owner of both children and parents thought was to the owner's interest. Under slavery there were no four levels of care for children in their relationship to parents. All children and parents were alike dependent upon the owner and could be temporarily or permanently separated from each other at his will. Of course there were humane, as well as selfish and cruel, owners but the attitude of a master toward slave children, so far as slavery influenced that attitude, was that of an owner to the thing owned. Children that are owned by a master tend to be used merely as means to the owner's ends, not as human beings whose lives are of value to themselves.

The Dependent Child under Feudalism

Feudalism lasted for centuries in all the countries of Europe from which, directly or indirectly, most people in the United States have come. Under feudalism the land itself claimed fealty: practically everybody had rights and duties in relation to some particular area, usually called a manor. Support came, as a rule, from that area of land to which a man and his family were attached by the feudal order. If parents died there was a certain claim for support of the dependent child from the product of the land his father had held. Nobody outside the manor had any obligation to support parents attached to the manor—or their children, if these became dependent.

Under feudalism every man, from villein, or peasant, up through the lord of the manor, to baron, duke, and earl, owed loyalty, food, raw materials, and the work of his hands in both peace and war to his immediate overlord, and all classes owed many of these things to the king. In return, from king down, through earl, duke, baron, lord of the manor, to peasant and villein, the man above owed protection against attack and an opportunity to get a living to all below him. Even the poorest parents and children belonged on some lord's landed estate and had some claim to support themselves thereon out of the products of scattered but definitely assigned strips of ploughed land; from pasturage upon the undivided common land; and from fuel rights in the forests. The lords of the manor got much of their living directly from the cultivation of their own demesne lands which were worked by the men below them in return for the right to cultivate the allotments granted by the lord of the manor. It was a system based almost entirely upon an exchange of personal services and goods, and very slightly upon money either in wages or in purchase prices for goods.

If parents and children became destitute and failed to get support on the manorial land where they belonged, whether because of injustice on the part of the overlord or because of the ravages of war, or from sickness, incompetence, Wanderlust, or other action of their own, the only help they could get was pure charity from kindly people, or from monasteries, abbeys, or churches.

Feudalism tended to hold men, women and children in the social status and locality of their birth. The attitude of adults toward children under feudalism was that children were primarily tributary to the welfare of the manor as a unit which, in turn, owed everything to the overlord according to the feudal system in general and the traditional customs of the individual manor in particular. Under slavery children were subject to their parents and the unregulated will of the slave owner. Under neither slavery nor feudalism could there be any real opportunity for children in general to be treated with discrimination, or with recognition of their individual needs, capacities, purposes, and plans. Only as their lives, their physical and mental abilities, and their welfare could contribute to the welfare of others, as well as to their own, were children under slavery and feudalism of any considerable importance. Both under slavery and under feudalism the personal and affectional relations of children to their own parents and to each other were a secondary consideration.

II. First Substitutes for Feudal Care

What became of dependent children in England when the feudal system gradually gave way to a different economic and political order? The answer to this question for England will throw light on the evolution of the care for dependent children in the American colonies.

Elizabeth was still Queen in England when our first colony was founded in Virginia in 1607. During the next two centuries there was a striking similarity between the methods that were developing in England for the care of dependent children and those that were in use in the American colonies and early states. Familiarity with the usages that came slowly to be substituted in England for feudal care of dependent children will therefore be useful in an attempt to see what processes were used in the early American settlements wherever the population was large enough to make the number of dependent children considerable.

The Passing of the Feudal Order

We have said that during the feudal period in Europe, whatever provision was systematically made for poor children was made in the various small local units of population called manors. Let us now try to find out how children upon the European manors were affected by the passing of the feudal order.

The passing of the feudal order was a slow process, taking two or three centuries in England. But by 1601, when a famous law called the Forty-third Act of Elizabeth was passed, the feudal attitude toward children, and adults as well, can be said to have been in theory exchanged for another. In actual practice, its passing has not everywhere been accomplished, even yet.

Now, for at least two hundred and fifty years previous to the Act of Elizabeth in 1601, notably from the time of the Black Death in 1348, a slow breaking down of the old feudal system of getting a living was in process. Although the causes were many, the chief agent in this breaking-down process was the greatly increased use of money. For example, payments of money came to be made for rent or limited ownership of land; as wages for service in peace and war; as a price for goods; instead of the tribute of food supplies and firewood to overlords, etc. To the degree that money payment was introduced, it tended to weaken the reciprocal personal obligations between overlords and vassals.

Everybody who came even to a restricted ownership of land through purchase, or to real tenant holding by paying rent in money—everybody who received full wages for his work and bought his living with the money earned, lost his direct claim upon an overlord for protection, and his chance to get a living or to receive support from the manorial community in case of sickness or poverty. It was no longer anybody's recognized business to care for the orphans and destitute children of parents who lived by what was called "money economy." All persons who had in any way become dependent upon "money economy" had ceased to belong fully to any landed estate and overlord and so lost all feudal right to help in days of sickness and poverty.

During the same period of two hundred and fifty years previous to 1601, while the feudal economy was breaking down, a long succession of laws leading slowly up to the Forty-third Act of Elizabeth was also being enacted. Most of these laws attempted in some way to stem the slowly rising tide destined to sweep away the feudal order. When men were scarce because so many had died from the Black Death, and there was a growing tendency by those who could work to demand higher wages in money, laws were passed to prevent increases in wages. When men had been shaken loose from their feudal ties upon the manor where they were born, and had begun to wander, to beg, and to seek their fortunes elsewhere, laws were passed to prevent wandering and begging. Penalties for these offenses became more and more severe, even to the extreme of branding offenders with hot irons. While the old feudal obligation, under which the lord of the manor had been responsible for the support of all those living on his lands, was passing away, some constructive attempts were made to meet the emergency by enacting laws to make the people of each locality support the poor by charitable gifts. But in spite of such attempts, more than two hundred years were needed for English lawmakers to see that feudalism was going beyond recall, and that they could not cure or control destitution by making laws which tried to push people back into the habits of an earlier day and which did not take into account the new economic order. Just before Elizabeth's time, another change had taken place, which thrust the problems of poverty and wandering and begging more and more upon the attention of all citizens: Henry VIII, father of Queen Elizabeth, had seized the monasteries and lands held by the Roman Catholic Church. To the degree that the Church itself became poor, it had fewer alms to give. Thus it was that two great factors converged during the years just preceding the reign of Elizabeth: one a growing number of wandering, unattached destitute people entitled to nobody's support, and the other the impoverishment of the Church which had previously, to some extent, mitigated their condition. This convergence of greater destitution and a lessened ability of church charity to meet the increasing need, radically altered the attitude of the English people and opened the eyes of the English lawmakers to the fact that a tax upon each community as a whole must be levied to care for the poor. Thus, when we try to trace the development of the care of dependent children, as well as of adult poor, in both England and the United States, we must go back at least to the Forty-third Act of Elizabeth in 1601, which enunciated for the first time the theory of the support of the poor out of public taxes.

Development of Varieties of Care Since Elizabeth

In effect this law said clearly for the first time: we law makers of England recognize that the feudal order, the charity of the well-to-do, and of the Church, can no longer be expected to carry the whole burden of the poor. The state recognizes that the final obligation now is not upon some of us in each community, but upon all of us. From now on, under the authority of the state, each community will collect taxes for the relief of poor people, including children, who cannot be supported by private benevolence. A summary of the law is as follows:

SLAVERY AND FEUDALISM

Poor relief is recognized in principle as a public concern. It is to be administered by individual parishes through overseers, who are to be appointed and constantly controlled by the justices (of the peace). The burden of relief is distributed by taxation. In the first instance, however, the nearest of kin (in case of children, parents and grandparents) are made responsible for the maintenance of their relatives; and in case a single parish is overburdened, the neighboring parishes may be called upon to contribute proportionately. The persons to be relieved are divided into three classes: children, able-bodied, infirm. The kind of assistance consists, in the case of children, in apprenticing them till their twenty-first or twenty-fourth year; in the case of the able-bodied by setting them to work (which they must perform, under penalty for refusal;) in the case of the infirm, in maintaining them, with power to place them in poorhouses.[1]

In short, each local community, now called a parish instead of a manor, could tax itself to care for destitute children in any one or all of four different ways:[2] (1) set them, and adults as well, to work directly upon "flax, hemp, wool," etc., which the overseers of the poor of the parish were empowered to buy for this purpose; (2) apprentice them; (3) care for them, especially those too young to work, together with infirm adults, either by "farming out,"[3] by "outdoor relief,"[4] or (4) in poorhouses. How many poorhouses were built during the seventeenth century we do not know. What we do know is that poorhouses having been authorized by the Law of Elizabeth in 1601 (the law was later changed so as to in-

---

[1] Aschrott, (Preston-Thomas) and Henry Sidgwick, *the English Poor Law System*, London, 1912, pp. 7-8.

[2] It is not our purpose here to trace the development of relief for adults, except as it throws light on the care of dependent children.

[3] To "farm out" means to give children or adults to a person for care, usually in the caretaker's own home, for a definite sum of money per week, month or year. If there were several bidders, the one bidding lowest was accepted by the local poor law officials.

[4] "Outdoor relief" then meant in England relief given by community poor officers to persons in their own homes, instead of these being made to go to the public almshouse.

clude in them the care of the able-bodied poor), one such, called a workhouse, was built in Bristol in 1697. From this date poorhouses were built in increasing numbers, so that by 1832 the Poor Law Commission found a mixed workhouse[5] (or poorhouse) in practically every parish, or at least in each group of parishes called a "Union." What we do know is, that as fast as workhouses were built in parish after parish, there were gathered into them the aged, impotent, diseased and derelict adults (during a part of the time also able-bodied adult poor) and those poor children who were not apprenticed or cared for with parents by outdoor relief.

Knowing these things, there is something else that we must bear in mind, namely that, while certain dates may be fixed for radical changes in laws and theories, the process of securing actual changes in method is slow—taking decades, generations and sometimes even centuries. It will be helpful later therefore to try to find out as well as we can how dependent children actually lived when cared for in different ways, times and places in England, in the American colonies, the early states, and even in our present states as late as the nineteenth century. The Elizabethan laws established the theory that it was the business of the community out of publicly collected taxes to care for children whom various privately supported agencies, as well as their parents, left dependent and neglected. How this theory affected the actual care of children it is our intention to find out.

Now it is evident that outdoor relief of children would not as a rule separate children from their own parents. From the time of Elizabeth (and earlier by private charity) down to the present, outdoor relief, both public and private, has meant, in the sense in which we are using the words, a supplemented home level for the children. On the other hand, the poorhouse care and farming-out of children have meant at least a temporary substitute (sometimes a permanent substitute) for the home level of care.

[5]A "mixed workhouse" means a home for the poorest of both sexes, all ages, good and bad, sick and well in both body and mind.

Indenture, which was primarily an organized system of industrial apprenticeship, has usually meant for dependent children a permanent substitute for the home level, at least until the child is grown. Since Elizabeth's day both in England and in this country, there has always been present in the problem of the care of the dependent child this question as to his relationship to his own parents. Shall the particular child be helped along with his parents, or shall he be temporarily or permanently separated from his parents? This question will reappear in later chapters which discuss in more detail what each alternative form of care really means to the children concerned. At bottom, there are involved, not only questions as to the kinds of food, clothing, shelter, etc., that the child may receive from his parents, as opposed to the kinds of these necessities of life he can get elsewhere, but also questions of love, the character-forming influences and other social and emotional factors by which the child would be surrounded while living with his own parents, compared with influences of these kinds to be found by him elsewhere.

CHAPTER II

INDENTURE AS A FORWARD STEP IN CHILD CARE

As we review historically the measures taken to care for dependent children, we find that the system of indenture takes on a special significance. Under the guild system of industry, long before the reign of Elizabeth, indenture had been in theory a pure business contract, aiming to give each of the parties thereto a fair bargain. The parents apprenticed a child, old enough to work, to a master workman, to live in his house, and to be taught his craft or trade. The master was to give the apprentice food, clothing, shelter, and training in a remunerative craft or trade, plus perhaps some extra payment in the form of clothes, or money at the expiration of the term of indenture.

The child was to give to his master obedience, loyalty and work that would grow more and more valuable over a period of years as the child approached maturity. When indenture was accepted by law in 1601 for the public care of dependent children, it still remained in theory a business deal from which the person accepting a poor child on indenture expected to receive from the child a full equivalent in work for the expense of his support, care and teaching. From its business origin and essential nature, indenture, then, has *never been well adapted* to the care of young children. How far this fact was recognized in the England of James I we cannot say, but in order to ease the mechanism of the indenture of young children, certain legislation was enacted by the Parliament of 1609-10. This law provided for the public control of moneys given by generous private contributors for the establishing of revolving funds from which advances were to be made to persons receiving on apprenticeship children who were too young at the outset to pay their way in work. Eventually the child's work was expected, not only to pay for his current keep, but also to enable his master to pay back into the revolving fund the amounts advanced to him.

A passage from Nicholls[1] throws light on the importance—in the eyes of the government—of these private gifts for the purpose of promoting the apprenticing of young dependent children:

The preamble (of an act of James I in 1609-10 providing for the right application of money given for apprenticing of poor children) recites that great sums of money have already been given, and that more is likely to be given in future, to be continually employed in binding out the poorest sorts of children as apprentices to trades and needful occupations, "which hath brought great profit into those cities, towns and parishes where the said moneys have been so employed"; and but for which such children would be brought up in idleness, "to their utter overthrow, and the great prejudice of the commonwealth." Therefore, in order that other well-disposed people may "be encouraged in bestowing money to the same good and godly purposes" it is enacted that all money so given shall forever continue to be used for such purposes only, and that corporations in cities and towns corporate, and in parishes and towns not corporate the parson or vicar, together with the constables, church wardens, and overseers of the poor for the time being, "shall have the nomination and placing of such apprentices, and the guiding and employment of all such moneys as are given for the *continual binding forth* [italics by the present writer] of such apprentices." Masters are required to give security for returning the money at the expiration of the apprenticeship, or in case of the death of the apprentice or the master; so that the *use* [italics by the present writer] of the money advanced and the *services of the apprentice* [italics by the present writer] are the master's only reward. There is no absolute payment with the apprentice, but the capital contributed by "well-disposed people" will remain under the control of the trustees, to be placed out and returned, from time to time as occasion requires.

From the above statement, it would appear that the money advanced to a master with an infant or young child apprentice was

[1] *History of the English Poor Law,* New York, 1898, Vol. I, p. 229.

merely to pay the necessary expense of maintenance until such time as the child could do enough work not only to pay for his keep but enough more so that the master could begin to pay back the money advanced. We do not know to what extent masters actually returned money so advanced with infants and young children. Obviously, to the extent that such repayments were made, the incentive to the master would be the greater to begin at the earliest possible moment to take out of the child in work the full equivalent for current and past expense for food and clothing.

As we study the growth of indenture of dependent children in England, therefore, two facts stand out:

First, that its purpose was to make some person or family definitely responsible for the support and care of dependent children, for whose welfare there was no longer any feudal or other community responsibility. Thus to make somebody responsible for the care of each stray, dependent and neglected child was certainly, in purpose, a step ahead.

Second, that the English used for this purpose of fixing responsibility a social procedure already commonly employed everywhere in giving industrial training to girls and boys old enough to work. Under indenture of the industrial form children were to pay for what they got in the matter of keep, and in training for a trade. When adapting this system to the needs of dependent and neglected children, the only change the English mind demanded was the establishment of an expense account for the accommodation of the master until such time as a young child grew old enough for the master to take out of him in work all current and past outlay for expenses.

In practically all of the American colonies, as in England, the same two facts stand out clearly with reference to indenture, namely:

First, unattached children and children whose parents neglected them or could not support them were to be attached to some person or family who would agree to be responsible for them.

INDENTURE

Second, the person assuming such responsibility and expense was to collect his whole bill from the child's work before the expiration of the term of indenture.

The first child placed out by public authority in Massachusetts was Benjamin Eaton. He was indentured in 1636 by the Governor and assistants of Plymouth Colony "to Bridget Fuller, widow for 14 years, shee being to keep him at schoole two years and to imploy him after in shuch service as she saw good and he should be fitt for; but not to turne him over to any other, without ye Gov'n consente."

It was the theory of the early community that every person should be attached to a family and that he should have some occupation. And this requirement applied to the children, even of fairly tender years.[2]

Along with this theory that every person should be attached to a family, went the theory, both in the colonies and in the England of the sixteenth, seventeenth and eighteenth centuries, that every dependent person must belong definitely to some town or place. The old definite feudal status upon the agricultural manor had passed away forever, but in the indenture of children, and in the locus of "settlement"[3] as applied to the poor generally, we may trace the effort of English communities to substitute for feudal methods some other definiteness of responsibility in the care of dependent persons.

Kelso traces this development of local territorial responsibility for the poor after they were shaken loose from the status of the feudal system.[4] He cites as typical of English towns a series of measures adopted in London, 1514-1524, to prevent begging and receipt of alms by all who did not belong in the city.

[2]Kelso, Robert W., *History of Public Poor Relief in Massachusetts 1620-1920*, Boston, 1922, p. 165.

[3]The term "settlement" was used to determine which of two or more communities in which a poor person had lived was responsible for his care. If his length of stay was such, according to the laws of the country, as to give a poor person settlement in town X, that town became responsible for his support.

[4]Kelso, *op. cit.*, p. 14.

Four surveyors were appointed to carry out these instructions. Another special officer was admitted to the office of Master and cheff avoyder and Keeper oute of this Citie and the liberties of the same of all mighty vagabonds and beggars, and all other suspecte persons, except all such as wore uppon thym the badge of this City.[5]

In the American colonies, once the "settlement" of a dependent child was acknowledged by a given town or local community, indenture offered the best opportunity for permanently easing demands on the treasury for the support of the child. To quote again from Kelso:

Cleaning off the account on the treasurer's book by a long-term indenture which for practical purposes amounted to the sale of the child with no guarantee of protection, save public indignation, against enslavement and abuse, was the constant effort of the early town authorities.[6]

The two indentures which follow, one from Virginia in 1686, and one from Massachusetts in 1747, are good examples. The Virginia indenture is for a girl of probably ten or eleven years, who can at once begin to give valuable service.

This Indenture made the Second of January in ye year 1686 between John Porter of ye one party, and Samuel Polly of ye other party, both of ye County of Henrico in James River in manner and form following witnesseth, that ye John Porter doth covenant, grant and agree to and with ye sd Samll Polly to take his daughter Mary Polly for ye full end and term of ten years from ye 1st month September in ye year 1685. In consideration ye sd John Porter shall use or maintain ye sd Mary noe other ways than he doth his own in all things as dyett, cloathing and lodging, the sd Mary to obey the sd John Porter in all his lawful commands within ye sd term of years above menconed as also att ye full end and term of years that ye sd John Porter doth bind himself his executors or administrators to pay unto ye said Mary Polly, three barrells of corn and one suit of penistone and one suit of good serge

---

[5]Cited in Leonard, *Early History of English Poor Relief,* Cambridge University Press, 1900, p. 25.

[6]Kelso, *op. cit.,* p. 168.

with one black hood, two shifts of dowlas and shoes and hose convenient. And ye said Saml Polly doth assure and bind firmly his sd daughter to ye said Porter for ye full end of ten years by these presents whereunto both the sd partyes have set their hands.[7]

It will be observed that this indenture is in essence a pure business contract between John Porter, an employer, and an employee, Mary Polly, the father Samuel Polly, acting for Mary Polly as her natural guardian. Mary is to work for John Porter for ten years and in return is to receive "dyett," "cloathing," "lodging," "three barrells of corn," "one suit of good serge with one black hood," "two shifts of dowlas," and "shoes and hose convenient." It may also be assumed that if Samuel Polly is a man of at least ordinary intelligence and paternal interest in his daughter, he will doubtless take pains to find out from time to time how hard Mary has to work and whether or not she receives her promised wages "in kind."

By the Massachusetts indenture the selectmen of the township of Leicester bind Moses Love, a poor child two years and eight months old, to Matthew Scott until the boy shall become twenty-one years old.

This Indenture made the fourteenth day of September Anno domini 1747 by and between Luke Lincoln, Benja Tuckor, Nathall Goodspeed and John Whittemor all of Leicester in the Covnty of Worcester selectmen of sd Leicester on the one part, Matthew Scott of Leicester aforesaid yeoman on the other part Wittnesseth that the above sd selectmen by virtue of the Law of this province them Impowering & with the assent of two of the Majesties Justices of the Peace for sd Covnty hereto annexed to put and bind out to the sd Matthew Scott & to his heirs Execvtors & Adminrs as an Apprentice Moses Love a Minor aged two years and Eeight Months with him & them to Live and dwell with as an apprentice dureing the term of Eighteen years

---

[7]Bruce, Philip Alexander, *Economic History of Virginia in the Seventeenth Century,* New York, 1896, Vol. II, p. 2. Quoted from *The Records of Henrico County* 1677-1692, p. 424, Virginia State Library.

and fovr months (viz) untill he shall arrive to the age of twenty-one years—he being a poor Child & his parants not being well able to support it. Dureing all which the sd apprentice his sd Master his heirs Execvtors & Adminrs shall faithfully serve at such Lawfull imployment & labovr as he shall from time to time Dureing sd term be Capable of doing and performing & not absent himself from his or their service without Leave & In all things behave himself as a good & faithfull apprentice ought to do and the sd Matthew Scott for himself his heirs Execvtors & Adminrs do Couenant promise and grant to & with the above sd selectmen of Leicester aforsaid & with their successors in the office or trust of selectmen of Leicester aforsaid & Inbehalf of sd apprentice that he the sd Matthew Scott his heirs Execvtors & Adminrss shall & will Dureing the term aforsd find and provide for the sd apprentice sufficient Cloathing meet drink Warshing and Lodging both in Sickness & in health & that he will teach him or cavse him to be tavght to read & write & siffer fiting his degree if he be Capable of Learning and at the Expiration of the term to Dismiss him with two suits of apparril one to be fitt for Lords days In Wittness where of the partyes to these present Indentvrs haue Interchangably set their hands & seals the day and year first written.
Signed sealed & Delivered in presence of
    Steward Southgate
    John Brown

                      Luke Lincoln (seal)
                      Benja Tucker (seal)
                      John Whittemor (seal)[8]

The indenture of this child hardly out of the cradle is also in form and theory a pure business contract between an employer and an employee (the selectmen acting for the employee as guardians), the work of the child to be paid for in "cloathing," "meet," "warshing," an elementary education and "two suits of apparril." How far Matthew Scott came to love Moses Love as his own son and to treat him as such, in spite of the business form and philoso-

---

[8] *New England Historical and Genealogical Register,* Boston, 1880, Vol. XXXIV, p. 311.

phy of the indenture contract, we can only surmise. How continuous, intelligent, and influential was the concern shown by the selectmen of Leicester that Matthew Scott, if a hard man, should at least live up to the letter of his contract with Moses Love during the eighteen years and four months the indenture was to hold, is also a matter for conjecture only. We know that in all the states, dependent children were indentured by the local township, city or county poor authorities. We know that in form and theory, indenture of a child pledged the work of a child as pay for his keep, for a minimum degree of education, and certain further payments in kind or money when the indenture was over. We know that the treatment the indentured child received depended upon himself, the tender mercies of his employer, the influence of the opinion of the neighbors, and the degree of interest the public poor officials took in him. We know that children differed widely in their ability to win for themselves love and justice from adults. Certain it is that employers were of all sorts from the kind, the generous and just, to the hard, the niggardly and cruel. We know that people hate to be responsible for the way their neighbors treat domestic animals and children. We know that local poor officials, however humane and faithful, are at least only human, that they are burdened with home and business cares of their own, and are called upon repeatedly to look after the urgent needs of destitute, diseased, sick and incompetent people. In view of the above facts, it is morally certain that the experiences of indentured children varied all the way from that of being virtual slaves to that of being real foster sons or daughters. The inevitable tendency of the system was to stimulate the employer to exact the pound of flesh from the indentured child, with no Portia at hand to see that more than a pound could be taken only at the employer's peril.

Nevertheless, the process of indenture offered to the homeless, destitute, and neglected children of the centuries following the feudal period, an open door to at least the possibility of a daily minimum of food, shelter and clothing. In modern psychological phrase, we may say that the process of indenture was in general better for the dependent child of the sixteenth, seventeenth and eighteenth centuries than homelessness and vagrancy, in that it gave the child a *certain degree of security*, a *feeling of belonging*, if only to a hard and poverty-stricken master—"a poor thing but mine own."

Further light is also thrown upon indenture by the following letter which ostensibly recites some of the woes, not of the child, but of the family to which a boy was indentured. Between the lines it is more pathetic than humorous.

R—— N. Y. April 14, 1844

To them what keeps the orpen asilum.

Madomes—The boy wat is of your orpen asilum i thort was a good boy takin him two munths tryol and i pay my muney bein a poor man an sined your indenshun for to keep him but wen i gets my muney pade he turned hiself and becom rite bad bein imperdent and disobeys and lyin and gous hookin and thievn bein constant in sellar and pantry and butry wen backs is turned an fillin hiself wen it ant no time to eat an plenty an good on my table witch made nede of fisikin whitch costs money an me a poor man an wen he took on the itsh an set all my family to skrashun witch ant no way pleasany an we ant use to it an so I want you should send for him and muney to pay his ekspens witch if you don't write sune i send him by sailin vessel of friend of mine an you have to pay tham or i get the law on you an my muney bak witch is a hard case bein hard com by an erned by swet of brow an me a poor man with big family an never no itsh before so I am

Yours afekshunly,
X. Y. Z.

You better make haste or you be sure i get that law on you an speke bad of your asilum.[9]

Of other evils of indenture and their persistence in later days when something better was possible for dependent children, more will be said in a later chapter.

---

[9]Written by a Hudson Valley Dutch farmer and published in *The New York State Charities Aid Association News*, November, 1927, p. 8.

Chapter III

THE ALMSHOUSE DOOR OPENED WIDER IN 1824

Every one who reads this is probably at least vaguely aware that there is a poorhouse somewhere within a few miles of him. Doubtless, also, he has a rather definite feeling of aversion to it, or of dread at the thought of ever having to live within it. In spite of these feelings, it is also probable that very few readers have ever been inside any poorhouse, or have any idea of what life in the "mixed poorhouse" has meant to children in England, the American colonies and most of our present states.[1] We shall later give some descriptions of poorhouses, or almshouses, where children have lived, and these will indicate that our aversion to them as homes for children or for grown persons has a good foundation. At present it is our purpose to show how intelligent and humane men could at one time think that there ought to be more of such poorhouses, bad as they always had been, and that everywhere they ought to open their doors wider, not only to adult men and women, but to dependent children as well.

The Yates Report of 1824

One of the most interesting and remarkable arguments for the establishment of an almshouse in every county of a state, for the use of both adults and children, is that of J. V. N. Yates, Secretary of State for New York in 1823-1824. Mr. Yates was authorized in 1823 by a joint resolution of both the Senate and Assembly of the State of New York,[2] "to collect from the several towns, cities and

[1] In a United States census report for 1923 *Paupers in Almshouses*, Table 61, p. 50. New Mexico was the only state of which it was said that there were no almshouses maintained within it.
[2] See *Annual Report of the State Board of Charities of New York*, 1900, which reprinted this *Report* from the New York State Assembly *Journal* of February 9, 1824. The page references which follow refer to this 1900 reprint.

counties of this state, such information as would be necessary to give a distinct view of the expenses and operation of the laws, for the relief and settlement of the poor; and also such information from other states, with respect to their poor laws, as would show the effect of those systems; and suggest improvements in our own; and that he communicate an abstract or digest of such information to the legislature."

Mr. Yates spent a "considerable portion of a year . . . in directing his enquiries to every source from which intelligence could be procured."

The report is in two parts. The first part is statistical and descriptive, giving in substance:

1. Number of paupers in cities, towns and counties of the state;

2. Costs for maintenance and relief;

3. Sums spent in costs and fees of justices of the peace, and overseers of the poor, and of constables in the examination and removal of paupers; costs of appeals from orders of removal; number of paupers removed; ratio of pauperism in each county; ratio of taxation for care of poor in several counties for the previous six years; extracts of letters from mayors of cities, supervisors and clerks of counties, overseers of the poor of towns, and other creditable sources; also the management, general success and effect of the various local experiments in the state, for the support of the poor—either by towns or counties in poorhouses.[3]

The second part gives a digest or analysis of the poor laws of most of the states then in the Union with extracts from official letters and documents, showing the operation and effect of those laws, together with a view of the state of pauperism in Europe, and brief extracts from works of American and European writers, illustrative of the evils of pauperism, and suggesting plans for their amelioration and removal.[4]

[3] *Op. cit.*, p. 940.   [4] *Op. cit.*, pp. 940-41.

THE ALMSHOUSE

The care of the poor as described by Mr. Yates in 1824 was as follows:

The poor of this state consist of two classes—the permanent poor, or those who are regularly supported during the whole year at the public expense; and the occasional, or temporary poor, or those who receive occasional relief, during a part of the year, chiefly in the autumn or winter.

Of the first class, according to the official report and estimates received, there are in this state, 6896; and of the last 15215, making a grand total of 22111 paupers. Among the permanent paupers there are 446 idiots and lunatics; 287 persons who are blind; 928 who are extremely aged and infirm; 797 who are lame, or in such a confirmed state of ill health as to be totally incapable of labor. . . .[5]

There are 8753 children of both classes (permanent and occasional poor) under 14 years of age, the greater number of whom is entirely destitute of education, and equally in want of that care and attention, which are so necessary to inculcate correct moral habits. It is feared that this mass of pauperism, will at no distant day form a fruitful nursery for crime, unless prevented by the watchful superintendance of the legislature.[6]

As a summary of methods Mr. Yates further states:

In most, or all of the towns and villages in the state, *where there are no almshouses,* the poor are disposed of by the overseers in one of three ways: *First,* the overseers farm them out at stipulated prices to contractors, who are willing to receive and keep them, on condition of getting what labor they can out of the paupers; or *secondly,* the poor are sold by auction—the meaning of which is, that he who will support them for the lowest prices, becomes their keeper; and it often happens, of course, that the keeper is almost himself a pauper before he purchases, and he adopts this mode in order not to fall a burden upon the town. Thus he, and another miserable human being barely subsist on what would hardly comfortably maintain himself alone—a species of economy much boasted of by some of our town officers and purchasers of paupers; or *thirdly,* relief is afforded to the poor in their own habitation.

[5] *Op. cit.*, p. 941.   [6] *Op. cit.*, p. 942.

The expenses for physicians and nurses, in attending paupers, *in towns where there are no poorhouses,* form a prominent article in the amount of taxation. Pauperism and disease, *except in an almshouse,* are generally found associated together, and hence it is, that this item of expense is so much complained of in the towns just alluded to.[7]

Difficulties Over "Settlement"

It should be noted that this study of the New York situation relative to the care of the poor—both adults and children—was more than two hundred years later than the Elizabethan Poor Law of 1601, which law, as we have seen, first authoritatively stated that the poor of England must be supported by each local community out of the proceeds of public taxes. What Mr. Yates found operative in 1824 in the State of New York was largely a reproduction of what England had been establishing between 1601 and 1824, namely, a local public responsibility for the care of the poor. This local, parish, town or county responsibility for the care of the poor which took the place of the feudal manor responsibility, is defined in many of our states—especially the eastern states—under laws, called "settlement laws." These determine which of two or more towns or counties, and sometimes states, in which poor persons have lived, is responsible for their support. According to these laws, a person who becomes destitute in a town or county after only a few weeks or months of residence, has no claim for support there but must be supported by the town or county from which he came, where he had lived longer and acquired a "settlement."[8]

Mr. Yates says:[9]

---

[7]*Op. cit.,* pp. 948-49.

[8]We use a similar idea in another connection to make length of residence the basis on which to determine where a voter may be allowed to vote.

[9]See pp. 1020-22 for illustrations. Other complaints related to the same difficulty between New York and adjoining states.

THE ALMSHOUSE

There were many reports of conflict between towns of a county and between towns and the county as to which town, or the county as a whole, should support individual poor persons—the difficulty arising from doubt as to place of legal settlement.

Mr. Yates further says in summary respecting attempts to avoid care of non-resident poor:[10]

1796 paupers, among whom were more than 600 children and 320 women, were removed (and many of them while sick and diseased) during the year 1822, to different parts of the state, under orders or warrants of justices, at an expense far exceeding $25,000; a sum if it had been applied for their support instead of their removal would have maintained 833 of those paupers for a whole year, being nearly half the number removed. From these orders of removal, there were no less than 127 appeals to the courts of general sessions of the peace, the management and defense of which cost the litigant parties upwards of $13,500—a sum equal to the support of 450 paupers for a year.

With regard to conditions in other states than New York Mr. Yates says:[11]

The information received from the other states of the Union [than Massachusetts, Connecticut, New Hampshire, Delaware and Pennsylvania] will not authorize any clear or satisfactory statement to be made of pauperism in these states, although it may be generally remarked, that in Rhode Island and Virginia it is less than in our own state, and that in Pennsylvania, Delaware, Rhode Island and Virginia *where the poorhouse system has prevailed for the greatest length of time, and to the greatest extent,* the ratio of pauperism, and the amount of expense is less than it is in any other state in which that system has been more recently or partially introduced.

In conclusion Mr. Yates makes these points among others. He says:[12]

---

[10] *Annual Report of the State Board of Charities of New York,* 1900, etc., p. 946.
[11] *Op. cit.,* p. 943.   [12] *Op. cit.,* pp. 951-52.

1. Removal of human beings like felons for no other fault than poverty,
seems inconsistent with the spirit of a system professing to be founded on principles of pure benevolence and humanity

2. The poor, when farmed out, or sold, are frequently treated with barbarity and neglect by their keepers. More than one instance has stained our judicial records, in which it appeared that the pauper had suffered such cruelty and torture from his keeper as to produce untimely dissolution.

3. The education and morals of the children of paupers (*except in* almshouses) are almost wholly neglected. They grow up in filth, idleness, ignorance and disease, and many become early candidates for the prison or the grave. The evidence on this head is too voluminous for reference.

Mr. Yates therefore recommended:[13]

The establishment of one or more houses of employment, under proper regulations, in each of the counties of the state, with a farm of sufficient extent, to be connected with each institution; the pauper there to be maintained and employed at the expense of the respective counties, in some healthful labor, chiefly agricultural; *their children to be carefully instructed, and at suitable ages, to be put out to some useful business or trade.*

It is confidently believed, that with such a mass of evidence before us *there can be no hazard in adopting the poorhouse system in every county in the state.* If, however, there is any county, whose small population, in the opinion of the legislature, would not at present warrant the expense, suitable provision might be made, either for exempting it from the operations of the proposed bill, attaching it to some other county, or directing some small building with a farm to be hired as a temporary poorhouse.[14]

Summaries of some sections of the law passed in 1824 on recommendation of Mr. Yates are:[15]

[13]*Op. cit.*, p. 956.   [14]Page 960.
[15]Summarized from—*Charity Legislation in New York, 1609-1900*, pp. 241-45. This is Volume III of *The Annual Report of the State Board of Charities of New York* for 1903.

THE ALMSHOUSE

An act making it duty of superintendent in each county (except in the counties already having almshouses) at their next meeting to direct the purchase of not more than 200 acres of land and to build thereon one or more buildings to be denominated the poorhouse of the county. Total cost not to be more than $7000. In October of each year supervisors were to choose not less than five persons to be denominated superintendents of the poor . . . who shall have exclusive charge of the poorhouse and everything relating to it.

It shall and may be lawful for the overseers of the poor of any town or city in said county, to take up any child under the age of fifteen years, who shall be permitted to beg or solicit charity from door to door, or in any street or highway of such city or town, and carry or send him or her to said poorhouse, there to be kept and employed, and instructed in such useful labor as he or she shall be able to perform, and supported until discharged therefrom by order of said superintendents, whose duty it shall be to discharge such child as soon as he or she shall be able to provide for himself or herself.

County to pay bills and collect from towns in proportion to the number of their paupers. Every sick, infirm or poor person to be supported until in sufficient health to gain a livelihood and then if he begs or is a vagrant he is to be treated as a disorderly person. Poor may be transported from town to town in county but not to another county. Other counties (those that were excepted) may vote at annual meeting to erect a county poorhouse, and may avail themselves of this act.

Philosophy of Mr. Yates

It should be noted that Mr. Yates not only advocated almshouse care of dependent and neglected children as a means to their education and moral training, but that he also depended upon indenture as the process by which children should be later removed from the almshouse and attached to individual families where they could pay their own way, for it was his plan that after the children of the poor had been "carefully instructed" in the almshouse, "at suitable ages they are to be *put out* to some useful business or trade." The point with Mr. Yates was, that as these poor children got no schooling, no moral training and no discipline with their parents, they should be gathered into the almshouse and given such instruction and moral training *before being indentured*. He thought that in the almshouse, children could be educated and set on the road to a life that would free them from permanent ignorance, pauperism and vice.

This was the theory of Mr. Yates in recommending almshouse care for the dependent children of New York State. What Mr. Yates failed to see was the effect upon these children within the almshouse of constant companionship with the adult persons whom he was also going to gather there. Some of these adults whom Mr. Yates found in need of care in New York State in 1823-24 were "idiots," "lunatics," the aged and infirm, the lame, those in a state of confirmed ill-health, and adult paupers of both sexes who could work. In a later chapter we shall look at some of the things which Mr. Yates and the people in general, both in Europe and America, had not realized up to that time. They had seen the debasing influence upon children of incompetent, neglectful and depraved parents. They had also seen that it was the duty of the public to give some form of care to children who were either homeless or in destitution and neglected at home, and they had devised the means of taking a part of the burden of such care from private charity and of placing it upon the public generally in the form of taxes. What they had not appreciated was the sodden, coarsening and debasing atmosphere of the mixed almshouse as a permanent or even a temporary home for children. Another thing that they had not glimpsed, and which we of today are only beginning to see, was the possibility of so understanding the parents as to use the affection between a child and even an incompetent and neglectful parent as an asset and a stimulus to both parent and child in their efforts to achieve character, self-support and family solidarity.

Chapter IV

REALITIES OF CHILD LIFE IN THE MIXED ALMSHOUSE

In the previous chapter, we have quoted the recommendations of Secretary of State Yates of New York in 1824 to the effect that every county should have its almshouse, and that the children should be gathered into it in order to give them schooling and moral education which would tend to make them good citizens. The reader is now invited to take a look at these mixed almshouses that had, since the last decades of the seventeenth century, been building in all the poor law unions of England; that had also, during the same time, been growing in number in most of the original thirteen states of the United States; and that Secretary Yates wanted every county in New York to build. The reader may see for himself how far the humane purposes of people in England and in the United States, including Mr. Yates with his new law in New York, actually helped, by gathering them into mixed almshouses, the children whom these persons intended to help.

The Mixed Almshouse in England

We are permitted to see the almshouses in England through the eyes of a Royal Commission of nine members appointed in 1832 and headed by the Bishop of London. The report of this Commission tells what they saw in the smaller parishes:[1]

In such parishes, when overburdened with poor, we usually find the building, called a workhouse, occupied by 60 or 80 paupers, made

---

[1] R. G. Nicholls, *History of the English Poor Law*, Vol. II, p. 248. Quoted from *Report of the Poor Law Commission*, 1834.
Alexander Johnson, *The Almshouse*, p. 141, also quotes a part of this report.

up of a dozen or more neglected children (under the care, perhaps, of a pauper), about twenty or thirty able-bodied adult paupers of both sexes, and probably an equal number of aged and impotent persons, proper objects of relief. Amidst these the mothers of bastard children and prostitutes live without shame and associate freely with the youth, who have also the examples and conversation of the inmates of the county gaol, the poacher, the vagrant, the decayed beggar, and other characters of the worst description. To these may often be added a solitary blind person, one or two idiots, and not unfrequently are heard, from among the rest, the incessant ravings of some neglected lunatic. In such receptacles the sick poor are often immured.

Mixed Almshouses in the United States

But we, in America, do not need to go to England for descriptions of poorhouse conditions. A select committee of the senate of the state of New York, under a Resolution of February 7, 1856, spent nearly five months visiting "poorhouses, workhouses, hospitals, jails, orphan and lunatic asylums, and other charitable and reformatory institutions supported by the state." Because their visits were made during the summer and autumn when the average number in the poorhouses is twenty-five percent less than in winter, they believed that they saw these houses at their best, rather than at their worst. Here are extracts from the findings of this Senate Committee:

[Outside of New York and Kings Counties (Manhattan and Brooklyn) they found in 55 almshouses 4936 persons of whom 1307 were children. 770 persons had died in a year. There were in these 55 almshouses 837 lunatics, 130 of them in cells or chains . . . There were also 273 idiots, 25 deaf mutes, and 71 blind.] The poorhouses throughout the state may generally be described as badly constructed, ill-arranged, ill-warmed, and ill-ventilated. The rooms are crowded with inmates; and the air, particularly in the sleeping apartments, is very noxious, and to casual visitors, almost insufferable. In some cases, as many as 45 inmates occupy a single dormitory, with low ceilings and sleeping boxes arranged in three tiers one above another. . . .

THE MIXED ALMSHOUSE

In one county almshouse, averaging 137 inmates, there were 36 deaths during the past year, and yet none of them from epidemic or contagious disease. . . .

A proper classification of the inmates is almost wholly neglected. It is either impossible, or when possible, it is disregarded. Many of the births occurring during the year are doubtless the offspring of illicit connections. During the last year, the whole number of births was 292. The indiscriminate association of the sexes generally allowed strongly favors this assumption. By day, their intercourse is common and unrestricted, and there is often no sufficient safeguard against a promiscuous intercourse by night. In one case the only pretense of a separation of the sexes consisted in the circumstance of separate stairs being provided at each end of a common dormitory, and a police regulation requiring one sex to reach it by one flight, and the other sex by another. . . .

The most important point in the whole subject confided to the committee is that which concerns the care and education of the children of paupers. There are at least 1300 of these now inmates of the various poorhouses, exclusive of those in New York and Kings Counties; enough in these nurseries, if not properly cared for, to fill some day all the houses of refuge and prisons in the state as receptacles for adult paupers. The committee do not hesitate to record their deliberate opinion that the great mass of the poorhouses which they have inspected, are the most disgraceful memorials of the public charity. Common domestic animals are usually more humanely provided for than the paupers in some of these institutions; where the misfortune of poverty is visited with greater deprivations of comfortable food, lodging, clothing, warmth, and ventilation than constitute the usual penalty of crime. The evidence taken by the committee exhibits such a filth, nakedness, licentiousness, general bad morals, and disregard of religion and the common religious observances, as well as of gross neglect of the most ordinary comforts and decencies of life, as if published in detail would disgrace the state and shock humanity. The committee hesitates to record in the pages of their report the particular instances which would amply justify their general condemnation of these misnamed charitable provisions for the *adult* poor. But with respect to *children* the case is far worse; and the committee are forced to say that it is a grave public reproach that they should ever be suffered to enter or remain in the poorhouses as they are now mismanaged. They are for the young, notwithstanding the legal provision for the education, the worst possible nurseries; contributing an annual accession to our population of three hundred infants, whose present destiny is to pass their most impressionable years in the midst of such vicious associations as will stamp them for a life of future infamy and crime. From such associations they should be promptly severed; and provision made for them either in asylums devoted to their special use, or in such orphan asylums as would consent to take charge of them for a fair compensation to be provided by the state, or by the several towns and counties properly chargeable with the expense. . . .

The education which the statutes provide for them is not suited to their particular case. Indoor instruction is often confided to unfit and vicious teachers; and the attendance of pauper children at schools in the vicinity of the almshouse is accompanied by a sort of disgrace attaching to their position which has a most unfavorable influence. Orphanage is not subject to the like stigma; and therefore to go from an orphan asylum to a public school does not expose the orphan to the same taunts and inconsiderateness that follow the pauper child who is the inmate of a poorhouse; which is generally reputed in its vicinity, as a habitation of vice and degradation, so low has it fallen from its original purpose.[2]

Eleven years after the above mentioned senate visitation of New York almshouses and forty-four years after Secretary of State Yates had recommended that children be gathered into these institutions, we are permitted to look again into the almshouses of New York State. Charles A. Hoyt, first secretary of the State Board of Charities of the state in 1868, describes them as he saw them. This State Board had been organized in 1867 and Mr. Hoyt

[2] The quotations are from "New York Senate Document No. 8, 1857," as quoted by Breckinridge in *Public Welfare Administration in the United States. Select Documents*, Chicago University Press, 1927, pp. 149-57. (This report is also reprinted in the *Annual Report of the State Board of Charities of New York*, 1903.)

THE MIXED ALMSHOUSE

visited in person all the county almshouses that, following Mr. Yates's recommendation in 1824, were now to be found in practically every county of the state. Here is one of Mr. Hoyt's descriptions:[3]

The poorhouse of Steuben County, erected in 1834, is located two miles from the village of Bath, the county seat. The principal building is constructed of brick, is two stories in height, and eighty by forty feet upon the ground. It is occupied by the keeper and his family and the more orderly portion of the paupers. . . . All the domestic labor of the house is performed by pauper inmates. There are several wooden outbuildings, one of which is used for children and aged females, and another as a schoolroom. Adjoining the latter is the wash house, the second story being occupied by male paupers. A high board fence encloses all the buildings. Within this enclosure to the front and right of the main structure is situated the lunatic asylum. . . .

At the date of visitation, June 29th, ninety persons were found present, the number being a trifle above the usual summer average. In winter, the number is often much greater, and not unfrequently two hundred persons are crowded into the institution. Of those present two were colored, forty-three native and forty-five foreign born, and five-eighths of the entire number were males. Twenty-five were over fifty years old, and *twenty-one* were *children* under *sixteen years of age*. Fourteen men and sixteen women were insane. The sexes are separated at night, but *mingle with one another during the day— the arrangement of the buildings rendering classification impracticable*. The children are taught in a week day school the entire year, and a sabbath school is maintained a portion of the time. Religious services are occasionally held in the house and Bibles are furnished for all the inmates. It was observed, upon examination, that a large number of those present were of the lowest order of paupers, several were middle-aged and able-bodied, and they were represented as slothful and depraved. *The children, when out of school,* necessarily, *associate more or less with* them, and the efforts made for their *moral training, in a great measure,* must be lost in the influences surrounding them. It

[3] *State Board of Charities of New York, Second Annual Report,* 1868, pp. 158-60.

was stated by the keeper that within the first three years, eleven illegitimate children had been born in the house.

Seven years after Mr. Hoyt, as Secretary of the State Board of Charities of New York, made his rounds of the county almshouses, another New York man made the same round of visits in the official capacity of a member of the same board. This was William Pryor Letchworth of Buffalo, a man of wealth who had given up his business, and thenceforth until his death devoted himself with distinguished ability to social service. Here is a picture of the Steuben County almshouse and its inmates, as Mr. Letchworth saw them in 1874. His description makes our picture of the almshouse experiences and associations of children more definite than either the English report or that of Mr. Hoyt:[4]

At the date of October 28, 1874, there were in this poorhouse fifteen (15) children. Ten (10) of them were boys and five (5) were girls—six of the number were under two years of age. . . *Five of the children were born in the poorhouse.* The longest time any one had been there was five years. . . Six were under two years of age; seven between two and ten, and two were ten and less than sixteen. Four were defective. . . .

These children were found in different parts of the poorhouse establishment *as is usually the case. Four* of them were in a ward with women paupers. Among these was a girl of eight or nine years old. One of these women had a child of her own in the same room, and among the children. She had been an inmate twenty months; had a very irritable temper—so violent that she could not retain for any length of time a home outside of the poorhouse. She was strong and healthy, and a woman of very debased character. *Such was one of the hourly companions of these young girls.*

A second group of children—boys—were found in the workhouse. They were intermingled with the inmates of the workhouse, around the cauldrons where the dirty clothes were being boiled. Here was an insane woman raving and uttering gibberings, a half crazy man was

[4] *Annual Report of the State Board of Charities of New York,* 1875, pp. 233-34.

THE MIXED ALMSHOUSE

sardonically grinning, and an overgrown idiotic boy of malicious disposition was teasing, I might say torturing, one of the little boys. There were several other adults of low types of humanity. The apartment of this dilapidated building overhead was used for a sleeping-room, and the floor was being scrubbed at the time by one of the not over-careful inmates; it was worn, *and the dirty water came through the cracks in continuous droppings upon the heads of the little ones,* who did not seem to regard it as a serious annoyance. The discomfort was immediately checked when observed by the keeper.

The third group were *in a back* building *called the insane department. They were the most promising children of all,* and yet the place was made intolerable by the groanings and sighings of one of the poor insane creatures, who was swaying backward and forward. She was a hideous looking object, and a great portion of her time was passed in this excited condition. *The children are not sent to school, neither is a school sustained upon the premises, the number being too small to warrant the hiring of a teacher.* Sad indeed is the lot of one born in destitution, bereaved of natural guardians and forced unwillingly upon the charities of the world but when, in addition to this, the purity, sweetness, and innocence of childhood are subjected to such soul-chilling influences, the deepest fountains of pity are stirred within us, and we hear tender voices of humanity pleading in tones which should reach the inmost chambers of legislative committees at the capital.

It would be unjust to leave this description with the inference that the superintendents and keeper were at fault for this unhappy condition of the children. The property of the county had the appearance of being well cared for, and the house was cleanly and in order; but *in this as others less aggravated, no separation of the children from the older inmates is practicable.*

Here also are some more general statements of Mr. Hoyt relative to children in the almshouses of New York, made in his report of 1868 after he had completed his visits to all the almshouses of the State:[5]

[5] *Annual Report of the State Board of Charities of New York,* 1868, pp. 76-78.

But few of the poorhouses of the state, owing to their arrangement, admit of a proper classification of their inmates. The authorities, most of them, aim to keep the sexes separated at night, but this is only partially accomplished. *During the day there is an indiscriminate and unrestricted association of all classes, including the aged and respectable, children, insane, idiotic and blind; together with the middle-aged, able-bodied, slothful, debased and profane of both sexes.* In most cases, they partake of a common fare at a common table, and not unfrequently share with one another a common dormitory. The effects of such an association can be better conceived than described. Its fruits will be reaped in a large increase of pauperism and crime, coupled with grievous and burdensome taxation. *During the year 304 children were born in these establishments, a large proportion of whom were illegitimate;* and 799 of their inmates absconded; many of them to become, quite probably, a public charge, as vagrants or criminals. . . .

But little can be said commending the *morale* of these establishments as a class of institutions. The houses are generally partially supplied with Bibles, and religious services are maintained regularly every Sabbath, and the expenses in connection with the same are met by appropriations made by the board of supervisors; but in the majority of cases, the work is purely charitable, being performed by benevolent clergymen, residing in the vicinity of the institutions. . . .

The children are generally taught in week day, and in some instances, in Sabbath schools. Occasionally they are instructed in district schools, but not unfrequently pauper children are denied admission to such schools. In some counties the practice prevails of sending pauper and destitute children to orphan asylums and homes for the friendless, the authorities contributing towards their support. *These institutions now afford accommodations for nearly all of the homeless and destitute children of the state,* and as they are accessible without any material increase in the cost of their support, the practice of retaining them in county poorhouses is inexcusable. . . .

During the year I have called the attention of the county authorities, so far as practicable, to the condition of the children in the poorhouses, and urged their removal *to orphan asylums;* in several counties, they have quite recently been transferred to these institutions upon terms

THE MIXED ALMSHOUSE

highly satisfactory to all concerned, and it is anticipated that considerable can be accomplished in this direction in the course of the coming year. Those in charge of these institutions express a readiness and desire to receive the children now in poorhouses, without reference to locality, to the full extent of their accommodations, and at prices that shall not be burdensome to the counties.

Taken together, the statements of the English Royal Commission, of the New York Senate Committee of 1857, and those of Mr. Hoyt and Mr. Letchworth, permit each of us to visualize what it would mean to a little boy or girl whom we love to live in a *mixed almshouse*. If we can see so vividly what it would mean to a child whom we know and love so to live, we ought also to be able to visualize something of what it has meant to untold children, generation after generation, in England, the American colonies and most of the states of the Union.

When we come to describe the origin and development of some of the later methods of care for dependent children we shall see over and over again in the background the shadow and influence of the once well-nigh universal mixed almshouse system of care. Even today the shadow of almshouse care for children still rests upon some children in most of our states, although the almshouse is no longer so "mixed" as to its inmates as it once was.

THE REVOLT IN NEW YORK AGAINST PLACING CHILDREN IN ALMSHOUSES

The revulsion which we have observed against mixed almshouses for children was potent, at least from the first decade of the nineteenth century, in stimulating local groups of persons in different places to found institutions for dependent children, in order to keep them from the mixed almshouse. This revulsion finally found voice in such men as Mr. Hoyt and Mr. Letchworth, and in New York State it culminated in a law summarized as follows by the president of the State Board of Charities, in his report for 1875:[6]

[6] Birdseye, Cumming and Gilbert, *Consolidated Laws of New York*, 1909, Vol. 4, p. 4256, with reference to Laws of 1875, Chapter 173, ¶ 152.

Provided that on and after January 1st, one thousand eight hundred and seventy-six, no child over 3 and under 16 years of age, of proper intelligence, and suited for family care, shall be committed to any poorhouse of this state, and that all children of this class, shall within the time named, be removed from such poorhouses and provided for in families, asylums, or other appropriate institutions.

In some states there was also a slow segregation of children with special handicaps—the blind, the deaf, and the feeble-minded—within special institutions. This movement began with the Hartford [Connecticut] Institution for the Deaf in 1817, the Perkins Institution for the Blind in Boston in 1831-32, and the Massachusetts Institution for the Feeble-minded in 1848. The latter became famous in after years, under the direction of Dr. Walter Fernald, in Waverley, Massachusetts. Other states slowly provided special institutions for one or more of these specially handicapped classes. Without tracing the movement in any detail, we may bear in mind this form of segregating children from the mixed almshouse population. It takes its place with the other movements before mentioned as indicative of the growing trend of opinion against mixed almshouse care for dependent children. In addition to orphan asylums and various forms of foster family care to be described later, the trend away from almshouses resulted in state-wide laws demanding the removal of children from almshouses and forbidding that others be sent to them. The states which took the lead in legislation of this kind, according to Mr. Homer Folks,[7] were as follows: Ohio, 1866, passed a law authorizing the establishment of county children's homes; Massachusetts, 1872, separated destitute children from adults in the state almshouses; Michigan, 1874, opened a state Public School "to which all destitute children in the State who were public charges were to be removed and from which these children were to be placed out in families as soon as possible"; New York, 1875, passed a law "requiring the removal

[7] *Care of Destitute, Neglected and Delinquent Children,* New York, edition of 1911, pp. 73-79.

THE MIXED ALMSHOUSE

of all children over three years of age, not defective in body or mind, from poorhouses, and directing that they be placed in families, orphan asylums, or other appropriate institutions, and that the public authorities make provision for their maintenance"; Wisconsin, 1878, passed a law requiring removal of children; Pennsylvania, 1883, passed a law prohibiting retention of children "between two and sixteen years unless feeble-minded or defective, in poorhouses for a longer period than sixty days." Other states passing laws relating to the care of children in almshouses, these as a rule prohibiting care of children above infancy for more than two or three months, were: Connecticut, 1883; Rhode Island, 1885; Maryland, 1890; New Hampshire, 1895; Indiana, 1897; New Jersey, 1899;—in all, twelve states up to 1900.

Processions of Children Still Going in through Almshouse Doors

In spite of all these efforts, public and private, to get children out of the mixed almshouses and to keep them out, the following table of numbers of children still in almshouses at each decade since 1880, is challenging:[8]

Children in Almshouses 1880-1923

	1923	1910	1904	1890	1880
Number Inmates All Ages	78,090	84,198	81,764	73,044	66,203
Under 5 years	842	1,186	1,276	2,555	3,850
5 to 9 years	538	641	805	1,783	3,052
10 to 14 years	516	543	674	1,289	1,983
15 to 19 years	688	908	1,136	1,623	1,833
Total under 20 years	2,584	3,278	3,891	7,250	10,718
Total under 15 years	1,896	2,370	2,755	5,627	8,885

[8] United States Census report for 1923, *Paupers in Almshouses*. Table 7, p. 10.

Although this table shows a continuous decrease since 1880 both in the number of children under 20 and those under 15, still the total number of children passing through the experiences of life in an almshouse is large, even in 1923.

For example, the number of children of school age (5-14) in almshouses on January 1, 1923, was 1,154, enough to fill a great public school building with 28 teachers, each having 40 children, and one teacher having 34. The total number under 15 years would fill two huge congregate institutions for dependent children with 1,000 children in one and 896 in another.

The numbers quoted above for 1923 included only those children who were present in almshouses on the one day of enumeration—January 1. In the same report, we find that the total number passing through the almshouses during the year, and therefore having almshouse experiences, was more than twice as large,—namely for 1922, 4,476 under 15 years of age.

Almshouse experiences are not what we who read of these numbers would choose for children whom we personally love. The effect of these experiences is not less harmful to the children concerned, because we who read do not personally know them.

It would be of interest to know how many persons in the United States and in each of our several states realize the magnitude and the persistence of the problem of almshouse children in the United States as the second quarter of the twentieth century opens.

Thus far we have seen some of the reasons why the almshouse could seem to Mr. Yates better for destitute children than their neglect in families, and better than the outdoor relief of his day; also some of the reasons why, a generation later, the same kind of an almshouse could seem to Mr. Hoyt and Mr. Letchworth an indefensible school for pauperism and crime. "Time makes ancient good uncouth."

CHAPTER V

ORPHAN ASYLUMS AS A STEP FORWARD IN CHILD CARE

From the descriptions of almshouses which have been given it is easy to see that, for the dependent children of the late eighteenth and early nineteenth centuries, life by themselves in an orphan[1] asylum might be vastly better than life in a mixed almshouse. The care of dependent children in institutions designed for them was therefore a step forward. Interesting testimony to this effect is given by the members of the New York State Senate Committee of 1857, whose impressions of the almshouse care of children have been related in the previous chapter.

It is agreeable to turn from the consideration of the poorhouses and their mismanagement, to the examination of the orphan asylums, to which the benefactions of the state are contributed. The committee visited them all. Whether it be that the principal charge of these is confined to females, or whatever be the cause, it is certain that with less comparative expenditure of the public money an incomparably greater amount of comfort, cleanliness, kind treatment, health, and good education is secured to the inmates, than happens to be the lot of the paupers in our poorhouses.

The orphan asylums are twenty-six in number and contain 2816 children.

The founding of each of the 1558 such institutions in the United States, reported in the volume of the United States census on *Children under Institutional Care,* February 1, 1923, probably had its stimulus in the actual, though often misinterpreted, needs

---

[1] A misnomer because in most institutions a large majority of children, often 90 percent, have one or both parents living.

of one or more neglected and dependent children. Extracts from the early records of some of these institutions will move the reader by the stories of the awakening of human sympathy and of the struggle made in turn by each small group of persons to provide shelter, food, clothing and care for the children whose needs they had discovered and which they felt "called by Providence" to relieve.

I. Origins, Early Methods and Philosophies of Selected Institutions

Among the reasons for starting these institutions, of which the founders were conscious, were these:

(1) Refusal to place dependent children in whom they were personally interested in the local mixed almshouse;

(2) To save children from neglect, outrage and destitution in the streets and in squalid homes;

(3) To give children care under the religious auspices of their parents and thus to keep them from losing their ancestral faith;

(4) To provide care for negro children.

We are told by Homer Folks that previous to 1800 there had been founded in America seven institutions for the care of destitute, neglected and delinquent children, one under private auspices in each of the cities of New Orleans, Savannah, New York, Philadelphia, Baltimore and Boston, and also the municipal orphan asylum of Charleston, South Carolina.

1. *The New York Orphan Asylum Society*

The story of the early years of this institution will be given at greater length than that of the others, in order to bring to the attention of the reader a variety of problems of institutional care which in some form most of the other institutions also had to face.

In New York the agency referred to by Mr. Folks was not really an institution, but "The Society for the Relief of Widows with

Small Children," which was organized in 1797 with a membership of women. What greater stimulus could there be to the founding of an institution for dependent children than such practical questions in child care as the women of this society soon faced? One and another of the widows whom they were helping fell ill, some of them even unto death, and "on their dying beds bequeathed their helpless offspring to those who had proved their own benefactors." What could the women do with these little ones? They could put them in the New York City mixed almshouse of that day, on the site of the present City Hall Park, with its hundreds of other pauper children and other hundreds of adult paupers — insane, idiotic, aged, diseased and debased. They could not bring themselves to believe that thus their promises to dying mothers could be kept. They could have them indentured, but some were too young to begin to pay their way at once and, besides, they would lose touch with the little ones whom they had come to know as individual boys and girls, each with a name and personality. They could and did take some of them into their own homes. But that method had its limitations as to certainty and length of care for all the children who needed care as the years passed. We are told in the memoirs of Mrs. Joanna Bethune, Third Directress, that "the question as to how the children of deceased widows should be provided for caused great anxiety to the managers, as the funds of the Society[2] could not be used by them."

About this time a copy of the "Life of Francke" with a history of his Orphan House at Halle, Germany, fell into the hands of Mrs. Bethune; she with her mother, Mrs. Graham (First Directress) and her husband, all equally interested in the matter, made a careful study of the book. It was regarded by them as a means used by Providence to assist them in their benevolent difficulty. "I will remain with the widows," said Mrs. Graham, "but you, my dear Joanna, are younger: do you leave the active direction of the Widows Society, and devote yourself to our Heavenly Father's children—the fatherless and the

---

[2] The Society for Relief of Widows with Small Children.

motherless." After careful, and not hasty deliberation, their pious friends were called into council, especially Mrs. Sarah Hoffmann, whose excellent judgment strengthened by much experience in charity, and commanding social position, rendered it peculiarly desirable that the movement should be made under her auspices, and it was determined that an appeal should be made to the benevolent public of New York for the means and agencies necessary to the founding of an Orphan Asylum, which should receive under its protective roof all legitimate children left orphans by the death of both parents.[3]

A public meeting was therefore called and the New York Orphan Asylum Society was organized on the fifth of March, 1806. Mrs. Sarah Hoffman was chosen as First Directress, Mrs. Alexander Hamilton,[4] Second Directress, and Mrs. Bethune as Treasurer; there were also ten women elected as Trustees. Mrs. Hoffman resigned her position on the Widows Society to preside over the Orphan Asylum Board. Mrs. Hamilton and Mrs. Bethune continued in service, each in turn as First Directress, for many years; Mrs. Hamilton served until a few years before her death, which occurred in 1854; Mrs. Bethune until 1859, a period of fifty-three years.

As a temporary asylum a (two-story) frame house on Raisin Street (near Barrow) in Greenwich Village was hired and the first object of the Society's attention was the providing of shelter for those little ones already under their care. . . . A pious and respectable man and his wife were procured to instruct and take charge of the children in order to qualify these for a useful station in future life. They were to be taught reading, writing, arithmetic, plain sewing, and when of a suitable age, domestic business, but as a far more important object a well adapted plan was formed for their moral and religious instruction. During the first six months, twelve orphans were received into the asylum and comfortably provided for.[5]

[3]*Origin and History of the Orphan Asylum Society in the City of New York*, New York, 1896, Vol. I, pp. 3-4.
[4]Widow of Alexander Hamilton, statesman, killed in a duel by Aaron Burr.
[5]*Origin and History of the Orphan Asylum Society*, etc., Vol. I, pp. 9-10.

ORPHAN ASYLUMS

In April, 1807, the Society held their first annual meeting when "the orphans (then more than twenty in number) were presented to the view of their generous benefactors, comfortably clad, and wearing on their faces the guileless smile of health and happy youth."

Meanwhile plans were under way for a permanent building. "A site of liberal size, nearly one acre, was contracted for not far from Mrs. Bethune's place near Greenwich Village, and on the 7th of July, 1807, the cornerstone was laid. It was to be of brick, fifty feet square, and was planned to accommodate 200 children."

The annual report for 1808 says that they had 53 children under their care and were planning to move into the partly finished building by May, 1808. At that time they expected "to have basement story ready and one or two of the upper rooms and to enclose the garden lots with a suitable fence." Their water supply was from a cistern, and a well in the yard, with a pump. They evidently burned wood at first as several loads of wood are mentioned as gifts. In 1813 mention is made of finishing the school room. In 1818-19 they finished rooms in the "garret for the further accommodation of the children." "The yard was paved; there was a root house and a new stoop and pump." A scullery was built in the rear "where all the cooking, baking and washing is performed. . . . The kitchen is now left free for cleaner work, and the smaller children; and a large apartment to be occupied as a school room for girls, who are there instructed by the governess and her daughter in such branches of education as are suitable for females in the humbler walks of life."[6] "The record also states that the orphan family (of 139) had with difficulty been accommodated before the building of the outside kitchen. The school room in particular was too crowded for health or improvement."

In 1821, when there were 152 children in the asylum, we are told that "the present accommodations are too limited, and an addition to the house is deemed requisite."[7] The addition of a wing was proposed:[8]

[6]*Ibid.*, Vol. I, pp. 99-100.   [7]*Ibid.*, Vol. I, p. 114.   [8]*Ibid.*, Vol. I, p. 114.

As many friends of the institution have expressed anxiety respecting the safety of the building from fire, it may be proper to mention for the satisfaction of those who have not visited the asylum that the kitchen is a separate building paved with brick and ovens heated by coals. Coals are also used for warming the school room; its dormitories extend the whole length of the house, and a staircase leads from each and opposite corners. The smallest among the children sleep on the first floor under the immediate care of the superintendent.

It is not entirely clear whether the house had a basement and first and second floors, or only a first and second floor. In any event, the reader will find it an interesting exercise in house planning to work out an arrangement to shelter, feed, school and "play" 152 children in a building fifty feet by fifty feet, and having not more than three floors.

In 1825 the *Annual Report* says: "Twenty years have now elapsed since the Orphan Asylum Society commenced its operations in the city of New York. . . . After struggling with many difficulties the Board of Directors have at last the satisfaction of announcing to their patrons that the Asylum at Greenwich is completely finished with sufficient accommodations for their large family (161 children). During the past year many necessary comforts and conveniences have been added, which their limited means did not permit them formerly to enjoy."[9]

The wing which had recently been built was "of brick 59 by 28 feet, and contains a wide staircase, a school room for boys and dormitories over the whole."[10]

Keeping in mind the fact that the children received were to be whole orphans, who were legitimate, it will be of interest to look a little more closely into the methods of the institution in caring for the children who one by one and in twos and threes entered the door of the asylum, stayed for a while within the walls and about the enclosed acre of ground, and then went out by ones, twos and threes to all that life had yet in store for them. The mis-

[9]*Ibid.*, Vol. I, p. 136.   [10]*Ibid.*, Vol. I, p. 119.

ORPHAN ASYLUMS

sionary spirit of the enterprise is shown by the Constitution, which reads in part:

Amongst the afflicted of our suffering race none make a stronger or more impressive appeal to humanity than the destitute orphan. Crime has not been the cause of its misery, and future usefulness may yet be the result of its protection. The reverse is often the case of more aged objects.

God Himself has marked the fatherless as the peculiar subjects of His divine compassion. "A father of the fatherless is God in His holy habitation." "When my father and mother forsake me, then the Lord will take me up." To be the blessed instrument of Divine Providence in making good the promise of God is a privilege equally desirable and honorable to the benevolent heart.[11]

From their original "plan" we also read: "A general meeting of the Society shall be held once every year; . . . the orphans shall be introduced and the gentlemen subscribers requested to attend." The duties of the elected officers included a weekly visit to the asylum, in rotation.

[From the Constitution and By-Laws, we have selected these provisions and rearranged their sequence:][12]

INTAKE AND CARE

No children were to be received until examined by a respectable physician and pronounced free from infection or incurable diseases.

Relations or friends of orphans shall on placing them in the asylum, renounce all claim to them in future years.

The orphans shall be educated, fed, and clothed at the expense of the Society, and at the Asylum. They must have religious instruction, moral example, and habits of industry inculcated on their minds.

INDENTURE

As soon as the age and acquirements of orphans shall, in the opinion of the Board of Directors, render them capable of earning their living,

---

[11]*Ibid.*, Vol. I, p. 16.   [12]*Ibid.*, Vol. I, pp. 18-20.

they must be bound out to some reputable persons or families for such object and in such manner as the Board shall approve.

A book shall be kept at the Asylum in which applicants for children shall insert their names, occupations and references for character, which shall be laid before the Board. At the monthly meeting a committee shall be appointed to make necessary inquiries. One month's trial shall be allowed, at the expiration of which, should the employer not be satisfied, or the child with his place, they shall be permitted to choose again, but no child shall be admitted into the Asylum after being bound unless the judgment of the Board deem it expedient.

In 1809 there is this further statement as to plans for indenture:[13]

The Board having been empowered by the Legislature at their last session to bind by indenture, without taking the parties before the police, their plan is to bind the girls as servants from the time they can read and write till they are eighteen; and the boys when equally instructed are to be put out as servants until the age of fifteen, at which time they are to be returned to the Trustees of the Asylum who will bind them as apprentices to virtuous mechanics in the hope of their becoming useful and happy members of the community, and perhaps the future benefactors of the institution which nurtured their helpless infancy.

In 1810, after reporting progress in paying debts they express the hope that, with only the annual expense to meet, "without taxing the community unreasonably, this Society will furnish it with a number of useful artisans and faithful servants, and they humbly hope, be rendered instrumental in gathering many a wandering lamb into the fold of heaven."[14]

Philosophy as to the work of children.—In many of the annual reports are statements in detail of the work done by boys and girls while in the asylum. That of 1821 is unusually good because the statement begins by giving an illuminating expression of the purpose and philosophy of the managers in setting the children to work. During the year they state that

16 boys have been bound to farmers or mechanics and 16 girls

[13]*Ibid.*, Vol. I, p. 31.   [14]*Ibid.*, Vol. I, pp. 37-38.

placed in respectable families, 10 boys and girls have been received into the institution, and there now remain 128 children dependent upon you for the necessaries of life. *In order to inure the boys to hardship and fatigue* [italics by the present writer] they are required to cut all the wood, draw all the water, etc., and are taught to cultivate the grounds belonging to the asylum which have yielded a very large supply of vegetables of various kinds. There have been raised the past year, 2000 heads of cabbage, 150 bushels of potatoes, 100 bushels of turnips, also beans, peas, parsnips, onions, etc. The girls are employed in work appropriate to themselves; they have within the last year made 550 garments of different sorts, 40 pairs of sheets, 18 mattresses, besides quilting 13 bed quilts, repairing their clothes, knitting, assisting in washing, ironing, and every variety of housework. Although care is taken to give them habits of industry, the culture of their minds is not neglected.[15]

Religious education and duties of members of staff.—A similar statement in 1824[16] goes into detail as to one of the ways in which the "culture of the mind" was developed. It says: "The boys have committed to memory 8881 verses of Scripture and 3103 verses of hymns. The girls have committed 4805 verses of Scripture and 6208 verses of hymns; nearly all the children can repeat the Mother's Catechism, the Creed, and the Lord's Prayer."[17]

There is printed in *The Origin and History of the Orphan Asylum Society* from which we have been quoting (pages 23-30), a series of Rules and Regulations designed to control in great detail the work of all employees. These rules are such as were in vogue in 1896, the date of compilation, and probably reflect the experience of the preceding ninety years. They are printed with the Constitution and Articles of Incorporation, as if they had been in force from the first. In any event, they are in harmony with what we know of the institution and the spirit of its managers. In one respect they could not have applied to the first years, for the number of teachers and caretakers is larger than was true of the asylum at first.

[15]*Ibid.*, Vol. I, pp. 107-8. [16]Several other reports give similar statements.
[17]*Ibid.*, Vol. I, pp. 126-27.

These points may be[18] noted as helping the reader to visualize the daily and weekly life of the children:

The superintendent shall attend church with the children on the Sabbath and daily conduct morning and evening worship at the asylum at which all members of the family shall be required to be present unless necessarily detained.

He shall admit no visitors to the Asylum on the Sabbath, nor allow any inmate to visit relatives or friends, except by permission of the Visiting Committee of the month.

The superintendent shall direct that the persons of the boys are kept clean, and their clothes in good order; and in detailing the large boys necessary for domestic or outdoor work of the asylum, shall endeavor to so apportion the work that all may have equal educational advantages; and if the services of a boy be required during school hours, a written request shall be made to the teacher.

At meal hours he shall direct that the children enter and leave the dining room in regular order; that a blessing be asked, and thanks returned; that the caretakers are all present to enforce the table rules and preserve order; and the children wash their hands and faces after each meal.

Among the duties of the matron were these:

She shall supervise all females employed in the asylum.

She shall employ a suitable woman as sick nurse, and place all sick children in her care. [This was not the case in the first years.]

She shall direct that each bed in the asylum be provided in summer with two sheets and a spread, and with sufficient blankets in cool weather and winter, and also be brushed and washed when necessary, and furnished once a week with a clean sheet; she shall also direct that all children on rising shall open their beds, and after breakfast make the same under proper superintendence.

She shall provide for each child four shirts or chemises, two suits of clothing, and four pairs of stockings, all marked with the respective names or numbers.

[18]Selected and abbreviated from *Ibid.*, Vol. I, pp. 23-30.

ORPHAN ASYLUMS

She shall direct that the children are neatly attired at morning prayers and suitably dressed during school hours, and that all are provided with extra aprons while working, or at play; that all underclothes are changed twice a week, and that all children are properly bathed and their hair cut, or combed as may be necessary, every Saturday. [In assigning girls for work she was to observe some rules already cited for the superintendent in work of boys.]

The teachers are to have general supervision of children during school hours which are 8.30 A.M. to 10 A.M., from 10.30 A.M. to 12 M, from 1.30 P.M. to 3 P.M. and during those hours no children shall leave the school rooms without permission. On Friday afternoon school shall be dismissed at 2.30 P.M.

On Wednesday and Friday afternoons of each week, the teachers shall instruct in singing the girls under their charge, and as all the children leave the asylum at a comparatively early age, the teachers shall endeavor, principally to instruct their pupils in reading, writing, spelling, arithmetic, grammar and geography.

No teacher or employee of this institution shall, under any provocation whatsoever, strike or maltreat a child under the care of the society; any such act will peremptorily forfeit the offender's position.

The superintendent is permitted to inflict corporal punishment upon the boys, but is directed not to adopt this extreme measure unless, in his judgment, it is necessary for the maintenance of good discipline. The offending child's teacher and caretaker shall always be present when such punishment is inflicted.

The same power is permitted to the matron with regard to the girls.

Teachers and employees of this institution will receive their friends and relatives in the parlor, no visitors being allowed to pass through the house, except by special permission of the superintendent or matron.

In 1836, when the first building had become inadequate, the same managers bought for $17,500 nearly ten acres of ground at Seventy-fourth Street and Riverside Drive (a part of which site is now occupied by the residence and grounds of Charles M.

Schwab of the Bethlehem Steel Company). On this new site they built a "noble building for extensive accommodation," the cornerstone for which was laid in 1836.

A boy's story of a day in the institution.—To help the reader to visualize still more clearly the daily program of children in the New York Orphan Asylum, a letter is here given which was written to the author in 1916 by a young man who had lived in the building at Seventy-fourth Street and Riverside Drive:

We had to arise at 6 o'clock in the morning the Bell rang the Big Bell for all to arise. Then we had to wash and get in Line by Six Thirty and we had to show our hands and faces to see if they were clean. We were arranged according to sizes. Then we had to march in the Dining room and the Girls on one side and the boys on the opposite side. After Breakfast we had to go in the assembly room and hold services. We had to sing Hymn without Hymn book and repeat Chapter of the Bible 23 Epistle, 14 chapter of John, Psalms 1. Ten Commandments, Beatitudes and we had to study the Hymn in the Class when we had the Day School in order. After services in the morning we had to make the Beds and Clean up. Then it was 8 o'clock and time for Day School to begin. We never had any after lessons to study. We had very bright teachers they must of bin College graduates. One thing we Lack and that was grammar. We had the best Education far superior than the Day school had. 12 o'clock was the limit for the morning Session and we all had to assemble and get Clean and go to Dinner.

After Dinner we had to go to School again and it was until 3 o'clock. After school Hours we were allowed to play until 5 o'clock. And we Heard the Bell ring and we had to come in. And we had to wash and get clean for supper. We heard the bell ring for 6 o'clock. And we had to march two by two in the Dining room. After Supper we had to March into the assembly and Sing Praise and repeat the Different Chapter in the Bible together. Then we went to our Play room until it was Bedtime. One thing that impress me most was the religious exercise we had to go through. The Care Taker and Lady Caretaker would tell the boys and girls story before going to Bed. P.S. We were allowed to write Home once a month and the Teacher would examine our letters before they were mail.

The social philosophy of the trustees as sung by the children.—
It may help the reader still further to imagine the life of a child in this institution and to breathe again its atmosphere if we revive a song which the children were accustomed to sing at the annual meetings. The song is first mentioned as sung on June 9, 1836, in connection with laying the cornerstone for the new building overlooking the Hudson. After the ceremonies usual to such an occasion the children then

sang with one accord a beautiful hymn, descriptive of their orphan situation, the kindness they daily received, and the gratitude they felt toward the friends that had fostered them during the helpless years of infancy. Their soft and solemn notes created a thrilling interest among the spectators, and the big tear was seen to race down the cheek of the hardy bystander and workman, who would have disdained to turn his back upon the roaring cannon's mouth.[19]

Here is the hymn; it is typical of songs used by similar institutions at about the same period:[20]

GIRLS

Again the happy day has come,
When we may leave our pleasant home,
Our much-loved friends with joy to meet;
Brothers, with song their coming greet.

BOYS

Yes, sisters; yes, our friends are here;
They come to dry the orphan's tear,
Their love our peaceful couch has spread,
Their care provides our daily bread.

[19]*Ibid.*, Vol. I, pp. 199-200.   [20]*Ibid.*, Vol. I, pp. 241-42.

GIRLS

Oh, brothers, when our parents died,
Who did these faithful friends provide?
Who first their generous hearts inclined
To be to helpless orphans kind?

BOYS

Sisters, it was our Father God
Beheld us from His bright abode;
'Twas He inclined their hearts to feel
And gave them means our woes to heal.

GIRLS AND BOYS

Oh, may we still their kindness share,
And well regard their pious care;
And when life's changing scene is passed,
Rejoice with them in heaven at last.

From the expressions by the directors of their philosophy of work—"in order to inure to hardship and fatigue"; from their frequent references to the binding out of children as "artisans and servants"; and from the spirit of this song which stresses the children's helplessness and dependency, the reader can judge for himself how much conscious purpose there was to discover and develop each individual child.

The health problem.—One of the problems frequently mentioned in the New York Asylum reports of the first decades is that of the health of the children.

Infectious and contagious diseases mentioned before 1836 are as follows: in 1811, whooping cough,[21] in 1819, measles and whooping cough, of which last two children died.[22] In 1824, one child died of scrofula and consumption, another from inflammation of the lungs, another of whooping cough and consumption, while 39 children had whooping cough, and 24 remittent fever. All of these recovered. Colds and fevers prevailed the whole of the winter.[23]

[21] *Op. cit.*, p. 50. [22] *Op. cit.*, p. 94. [23] *Op. cit.*, p. 125.

ORPHAN ASYLUMS

In 1825—60 children had the measles and 2 died.

In 1826, 1827, 1828 and 1829 respectively 3, 5, 5 and 10 children died—the last number being the largest ever reported in the equal period of time. In 1830, 4 died. In 1834, only 2 died.

In 1835 one woman teacher and three children died of cholera. "The neighborhood was exceedingly sickly, and other diseases followed in the train of cholera . . . and in all 18 children died."[24]

Health conditions and the need for fresh vegetables and pasturage for cows seem to have been determining considerations in the purchase of the Hudson River property.

Until nearly the year 1900, children were cared for in the congregate building (once rebuilt and enlarged) at Seventy-fourth Street. The Asylum then removed to a cottage institution at Hastings-on-the-Hudson. Dr. R. R. Reeder, who became superintendent in 1898, just before the old congregate building at Seventy-fourth Street was abandoned, has written a fascinating story of the experiences of the children after they were moved to the cottages at Hastings-on-the-Hudson. This book, *How Two Hundred Children Live and Learn*,[25] is now out of print and should be carefully preserved by those persons and librarians who have it. If the reader of this chapter can get access to a copy, he should read it. It gives a picture of institutional life that many people think too roseate[26]—certainly very different from that which children lived in the first simple, unfinished congregate building opened by the New York Orphan Asylum Society in 1808. Clearly, for the children at Hastings, life was far richer than for the earlier inmates, either of the congregate building in Greenwich Village, or of that at Seventy-fourth Street. It must also be clear that life in this institution, at whatever stage, has been more wholesome than it could possibly have been in the old mixed almshouses that were

[24]*Ibid.*, pp. 183-84.
[25]The substance of the book was originally contributed in a series of articles, 1903-1908, Vols. XI-XIX, in *The Charities and Commons*, which name the predecessor of *The Survey* then bore.

so universal during the first three-quarters of the nineteenth century in both this country and in England.

2. *Some Further Institutional Origins*

The first annual reports of orphan asylums founded fifty or more years ago give new and challenging impressions of the sufferings which neglected children endured at an earlier day, as well as inspiring glimpses of the love for children and the missionary zeal shown by those who took the lead in founding each particular institution. The whole situation may not have been studied with scientific intelligence, so as to approach the best standard of practices of the day, or with a view to avoiding duplication of local undertakings, but there can be no doubt that what a friendly critic has described as "heart action" was the basis of many of these pioneer efforts. The extracts now to be given from the records of several more of these early institutions for dependent children in different parts of the country present interesting and instructive evidence, not only of the "heart action" above mentioned, but also of the part played in the situation by the presence of children in the local mixed almshouse. There are glimpses to be had of the daily program of children in the institution; the method of intake by surrender, and of outgo by indenture, that were the rule in those days; and finally there is the illuminating disclosure of the social philosophy and child philosophy practised by these early "child benefactors."

3. *The Boston Female Orphan Asylum*[27]

We are told that Boston in 1800 had only 20,000 inhabitants, and that its only public charities, beside the Almshouse, were the

---
[26] For Dr. Reeder's later views on institutional care, see *The Survey* for April and October, 1925, and January, 1929.
[27] See *One Hundred Years of Work in Boston,* published in 1919 by the "Boston Society for the Care of Girls," which had succeeded the Boston Female Orphan Asylum.

Boston Marine Society (founded in 1742), the Boston Humane Society (founded in 1785), and the Boston Dispensary (founded in 1796).

Mrs. Samuel Stillman, wife of the pastor of the First Baptist Church, down in the North End, was stirred to action by the story of a little orphan girl who had become the victim of an unscrupulous man. Mrs. Stillman had seven children of her own, and she felt that many other young girls must need the care that was lacking in the case of the orphan girl whose story she had heard. She therefore urged her friends to help her start an asylum for orphan girls. Information about institutions for children in Europe was gathered with the help of Mrs. Ozias Goodwin and of her husband. Mrs. John Adams, "Lady of the Late President of the United States," headed a list of three hundred subscribers secured in a single year. At the first annual meeting, September 25, 1801, "five hundred dollars were collected for the orphans, twelve of whom were present neatly dressed in blue." At a similar annual meeting in 1807 the degree of understanding of child psychology shown by those in charge of the institution is revealed by the following incident. The Reverend Jedediah Morse of Charlestown, who had preached the anniversary sermon, closed with this appeal in the presence of thirty orphans:[28]

> What more shall I say? Let your eyes plead for me. *Look at these dear orphans. They live on your bounty. They need its continuance. You see how happy they are; what prospects are before them in life. Contrast these with their former condition and prospects.* Can you describe the feelings excited in your minds by the happy change they have experienced? Think now of other orphans who are sighing for such a change; and can you withhold from those respectable, faithful, benevolent Managers, the necessary means to produce it? No; melted and convinced by what you see and hear, that it is your duty to act, you are ready eagerly to enquire, "What can we do?" "What is expected of us?" While your hearts are thus affected you are ready to do

---

[28] *Anniversary Sermons*, Boston Female Asylum, p. 22.

anything in support of such an Institution. It is well. Yield to the generous impulse. Give liberally under your present impressions. Sow bountifully, and you shall reap bountifully. Never shall you have cause to repent your liberality.

On September 20, 1816, during the annual meeting held in Hollis Street Church, the orphans themselves sang this "Hymn," obviously composed for such occasions:

1

With cheerful notes begin the strain,
    To Charity so justly due;
And gratulate this Orphan train,
    On the best hopes they ever knew.

2

No more complaining fills the street,
    Of children who deserted roam,
For here the *houseless vagrants* meet
    A benefactor and a home.

3

And girls defenceless, wretched, poor,
    Snatch'd from the haunts of vice and care
From ill examples here secure,
    Instruction and protection share.

4

Train'd soon in wisdom's pleasant ways,
    And taught to be discreet and good,
Virtue will be, through all their days,
    From habit and from choice pursu'd.

5

Then, as they praise each Patroness,
    Who bounty and assistance lends,
Join them in prayers that God would bless,
    The Institution and its friends.

CHORUS

We join in prayers that God would bless
    The Institution and its friends.

Abuses under indenture in Boston in 1844.—Passing over the intervening years to 1844 we find a contemporary description of the use of indenture by this Boston Institution and of the selfishness, harshness, and dishonesty frequently shown by the mistresses to whom girls had been indentured.[29] The description is of special value because it shows clearly the steps by which an elementary system of checks upon the mistresses came to be devised.

The greatest care is always taken in selecting places for those who are old enough to go into families. And this might seem easy to do, as applications for the children always greatly exceed the number to be placed out. Yet it cannot be denied that the most difficult duties of the managers in regard to them often occur after they leave the Asylum. It is true that instances of mutual satisfaction—of good treatment on the one side, and good conduct on the other greatly preponderate. But cases of an opposite character were presented often enough to induce managers to consider, whether they did not in part arise from some cause that might be removed.

In the *"olden time"* [italics by the present writer], when the regulations for binding out the children were adopted, it was very much the custom for the mistress of a family to take from poor, though often respectable parents, a young girl to clothe and instruct until she should be eighteen years old, in return for her services. Sometimes this was done by indenture, and sometimes by simple verbal agreement; and from such agreements faithfully observed, have arisen many connexions productive of mutual advantage through life. The Asylum children then, were placed out on conditions perfectly according with prevailing customs. And nothing more was required in their indentures, than kind treatment, suitable clothing and instruction, and when they should be eighteen years old "two suits of clothes, one proper for Sunday, the other for domestic business."

But *"times are changed"* [italics by the present writer]. The increase of wealth and variations in the forms of society, have at the same time increased the demand for service, and removed the mistress of a family farther from that direct supervision of those who perform it, which is

---

[29] *Reminiscences of the Boston Female Orphan Asylum,* 1844.

so especially important to the young. *Now a girl, long before she is eighteen, can obtain wages, enable her to indulge that love of dress, which is a prevailing folly, and give a feeling of that independence, the desire for which, is often most strong in those who least know how to use it.* [Italics by the present writer]. It was not then perhaps strange that the girls should, during the last years of their apprenticeship, feel dissatisfied, at seeing others possess apparently greater advantages than themselves. And that some forgetting the destitution of their early childhood, the advantages of a permanent home, thorough instruction in domestic affairs, and the power of securing friends who may be of incalculable benefit to them through life, should be tempted by the precarious, and often delusive good of having an earlier command of wages, and imagine that mere food and clothing and teaching, are insufficient compensation for the work for which they see others obtaining a recompense which seems larger.

It is true that domestic labor commands a larger remuneration than formerly; and it seems but just that these girls should have their share in the advantage. It is true that some who apply for them may have little other purpose than that of obtaining a selfish convenience; the most service at the least price at which it can be procured; that in the idea of *servant* some may have lost sight of the *child,* of one needing all the instruction, forebearance, encouragement and restraint that youth always requires. That disappointed in their expectation of finding an obedient and useful domestic, some become impatient and unmindful of their obligations.

These considerations led the managers in 1842, to review their form of indenture, and the following additional requisitions were inserted in it: First, that a written report should be required once in a year, relative to the health, character, and well-being of the apprentice.

This condition would, it was hoped, be a security for kind treatment toward the girl, and at the same time a restraint and incitement to her.

Secondly, that the sum of fifty dollars should be substituted for the clothing formerly required at the expiration of apprenticeship; this sum to be paid "unless the apprentice shall have been guilty of such gross misconduct that the Board of Managers shall be of the opinion that she has forfeited her claim to it."

The third, and last alteration is, that a penalty of one hundred dollars is incurred in fulfilling the conditions of indenture. This will be readily perceived to be a necessary guard to the institution.

But after all the precautions that can be taken, much must be left to individual conscience. The following appeal to those to whose care these children are committed is copied from the report of 1842:

"You take a *child;* you must not expect to make her, without care, and instruction and patience, a useful domestic. Encourage what you may find good in her, and in punishing her faults, consider how you should endeavor to correct those of your own children; for is not One the Father of us all? And on no occasion should you feel authorized to throw her off from your protection, or permit her to leave it, without the consent of those by whom she was put in your care."

3. *The Second Annual Meeting of The Cincinnati Orphan Asylum in 1835*

Meanwhile the Middle West was discovering the need for institutional care of dependent children. The second anniversary of the founding of the Cincinnati Orphan Asylum, in Cincinnati, June, 1835, was marked by prayers and hymns which show that New York and Boston had no monopoly of poetic inspiration and were not alone in the desire to have their benefactions counted to them for righteousness, not only by the children but by God himself. In an old report the following appears:

About fifty smiling orphans, neatly dressed, were arranged in front of the pulpit. None could think of their past history and their present comfort without invoking the blessing of God upon their benefactors.

The last stanza of the hymn the orphans sang was:[30]

> O let thy love descend on those
> Who pity to us show;
> Nor let their children ever taste
> The Orphan's cup of wo.

---
[30]Quoted in a letter to the writer by a worker in the institution, November, 1928.

4. *The New York Colored Orphan Asylum*

The part played by the almshouse and jail in the founding of the above institution is shown by this account of its origin:[31]

The Colored Orphan Asylum and Association for the Benefit of Colored Children was founded in the year 1836 by two young Quakers, Miss Mary Murray, eighteen years old, and Miss Anna Shotwell, twenty-eight years old, as a protest against the then existing system of keeping destitute colored children in the jails and almshouses.

It was the design of all interested to establish this Asylum and Association on the basis of enlarged Christian charity, without sectarianism or party spirit, and entirely independent of the exciting questions that agitated the public mind in relation to the colored race.

The concurrence of many persons of wisdom and benevolence in the expediency of the undertaking, and a number of very liberal donations and subscriptions, enabled the Association to prosecute their plans, and during the winter of 1837 and 1838 an attempt was made to hire a house for the accommodation of the orphans. Such, however, was the force of prejudice, that no dwelling could be obtained for the purpose and thus situated it became necessary to purchase.

A suitable building was eventually procured in Twelfth Street, near Sixth Avenue, for the sum of Nine Thousand Dollars. The Trustees of the residuary estate of the late Lindley Murray, granted One Thousand Dollars toward this purchase, which enabled the Association to complete a payment of Three Thousand Dollars, allowing Six Thousand Dollars to remain on the mortgage. This, while it laid the foundation of the institution, completely exhausted its funds and the Asylum opened its doors at a time of great pecuniary pressure, with an exhausted treasury.

Notwithstanding the adverse circumstances, the managers ventured to admit a few children, and engaged a person to take charge of them. Donations of furniture, provisions, etc., were liberally supplied, and up to this moment the barrel of meal has not wasted, nor the cruse of oil failed in their humble household.

---

[31] From a manuscript by Lillian Sadler, based on data in the annual reports of the New York Colored Orphan Asylum; now in the hands of the present writer.

A promise of Five Hundred Dollars towards education from the Manumission Society, Three Hundred and Seventy-five of this amount was received, which authorized the formation of a school which should extend its benefits to colored children. During the summer, the day-school contained nearly forty children.

The number of orphans gradually increased. The managers congratulated their benefactors on having extended their fostering care to twenty-three destitute children. Most of these were rescued from scenes of misery. A few were taken from the almshouse, with cordial approbation of the Commissioners, where they were found in circumstances under which the managers deemed themselves justified in admitting them into the orphan asylum.

5. *The Northern Home for Friendless Children*

The extract which follows is from the 1859 report of the Northern Home of Philadelphia, founded in 1853 and incorporated in 1854. It will be noted that one motive in the establishment and maintenance of the institution is to prevent the final resort of the children to the almshouse and to a pauper's grave.

Let the friends and patrons of the Northern Home for Friendless Children accompany us in imagination to some of the localities familiar to our Managers, who go out into the lanes and alleys, the courts within courts, seeking for these children who, in their ignorance and destitution, but for this seeking, would not be found at all. Look at that *Street*. Whatever you have read of the "Seven Dives of London," of the "Wynds" of Glasgow, of the subterranean dens of Liverpool, of the "Five Points" of New York, will also find its counterpart in a good degree in various localities here in Philadelphia—the same filth, the same poverty, the same dilapidation, the same pestilential atmosphere.

Look at that *Grocery:* that fatal row of barrels on the shelf, and of decanters on the counter; see spread out in that window in disgusting profusion the broken food that has been collected from door to door and sold or exchanged by various beggars, male and female, old and young, for *Rum* [Italics in original.].

Go up that *Court:* see how it swarms with population, like a leaf with vermin; ragged, barefooted children at every step, without hats, without bonnets, unwashed, uncombed, uncared for either in mind or body, gambling, blaspheming, fighting, crying, and feeding on garbage.

Enter that *Room:* the only furniture a stove, and a bottle and in one corner a bundle of straw or rags; no bedstead, no table, not even a chair or a stool; the accumulation of dirt upon the floor so thick and of such long standing, that whether it is wood or brick you cannot tell.

Go down into that *Cellar:* water oozing through the crevices of the floor; walls thick with mildew; vice is there, poverty is there, disease is there in all its horror; there is a drunken father, a drunken and abandoned mother; there is the thief, the gambler and perchance a murderer; and there too are little *children. Is* that, *Can* that be, a proper place for them? Is not the influence of such a *place* upon their character equally fatal as the supposed effect of the evil birthday among the heathen? Where every word is an oath or a lie, or connected in some way with profanity or impurity, is that the language with which their little tongues should be familiar, with which their minds and hearts should be brought in constant and deadly contact?

Are the influences of that corrupt and degraded street the only influences that are to be thrown around them?

Is their pilgrimage to be the same melancholy pilgrimage of so many hundreds of thousands before them? Must they too find their way to the grocery, and then to all the various haunts of *vice* and then, to *prison,* and then to the *almshouse* and at last *receive* a pauper's burial in *Potters Field?*

Somebody must consider these questions. *Somebody* must answer them. Society cannot do it in the aggregate. It must of course be answered by the individuals who compose Society, and thence the originators of the Northern Home and other Homes for Friendless Children.

6. *Connecticut County Homes*

Of early child welfare work in Connecticut, and of the part played therein by almshouses and orphan asylums, Mrs. Virginia T. Smith of Hartford gives testimony in a paper read before the

ORPHAN ASYLUMS

National Conference of Charities and Corrections in 1893. Mrs. Smith says in part:[32]

> The work of prevention for neglected children began in Connecticut a little more than sixty years ago. Before that time the poorhouse sheltered all children friendless and homeless, except as boys and girls were "bound out" on farms or as apprentices to trades or to housework. Poorhouses have kept their hold on children, in spite of the multiplying preventive measures of the state, until within the last ten years, since which time it has been forbidden by law that they should remain in them after they were two years of age.
>
> Back in those days, for the children of the poorhouse, for those bound-out, and, in fact, for all children of ordinary grades, the maxim that "children should be seen and not heard" was adhered to; for beyond being instructed to repeat the Catechism, to read aloud in the New Testament, write, and study 'rithmetic, to tell one's name and age in a clear voice, and to "curtsey" by the roadside to carriages passing, there seems to have been little education to anticipate.

7. County Homes in Indiana

In Indiana, as in Connecticut, the growing dissatisfaction with care of children in almshouses led to a provision for them under public auspices in County Children's Homes. Of this Indiana situation we are told:[33]

> The statutes of Indiana prior to 1875 contain little mention of dependent children. A law passed in 1795 and another in 1821 gave township overseers and county "directors of the poor" respectively the right to bind them out as apprentices. The only institutional care other than that for the children of soldiers and sailors was provided by the county poor asylums. An investigation conducted in 1880 disclosed the fact that

---

[32]*Report of the Committee on History of Child Saving*, 1893, p. 116. This is a special volume among the *Reports of the National Conference of Charities and Corrections*.

[33]Amos W. Butler, *Indiana, A Century of Progress, A Study of the Development of Public Charities and Corrections, 1790-1915*, prepared for the Indiana Board of State Charities, Indianapolis, 1916, third edition, p. 4.

there were seven hundred children under sixteen years of age in such institutions. In 1875 county commissioners were permitted to subsidize private orphanages at the rate of twenty-five cents per day per capita. The children thus maintained were to be furnished with homes as expeditiously as practicable. The Widow's and Orphan's Asylum of Indianapolis (now the Indianapolis Orphans' Asylum) incorporated in 1851, was one of the first to receive this subsidy. Still further provision was made for this class in 1881 when county commissioners were authorized to establish orphan asylums. A home for county children was opened at Spiceland, Henry County, June 8, 1880.

8. *The First County Children's Home in Ohio*

Laws permitting township trustees to "bind out" orphan children, who were by the public frequently called "pauper brats," and also laws permitting the incorporation of private orphan asylums, were passed as early as 1824 in Ohio. The alternative forms of public care were jails, infirmaries (mixed almshouses), and two state reformatories. "In 1877 there were 2273 children under 16 years of age under care in the infirmaries. They were dumped into jails festering with crime, disease, insanity and other evils, or sent off to the two state reform schools."[34] It was from such tragic inadequacy in the care of dependent children that the Ohio County Children's Home plan was born and nurtured.

Miss McClain tells the story thus:[35]

The story of "Aunt Katie Fay," a southern Ohio woman of the Civil War days, a pioneer, resourceful, dauntless, visionary and faithful to her vows to get the children out of the wretchedness of the infirmary into a "Children's Home" rivals the story of Paul in his establishment of the first church in Antioch. She came to the Washington County Infirmary, she saw "twenty-six children of every condition amid older people of the vilest and most profane characters" (quoting her own words) and she

---

[34] The writer is chiefly indebted for the data of this section to pp. 10-11, *Child Placing in Ohio*, by Esther McClain, Division of Charities, Ohio Department of Public Welfare, Columbus, 1928.
[35] *Ibid.*, p. 11.

started to conquer public opinion and prejudice by taking several of these children, nine to begin with, and later reaching the number of thirty-five, into her "Children's Home." She saw beyond the institution, however, and visualized child placing of the right kind for these children. Her success in finding good foster homes was a surprise to many, and the finding of permanent family homes became an important part of her work. From a private enterprise, she later sought legislation to make "Children's Homes" public institutions, and after one defeat in 1864, a bill was passed in 1866, "An Act for the Establishment, Support and Regulation of Children's Homes in the Several Counties of the State of Ohio." Thus Washington County at Marietta acquired the first "Children's Home" in the state.

9. *The Michigan State Public School*

The unsatisfactory care of children in almshouses was a stimulus, not only to the founding of private institutions and public county houses for children only, as in Connecticut, Indiana and Ohio, but also to the Michigan State Public School, or state institution for dependent children.[36]

In 1869, Governor Baldwin, after visiting several poorhouses, appointed a commission to investigate the subject of charitable, preventive and reformatory institutions. The commission made a two year exhaustive study of dependent children in the county almshouses, and the methods of caring for such children, public charges, in other states. They reported that there were about 600 children under sixteen years of age in the poorhouses of Michigan, pointed out the degrading influences of such surroundings, recommended their removal and the adoption of one of the following plans: first, a state placing out agency by which dependent children should be removed from the county poorhouses and placed directly in private families; second, the removal of children to private orphan asylums to be supported therein at state expense until

---

[36] The paper from which this extract was taken was written by Miss Gertrude Quinlan and is now in the files of the present writer. See also G. A. Merrill, "State Public Schools for Dependent and Neglected Children" in *Report of Committee on History of Child Saving,* 1893, pp. 204-226.

placed in families; third, the establishment of a state primary school "after the plan of that at Monson, Massachusetts." The commission also urged the importance of supervision of adopted or indentured children. The legislature of 1871 to whom the report was submitted went a step farther and passed a law creating a state public school for *dependent children* to which all destitute children in the state who were public charges were to be removed and from which they were to be placed out in families as soon as possible. The State Public School was opened at Coldwater in May, 1874. Michigan therefore was the first state to establish an exclusive state system for the care of all destitute children who became public charges.

Subsequent legislation authorized the commitment to the School of neglected and ill-treated children. Two years after the Act establishing the public school, i. e. in 1873, the legislature provided that each county should have a county officer or agent appointed by the governor to investigate applications from families desiring to receive children and to visit children placed in homes in his county from any of the state institutions. There was also one state agent appointed by the Board of Control with the same duties.

10. *The Jewish Foster Home and Orphan Asylum in Philadelphia*

Not only to rescue children from poverty and wretchedness, but specifically to save Jewish children from losing their ancient religious faith, was a motive for founding the above institution.[37] The motto of the home is:

> In deeds of love, unselfish, great,
> Men must their faith attest;
> To God this Home we dedicate,
> Through love it will be blessed.

[37] The account which follows is based upon a manuscript now in the files of the present writer, written by Miss Pauline Gallub, who acknowledges indebtedness to S. M. Fleischman, *The History of the Jewish Foster Home and Orphan Asylum of Philadelphia, 1855-1905*, published 1905. The Rebecca Gratz named was the unconscious prototype for the Rebecca of Scott's Ivanhoe. See Philipson, *Letters of Rebecca Gratz*, Philadelphia, 1929.

For years Rebecca Gratz had been secretary of the Philadelphia Orphan Asylum, and for many years had she seen Jewish children accepted by this non-sectarian organization—non-sectarian in name, Christian in religion and education. Raised as Christians, indentured to Christians, they returned when young men and women, to their parents or relatives and found themselves among a people of whose culture they had little or no knowledge, for whose faith and religious principles they had no sympathy, and whose manners and customs were strange to them.

Many were the times, too, when she saw Jewish widows and widowers struggling daily with their orphans but unwilling to "barter the spirit for the body."

Miss Gratz began to write about the plight of these dependent Jewish children in *The Occident;* also to stir up her personal friends, and to hold meetings in the synagogues. After five years of desultory effort a fund of

$140.87 had been collected through the newspapers. The few signs of enthusiasm and interest had waned and there the fund would have remained had not the interest of a few noted women in the Jewish community been awakened. Walking leisurely down Chestnut Street, three ladies were aroused by the miserable sight of a number of ragged children selling matches. They began to discuss the poverty-stricken condition of these children and decided that some means ought to be found for providing care for them. They recalled the appeals written in the "Occident" by the "Daughter of Israel," recalled also that a small fund existed and decided to appeal to Rebecca Gratz for assistance.

In February, 1855, an informal meeting was held and the Ladies Society was formed. Later a constitution and by-laws were drafted, prefaced by the preamble—"Deeply impressed with the necessity for providing a home for destitute and unprotected children of Jewish parentage, the ladies of the several congregations have associated to form an institution denominated the Jewish Foster Home, wherein the orphans or children of Indigent Israelites may be rescued from the evils of ignorance and vice, comfortably provided for, instructed in moral and religious duties and thus prepared to become useful members of society."

On May 1 of that year a house located at 799 North Seventh Street was opened with five children. After twenty years of struggle the Ladies Society transferred their administrative powers to the men "with particular reference to obtaining financial assistance and performing executive duties."

At the time of the inception of the Jewish Foster Home there existed only two other foster homes in the United States for the care of Jewish children—the Hebrew Orphan Asylum of New York City, founded in 1822, and the New Orleans Jewish Orphans Home, founded in 1855. The children in the home were drawn from New York, the southern part of the United States, and the inner parts of Pennsylvania; but the majority came from the city of Philadelphia.

11. *The Hebrew Sheltering Guardian Society*

The second institution for Jewish children in New York City was the Hebrew Sheltering Guardian Society founded in 1879, the motto of which is "Shelter us under the shadow of Thy wing." We shall have occasion in our last chapter to mention the work of this institution and its Home Bureau in the twentieth century. At the time it was founded, there was in New York City only the Hebrew Orphan Asylum to care for dependent Jewish children under Jewish auspices. This one institution was thought, by those who took the lead in founding The Hebrew Sheltering Guardian Society, to be inadequate to the needs of Jewish children. When the new Home was opened, Mrs. P. J. Joachimson, president, made this statement as to its origin and purposes:[38]

This new home for Jewish children who otherwise would be unprotected or be found in institutions of other denominations, is now, under God's favor, open to your inspection. We trust that you will be pleased with the arrangements for the comfort of the children. We have endeavored from the start to bring into operation all the improvements found in the best institutions of this class. We will endeavor to make good and reputable members of the community of these little ones by

---

[38] *First Annual Report,* Hebrew Sheltering Guardian Society, pp. 3-4.

properly educating them. My own experience in connection with charitable institutions has convinced me that unless we take care of our children, they become lost to our religion, and that it is the duty of Jewish men and women to be very vigilant to prevent such consequences. Our Holy Writ instructs us that when King Pharaoh's daughter saved the infant Moses, recognizing him as a Jewish child, she immediately sent for a Jewish woman to nurse him. This is a lesson to us this day, and we have to take care and nurse the neglected and abandoned Jewish children because we are Jewesses. . . .

It is our benevolent purpose and religious aim to take care of such Jewish children as by law are required to be placed in an institution removed from all vicious influences, and from which the inmates are to be prepared to go forth into the world properly educated to elevate themselves in the ranks of society by honest industry and moral worth.

And after ten years the president of the Asylum remarked that without the work of the institution, "1493 Jewish children would have been lost to our faith—placed, that is, in other non-Jewish institutions."

12. *The New York Catholic Protectory*

In the next chapter there will also be reference to the part which a desire to safeguard the religion of Catholic children played in the founding of this institution.

II. ORPHAN ASYLUMS AS THEY SEEMED TO INMATES AND NEIGHBORS

To remove children from the mixed almshouses, where they were in close contact with adults representing every degree of depravity of character and defectiveness of mind and body, and to house them in so-called orphan asylums in groups by themselves, was obviously an advance in child care. However, it is probably difficult for most of us to visualize the actual life of children in orphanages and to imagine how life (both the bitter and the sweet) in these institutions seemed to the children themselves. The statements which follow are by former residents in institutions. They have been given to the writer in answer to his request that they who had experienced institutional life should state fairly and without exaggeration just what happened to them as children, and how they felt. The first is by a man who is a national figure but who, to protect some of those from whom he differed and who are yet living, from indiscriminate criticism, prefers not to have his name used.

Life for the typical boy in an institution at the time when I was in one, meant essentially shelter, the actual necessities in the way of clothes, and food which primarily served the purpose of preventing starvation, rather than scientific or, may I say, common sense nourishment. The attitude of those responsible for the institution was that the boys and girls were unfortunate objects of charity, and therefore should be content with whatever was done for them.

I demonstrated to the satisfaction of the Board of Managers where I was, based upon thirteen years of experience, that aside from the bread and milk bill of the institution it cost more and involved more labor and trouble to prepare the meals for the limited staff of employees than it did for the one hundred and eighty children in the institution. The limited educational program, covering primarily the "three R's," and the unwillingness to accept the opportunities of the public school system of education reflects the institution's attitude of not wanting to be bothered with having the children think too much of their education. While I managed, with the aid of friends from the outside, to break through this tradition and secure for myself and many others the privilege of going through public school from the fifth grade, it so greatly upset the routine of the institution as to make the practice very unpopular and very difficult for the boys and girls who were involved.

Well do I remember the amazement of the matron and the ridicule she heaped upon me when I ventured to urge a plan of giving me an opportunity of entering high school. Her question as to "who had ever heard of an orphan boy having a high school education" reflected the attitude of the institution towards me as an ambitious boy, as well as the others in the institution. For the most part the boys who were in the institution during my experience were indentured out to farmers or mechanics or others, without any obligation of adoption or relationship other than that of apprentice. Fortunately, for me, because of my lameness, I was not eligible, although very definite efforts were made to have me taken by a number of different people. I remember one, a tailor, who was made to believe that I could more than earn my board because of my experience in sewing. In other words, the institution did not mean opportunity to the boys. It did not mean preparing them for life's responsibilities and opportunities. It meant, primarily, treating them as so many paupers dependent upon charity, under conditions which would not tolerate anyone inquiring too closely as to whether everything was being done that should be done for the individual boy. What a difficult time those who indicated such interest had!

I do hope this will not be interpreted as a lack of appreciation for the good intentions of the lady managers and those who contributed to the support of the institution. Bless their souls! Their ignorance of actual conditions because they thought it more charitable to pay their fines rather than visit the institution; the lack of development of standards through conference and exchange of ideas on the part of institutional leaders; and the willingness of the general public to assume what was done in the name of charity is done wisely and scientifically, are some of the contributing causes for the lack of efficiency in the management of the institution, but no one should be permitted to challenge the sincerity and devotion of the good people who served as members of the Board of Lady Managers and those who contributed to the support of such institutions.

The next statement is by a Lutheran minister in Pennsylvania, who says of his story:

This picture, while it has a touch of prejudice, is not an unnaturally dark picture. I have not exaggerated any one part. In fact, some of the darker details I have purposely left untouched.

Henry Adams in his autobiography says: "Boys are wild animals rich in the treasures of sense." Perhaps it was the sense of sight which was strongest in a delicate, timid, young lad as he stood one cold February morning between two gentlemen of the church, looking up at a huge, dismal brick building, pitted against a dark, grey sky, surrounded by black, dead, leafless trees. It was an orphan asylum (orphan home—being a term used to hide reality). It was to be this boy's future home—for how long—no one had even a dim notion, nor did it matter much. Perhaps "walls do not a prison make" but to a homeless lad of nine this scene was not cheerful nor to his liking. . . .

Sad, disappointed, afraid, yet eager was he to see more of this huge thing, so he followed the two men through the narrow doorway. There along a long narrow hall stood a line of boys, lined up according to height, all standing erect without a smile. Watching them was a tall, military-looking German (not forgetting the mustache and glasses). He was the superintendent—my future master. Although he greeted me kindly, my interest was in that long line of boys, who had somehow sensed a new arrival, and were craning their necks for a sight of him. I have often wondered since if that was the first time I became conscious of myself. There I stood—a thing apart—something to be looked at, out of curiosity and even hostility—for boys in an orphan home are strangely self-centered. But whether I had thoughts at that time, I know not. If I did they would be rudely halted by the clanging of a loud bell, which I discovered meant dinner.

I soon found myself in the largest room I had ever seen, where there were dozens of long tables, around which crowded hungry boys and girls. It was in the jangling of knives and dishes that I found a sense of relief, of forgetfulness, and even managed to eat. The meal ended with some sort of an unintelligible German prayer.

My two guardians were soon closeted behind a door on which was nailed the imposing word "office," while I was left to wander as I saw fit. To escape curious glances and open mouths, I wandered into all the empty rooms, and to my delight soon discovered a library. If I had any thought that this room might prove a refuge for me, I was doomed to disappointment; for I afterward learned that it was only on special occasions and with special permission that a book could be used. Even in 1913 all the homelike things and kindnesses of such an institution were but a show and a sham to allay the suspicions and idle curiosity of visitors and social workers (that radical and hated class). No, kind reader, think me not unjust in speaking so. Since 1913 this institution, with all others of its kind in the State of New York, has come under the supervision of the state welfare department. The shams that were are now beautiful realities. The prevailing idea of the trustees has changed from "Anything is good enough for these children" to "Nothing is too good for children, especially under such circumstances."

It was not long before my friends came to shake hands and bid me goodbye with all kind wishes. As the heavy door closed, a new chapter in my life opened. Life was now begun in earnest.

During those next few weeks of readjustment and the making of friends, I experienced all the pangs of loneliness and homesickness, and even developed perhaps a certain stoicism, which went a long way in helping me through my first year in the ministry.

The superintendent I found to be a kind but stern man, a military man of Bismarck's day, and a priest for form and order. Often during those following years did I feel the smarting raps of his rubber hose across my back. For I was a thorough child, and soon found myself up to all the pranks and mischief of animals restrained by the lash.

In an institution the individual counts for nothing! Nor is the welfare, temperament, or disposition of any one child taken into consideration. What might be good or healthy for one is taken to be good or healthy for all. Life must be uniform, logical, and conventional. Thus life becomes stereotyped. The duties, tasks, and experiences of one day become the duties, tasks, and experiences of all the other three hundred and sixty-four days of the year. The activities of every hour are planned. Let me give you a little more intimate insight into the actual working and daily routine of this life as I experienced it.

At six o'clock in the morning our day began. For what reason I have never been able to find out except the old proverb "Early to bed and early to rise makes a man healthy, wealthy and wise." Ten minutes was allowed for dressing, after which we were all marched down to that same narrow hall for our morning calisthenics. Here it was that I tasted the first bit of cruel and torturous punishment I had ever known. If anything (such as a cut while shaving) had aroused our master's German ire, he would make us stand in a long line and hold out our arms horizontally until our faces assumed all sorts of agonizing twists. Anyone who has ever tried holding out his arms any length of time knows the meaning of such an experience.

Promptly at seven o'clock we were marched to our morning bowl of oatmeal, dry bread and coffee, which was served between German prayers and devotions. For religion held an important place in the daily routine, as we shall see later. Then we were brought back to our dormitories and each had to make his own bed. Perhaps you are interested to know how the work was done. Who was to wash all the dishes? Who was to clean all the rooms? Obviously outside help could not be brought in and paid to do such work. So the girls were given the work of the dining room and kitchen; while the boys with pails and brooms proceeded to sweep and scrub the floors, dust, and clean the windows. The smaller boys and girls, not able to do either, were fitted out with needles and thread to learn the art of sewing. "Useful training" was the argument. And it was that; for it assured me a place in the kingdom of bachelordom.

School was not neglected. That they held the idea that education was the panacea for all evil, I doubt. At least they knew that illiteracy was not necessary. Two teachers divided the work between them, each taking four grades. Recitation was the method of instruction. While one class recited, the next class studied. Whether that method was good or not, I cannot say. All details are hazy at this time, except the picture of that green-walled room with its many benches. Yet it enabled us to pass the New York State Regents examination, not a mean accomplishment. One morning the superintendent surprised us at devotions by telling us that we were to have two new teachers, and we were to obey their every wish. He ended by saying, "A new broom sweeps clean." Mayhap that amused us, at least we decided to prove it. We did, to our own sorrow.

From 4.30 to 5.30 in the afternoon we were free; at liberty to do as we wished, provided we wished not the impossible and stayed within the bounds of the fence. Football, baseball, "shinny" (an orphan boy's game of golf) fights, flying kites, all came in turn as the seasons and king of sports decided.

At six o'clock food and prayers. Then to study, or possibly to read a good story, if no one was watching. Until at eight o'clock that dismal, haunting bell sounded for the last time. Soon a strange solitary silence. The spirit of night and of sleep had again spread her dark heavy mantle over her children.

Summer and vacation to most boys means, as it meant to Henry Adams, "rolling in the grass, or wading in the brook, or swimming in salt ocean, or sailing in the bay, or fishing in the creeks, or exploring the pine woods and hills"—but to my companions and me it meant three hours each morning of religious instruction in the German language, and then a hot summer afternoon's work of weeding or hoeing on the farm. The only real vacation was an occasional half-hour of sport in the "ol' swimmin' hole," or an afternoon in the hay fields. To lie on the top of a load of hay, with its sweet smell, and look up through the cracks of one's straw hat, at the blue sky, dotted here and there with lazy white clouds, was one of the most delightful sensations of my childhood.

Yet there was one day of the year when all had to be different—the day of all days for children—Christmas. On a Sunday afternoon about a month before Christmas we were all told to think of two presents we wanted Santa Claus (we knew there was no Santa Claus) to bring us, one for twenty-five cents and one for fifty cents. For the next few weeks we searched eagerly hrough all the available magazines and newspapers for advertisements of things wonderful, precious, and not exceeding fifty cents. We usually ended by picking out a knife or a belt. Then anxious waiting until Christmas eve.

Religion to a child is mostly a matter of sight and of hearing. The scene of that chapel on Christmas eve, with its soft music and the singing of "Stille Nacht, Heilige Nacht," with its two huge decorated Christmas trees on either side of a cleverly constructed village of Bethlehem in miniature, with angels and a lighted star, with shepherds watching their flocks on built-up hills of mossy stones, and Mary and Joseph in a lowly cattle shed kneeling by the manger, wherein lay the newly born Christ-child—that scene still haunts me at this date. Yet to a child it was quickly forgotten in his hurry and eagerness for the long-waited presents. For a few hours and days all else was forgotten—we were completely happy.

Would it be altogether out of place to speak of the religious training for a moment? For be it understood, this institution was under the control of the church, with all its stiffness and cold formality. Of religious education, such as church leaders today speak, there was none. All instruction was in the German language (of which most of us were completely ignorant), and consisted of constant memorization. Luther's "Small Catechism" was memorized from beginning to end, chapters of the Bible, and many hymns of the church. On one occasion we had to learn a long hymn which began

> Voeglein in hohem Baum

I could remember that first line, but the second line constantly eluded me until my youthful genius asserted itself with this result,

> Voeglein in hohem Baum
> Pick up a stone and knock him down.

But there was no need to rejoice in my ability as it got me into very serious trouble.

Thus religious education as a whole meant simply the memorizing of words without their meaning, without adapting any of the material to the needs of the child.

It was this same rigid religious conventionality which produced another failing, at least to my mind, as I now look back. It was the complete separation of sexes. Boys are kept as far as possible from the girls, and to be seen talking at any time to a girl meant severe punishment. This brought vague notions into a child's head—why should it be so? What was there wrong in it? The result was that after a boy or girl left the home at the age of sixteen there came a complete reaction. That strange desire coupled with complete ignorance brought disastrous effects. And many of those fine young lives have been spoiled or seriously handicapped. I know this from the lives of some of my companions.

So passed four years of my life with little or no variation. Until one morning I was called into that forbidding-looking office. What it was for I could not imagine, but I supposed I had done something wrong again. Can you imagine my surprise then, when asked if I would like to attend school in R——, to study for the ministry. I, who had never been out of B——, who had been in bondage and who longed to be free! I never heard the latter part of the sentence that limited my choice to the ministry. In fact, I didn't even think, I simply said "Yes." So one September morning, with a little grip in one hand, and the superintendent's hand in the other, I walked up that long lane for the last time as a child out into life. Another chapter had closed. What awaited me holds no interest here.

The next story explains itself:

STATEMENT BY AN ORPHAN ASYLUM BOY WHO BECAME A SUPERINTENDENT
E. J. HENRY

When I was about four years old, my father was drowned in the North River, New York City. My mother was not a success in managing her financial affairs and in a short time she had nothing on which to support her family. She had a sister in Cleveland who was a business woman, but no housekeeper. This aunt induced my mother to come to Cleveland and keep house for her, while she looked after the store. My mother accepted and started west. We were soon settled in the new home. I was a normal, healthy boy and full of mischief, and my aunt was not accustomed to children. Naturally, I was in the way. My aunt, unknown to my mother, went to the officials of the institution and found that by paying a nominal sum, they would take care of me. When she first broached the subject my mother absolutely refused to have me go and threatened to take me and go elsewhere, but pressure was brought to bear and she finally consented to place me in the institution temporarily. Of course, after I had been placed, everything went lovely at home and I remained in the institution.

I was very fortunate in this, that the institution in which I was placed was one of the best of its kind, but I will never forget the impression that was made upon me when I entered that large building. It was no "Daddy-Long-Legs" affair, for in those days people had the means to provide only the necessities.

When my mother and I were waiting in the room where they received children, I was frightened, wondering what kind of a place it was, and what they were going to do to me, as I had had the threat held over my head that if I were not a good boy, I would be put in an institution; but to my surprise, the matron was very pleasant and it impressed me that she was interested in me more than she was in my mother, which is a big asset to any matron. After taking my name, my mother's and the address, she told my mother that she could see me once a week and that they expected her to clothe me.

I then went down a long unfurnished hall to a large room, and there I found about twenty-five boys, averaging from six to fourteen years. I was the smallest boy in the department. There were no furnishings in the room, except a small table and chair, in which the governess, as we called her, sat. The floors were of rather rough boards, but very clean. It was the boys' job to do the scrubbing. As I was the smallest boy, no doubt I had the sympathies of the others, so I did not have a very hard time, but my mischievous trend often got me into trouble.

The Board of Managers of the institution were exceptional women; their hearts were in the work and they not only gave financial assistance, but personal service, and it was my very great privilege to get acquainted with them. Being the smallest, they called me the baby of the family.

When night came, we all had to be in our places in the playroom. We took off our shoes and stockings and placed them in front of the bench where we sat, before which we knelt for our devotional exercises. Then we formed in line and marched upstairs to the dormitories.

There were ten iron beds in this dormitory; two boys slept in each bed. The governess in charge had her hands full until all had gone to sleep. This dormitory was a very plain room—no pictures on the walls and no furniture except the beds.

In the morning when the rising bell rang, we all jumped up, dressed and marched downstairs where we washed and combed our hair. The dining room and kitchen were in the basement. We marched down single file, to long, roughly made tables, such as you see on picnic grounds; we had wooden benches to sit on. There was mush and milk for breakfast. At noon we would have soup and bread and water, or once in a while chopped meat made into a gravy to put on our bread. At night we would have bread and milk—and only one helping. We growing boys were never satisfied when the bell tapped to get up from the table—there was no danger of stomach trouble from overeating in those days. I never held this against the management, as I know they were working hard to provide even what we had.

There was about the same number of girls and their ages ranged about the same as the boys'. Very strict discipline was maintained. The girls' playroom was across the hall from the boys' and the playgrounds were separated by a high board fence. Sometimes there would be weeks at a time, when brothers and sisters in the same building would have no chance to talk with each other. This was rather hard on many of the boys and girls, but the management thought that was the way it should be done.

There was no such thing as playground equipment in those days, but when we were turned loose in what we called the play-yard we got busy digging caves, building shacks, and in fact, we constructed our own equipment and it worked. I really think if we followed that line of thought to a certain extent today, the children would appreciate it more. It is human nature for the boys to build and provide a shelter and the girls to look after their dolls and keep house. Give the boys material and tools to construct according to their ideas and the girls cloth and old dishes. You will see them a happy bunch of children and no accidents.

Our institution always believed in the public school. We never had a school in the building or on the grounds. Going to public school gave us a chance to mix with the girls and boys outside, although we always had a feeling that because we were in an institution, we were not entitled to the same privileges as those living in their own homes. I was in the institution about three years. They allowed me to go home to my mother for a couple of days about once in six months, as she was paying the large sum of $1.00 per week for my board. During that time, I saw many boys come and go. Some would come back and tell about the farm, the country, etc., and I thought it would be a wonderful thing if I could go into the country into a home, but my mother would not consent. The superintendent talked to her but she would not allow it, as in those days children were indentured or apprenticed and many of them legally adopted. Finally the superintendent took it up with me, thinking possibly I might have some influence with my mother. They told me of the beauties of the country, about the cows, horses, sheep and chickens, and naturally it "got me" and I coaxed and coaxed and finally persuaded my mother to allow me to go. She consented but with the understanding that I should not be given for adoption. Never will I forget the day I was called into the office and told by the superintendent that he had a very nice home for me in the country, with good religious people, a widow and her grown daughter. They wanted a little boy who could do the errands and small chores around the place and they thought that I was just the boy. It happened that at that time we had in the institution three or four very pretty puppies and one of them was given to me as a pet. I told the superintendent that if I could take my puppy, I would like to go, so he said he would write and ask if I could bring the pup. In a few days he told me that he had just received a letter asking him to send boy and pup. I was then ready to go.

It was on a beautiful October morning that we started. We took the train to a little country station and walked about a mile and a quarter to this farmhouse. I carried the pup under my coat. The superintendent, who was with me, carried my bundle—what clothes I had. I received a very cordial greeting by the family. They were good people, very religious and proud, but poor. The home had been investigated and visited before I went there and I have no complaint to make regarding the treatment I had. However, I always had a feeling of being dependent; that other children had the right of way. I think I have never overcome this feeling. I had to work very hard as I was the only man on the place, but the neighbors were very kind and by my helping them with such work as driving the team, etc., for three or four days, they would come and do a day's work and that is the way we got along. With the people with whom I lived, schooling seemed to be a second consideration. They did not think that a boy situated as I was really needed an education, as I would always have to work out, not having any relatives that could help me or give me prestige. This is a matter that should be very carefully considered today when placing children in foster homes.

There is a tendency to make the child feel indirectly that it is dependent, not only by the family, but by other people in the community. If such an attitude is detected, the child should be removed from that community, because sooner or later he will leave. If he cannot get away any other way, he will run away. This is one great reason why so many children leave their foster homes.

I earned my way while in my new home. As I look back and think of the work I did, regardless of the weather, I wonder how I stood it. What schooling I got while there was earned by my perseverance. I had to do all the chores in the winter weather, then walk one and one-half miles to school, and when I got home just about dark, do all the chores at night, most always by lantern light. However, I do not look upon it today as a hardship, but as the making of me. As I said before, school was secondary with the people with whom I was living, and that could be attended to if there was nothing more to be done at home.

You must remember, however, in those days, there was not the supervision we have now, but I am very happy to state that it was our institution that first started the follow-up system for children placed in foster homes. This was brought about by such cases as my own, as they came to realize, in my case as well as many others, that things would have been different with me had they visited the home and advised the people of their obligations to me regarding school. We also must bear in mind that in those days children in institutions were regarded much as the dwellers in poor houses.

I remained in this home until I was seventeen and then started on my own hook as a messenger boy in a nearby town.

While working in this capacity, I took up telegraphy and was just about ready for a position when I was persuaded to go into the mercantile business. Not having anybody to advise with, the wages offered me were responsible for my decision. I went to work as a clerk instead of a telegrapher. I worked in a dry goods store for about two years and from there I went into a shoe store. The wage offered was again the dominating factor. This position was with the John Wanamaker Company of Philadelphia. After a time the institution in which I had lived attempted to induce me to take up the work, but as I was still very young, I felt that I could not assume any such responsibility. The institution called me into its service three different times, but each time I would receive a call from the store in Philadelphia, offering me a better wage. The officials of the institution did not want to stand in the way of my advancement, but as I grew older, I thought more and more of the debt I owed to the children who were in the same position that I had been in in my early years. The institution again called me—this time to do the follow-up work of the children who had been placed in foster homes. It was then I really made up my mind that this was my work. I resigned from the Wanamaker Company and at a smaller salary took up the work with this institution, which I followed for ten years. At this time I was urged to take up Fresh Air Work and after due consideration resigned from the institution and accepted the Superintendency of the Children's Fresh Air Camp. While in this branch of the service we succeeded in interesting leaders in the Anti-Tuberculosis League in our Fresh Air Camp. We worked together and established what we called the Tent Colony for tubercular children. This Tent Colony grew to such a size that we finally turned it over to the city. There now exists a wonderful Sanitarium, built especially for the children afflicted with tuberculosis. I served as superintendent of the Fresh Air Work for over three years. The Orphan Asylum then requested me to take over the superintendency, which I did. My greatest reason for doing this was that I felt I owed the organization a great deal; that the surroundings of its then present site were not suitable for the work; that it had not progressed with the times, and I could not bear to think that this particular institution was falling behind, a follower, instead of a leader. So I returned to the institution and put all my energy and thought into the work, with the idea of moving out into the country. Today, my dreams have been realized and we have what is considered one of the finest institutions in the country. However, I have tried to emphasize that buildings are only a small part of the institution. The children need something far greater and we are trying to provide this great need— home, health and happiness . . . .

After all, I feel that my life has not been wasted, notwithstanding the handicaps that I had to overcome early in life, and what I have done I see no reason why others could not do—as well, if not a great deal better.

The Woman Who Was Neighbor to Children in an Orphan Asylum

And here is an illuminating story of a mother and her children who lived across the street from an orphan asylum and made friends through a picket fence with the children inside.[39] Out of such deep and spontaneous understanding of the feelings and needs of children has come and will always come the betterment in the processes of care for dependent and neglected children.

THE OTHER SIDE OF THE FENCE

About a mile from the "four corners," the center of the city, on a side street occupying a city block, was the Rochester Orphan Asylum. Two large three-story buildings connected by a frame structure stood in the middle of the square leaving two open spaces at either end to be used as playgrounds. These yards were entirely enclosed by a wooden picket

---

[39]From a letter to the present writer by Mrs. Theodore Steinhausen, a daughter of the woman who was the neighbor in question.

fence about four feet high. On the other side of the street there were a number of homes surrounded by lovely gardens.

The street was a private parkway with beautiful elm and maple trees. Many happy children played in the park. These were watched enviously by the little orphans from their world beyond the fence.

Across from the main entrance of the orphanage lived a family—mother, father and five children. These children have a happy memory of a mother who cared about the little ones living in the orphanage and who made her little ones care.

As one of these children, I can see my mother, leaving for downtown, cross the street and slowly walk to the corner on the outside of the fence. Depending on the time of day, there were few or many children on the other side, also walking to the corner. It was only a matter of a few hundred feet but that walk always took a long time—so much was there to tell "the mother on the other side." Those were the days of horse cars. The driver, seeing mother, would stop, clang-clang his gong, as much as to say, "I'll wait, but don't take too long."

The corner would be reached. Three or four children deep, pressing their little faces against the fence, would call "Goodbye, goodbye, what time are you coming back? We'll watch for you." And watch for her they did.

When the time came the children would just naturally be in that corner of the yard waiting. One street car would pass, perhaps two. "Here she comes!" some sentinel would shout at last. With glad greetings they would run to greet her and begin to walk slowly up the street with her always on their side of the fence.

Again there seemed to be so much to talk about. Not always, but sometimes, there would be a bag of animal crackers. A friend once asked me, "As a child, what seemed to you to be the biggest treat?" I said, "Animal crackers!" The reason I now know was that we five were often allowed to play "on the other side of the fence"! Mother had made us blue checked gingham aprons the same as the orphans wore, so the children accepted us and when there was a treat we, too, had our share. Mother must have been very wise because I do not remember animal crackers at home. I can only remember putting my hand between the pickets and closing my eyes waiting for the animal cracker to drop in my hand. Then the surprise, "I've got a bear!" "I've got a lion!" "I've got a monkey!" We would all get together, compare our animals and slowly begin to nibble, first one foot, then another and so on, always leaving the head until the last.

There were other treats, sometimes an organ-grinder with a real monkey that would climb over the picket fence, to the great joy of the children. Instead of mother paying the organ-grinder, by some magic she would produce many pennies to give the children for the monkey to collect. This always guaranteed a long performance. We never gave up our pennies in a hurry and the organ-grinder never left until he was sure he had every one.

Then one day "Frog-legged George" appeared with a popcorn wagon. He must have heard the news about the orphans' friend for at regular intervals the whistle of the popcorn man, the ding-ding bell of the waffle man or the sing-song "ice cream, penny a lick, eat too much and it'll make you sick" would bring mother to the door and if we were not already on the other side of the fence, we would hurry into our blue aprons and over we would run for these treats could only be had "on the other side of the fence." I have often wondered, "Did mother know?" These little ones looking out from an enclosure, fenced in, were allowed to go out only on special occasions, and then in uniform, marching two by two "like the elephant and the kangaroo," with some one at the beginning and at the end of the line. Looking out, as they did, into yards where there were happy children with mothers, fathers, brothers, sisters and freedom! Did she know that by giving them treats that we could only have by being on their side of the fence, somehow she evened up things just a little bit?

Another memory is of our regular attendance at Sunday afternoon service held in the orphanage. A vivid recollection is of mother's and father's return from a long vacation in Europe and their having to pass through an aisle of orphans who were lustily singing a welcome song. The raising of a new flag on our lawn was as much a matter of pride for the orphans as for us.

These memories could easily fill a book; their sharing of our Christmas tree—our sharing of their New Year's celebration. So on and on, until the second day of July the orphans were told that their friend would not walk on her side of the fence any more. We were much touched and troubled when the morning of July Fourth came, not to hear any celebration across the way. Father went over to beg the matron to do all in her power to help the children not to think of mother in sorrow but with joy. They could not, for they shared our sorrow. About a month later, chartered cars stopped at the corner of the street, the children walked down the street on the outside of the fence, were taken to a lake resort near Rochester and a very happy day was spent in memory of their friend.

One winter night two years later the orphanage was destroyed by fire and many lives lost. We were grateful that mother, the orphans' friend, was spared this suffering. The orphanage was never rebuilt, but as is many times the case, the tragedy resulted in ultimate good. The Rochester Orphan Asylum is now ideally located on the picturesque Pinnacle hills on the outskirts of the city. There are no enclosures, the children roam all over the hillside, but they will always need a friend "on the other side of the fence."

We have presented only fragmentary statements relating to the lives of dependent, neglected and destitute children in various cities, and only meager descriptions of the emotions which led a few persons in a few places to establish institutions where children could be gathered from mixed almshouses and the streets; yet it is hoped that enough has been given to enable the reader to sense the reasons for the trend, away from almshouses and toward the building of orphan asylums, that has been going on for over a hundred years.

It is hoped, also, that a few genuine glimpses have been given of the lives of children in orphan asylums, and of their usual way out of them, if not back to their own homes, then through indenture, into some other home where, with very little knowledge of their weal or woe on the part of those who had gathered them into the institution and sent them out again, they were well-nigh universally expected to pay their own way in work.

III. Summary

The Development of Institutional Substitutes for the Mixed Almshouses in the United States

The following statement[40] may serve to summarize the history of almshouse care for children and the growth of orphan asylums during the nineteenth century:

The building and maintenance of orphan asylums by private funds contributed by various groups of charitably disposed persons went on in the United States and in England during the whole time that the mixed almshouse itself was developing. Many such institutions were in charge of persons of a particular religious denomination and were really charitable agencies of the church itself. Such was the first orphan asylum founded in the United States by the Ursuline Convent in New Orleans,[41] to care for children orphaned by the Natchez Indian massacre of 1729. Such also was the Bethesda Orphan House founded in Savannah, Georgia, in 1738 by the Methodist preacher, George Whitefield, with funds collected in England.

An examination of the list of 77 orphan asylums and other institutional agencies for children listed by Mr. Folks,[42] and built from 1729 to 1851, shows that 31 bear names indicating connection with a single religious denomination. Four other institutions of the same list located in Philadelphia (1822), New York (1836), Providence (1838) and Avondale, Ohio (1843), were specifically for the care of colored children; two—Onondaga County Orphan Asylum, Syracuse, New York (1845), and Jefferson County Orphan Asylum, Watertown, New York (1848)—bear county names; a few others, like the Boston Female Orphan Asylum (1800), and the Washington City Orphan Asylum (1815), bear names of cities; and many others with various characteristic names

---

[40] Based largely on Folks, *Care of Destitute, Neglected and Delinquent Children*, 1911 edition.

[41] *Ibid.*, p. 9.   [42] *Ibid.*, pp. 52-55.

indicating functions and sometimes also supporters, evidently bear the name of the city only to indicate their location. Apparently some of the 77 were in part at least municipal; some were county; some racial; some strictly denominational, and others partially inter-denominational, in auspices and support. In a majority of cases undoubtedly their support was derived largely from private contribution, rather than from public taxes. But whatever their control and support, the significant thing here emphasized is that, beginning in the eighteenth century and developing with increasing rapidity during succeeding decades of the first half of the nineteenth century, separate institutions were growing up and in effect competing with the growing mixed almshouses as agencies for the care of dependent children. This growth of orphan asylums, largely under private auspices, continued more and more rapidly during the second half of the nineteenth century, as shown by the numbers of institutions founded during each decade of the century, and still in existence in 1923.[43] Not only were orphan asylums established and maintained for the destitute and neglected children who had no outstanding physical and mental defects, but special institutions were also gradually established for various classes of children with such defects. The tendency of all such institutions as fast as they were established, was to prevent some eligible children of each class from going to the mixed almshouses of their locality, and possibly to take out some who had already entered the almshouse.

All this segregation of children from the mixed almshouse, whether into orphan asylums or into special institutions for the deaf, blind, feeble-minded, etc., was plainly one step forward toward a recognition of the needs and capacities of these destitute and specially handicapped children as individuals. They were at least becoming recognized as a class of juvenile dependents, with needs somewhat different from the needs of adult dependents. The reader may, at this point, ask himself another question: "How

[43]See the Census report, 1923, *Children under Institutional Care,* Table 22.

far have such institutions really recognized the individuality of each child?"

Meanwhile, even within the circle of those who were administering the mixed almshouse itself, there were occasional signs of dissatisfaction and of change. For example, over a period of thirty-two years, from 1816 to 1848, there was a gradual separation of the dependent children of New York City from the other classes of the mixed almshouse population.[44] At the end of this period, 1,054 children were housed in ten new brick buildings erected for their shelter on Randall's Island. In short, a segregation of the children out of the New York mixed almshouse into a municipal orphan asylum had been effected. The name given to this group of buildings was "The Randall's Island Nurseries." Technically the children were still in the city almshouse, under the poor authorities of the city; actually they were in an orphan asylum consisting not of one huge congregate building, but of ten separate buildings. Under such conditions, an elementary schooling could be given to children of suitable age before they were indentured, returned to relatives, or otherwise restored to family life in the community. In Boston and Philadelphia a similar municipal segregation of children from other almshouse inmates went on. In Philadelphia they called the separate institution the Children's Asylum. The "Randall's Island Nurseries" of New York City, and the "Philadelphia Children's Asylum," are both examples of the process which was going on during the same period in England,[45] where the "separate" and "district schools" were being founded by a similar segregation of children from the mixed almshouses.

It should be pointed out, also, that in large cities, the desire to separate children from adults, or the purpose of isolating and controlling ophthalmia and other infectious and contagious diseases, were not the only motives operating; increasing numbers which had to be cared for in city almshouses had something to do

[44] Folks, *op. cit.*, 1911 edition, pp. 13-27.
[45] See below, Chapter IX, "Trends in England."

ORPHAN ASYLUMS

with the effort to segregate the children. Even grouped by themselves the 1,154 children who were finally installed on Randall's Island in New York City made a large institutional group.

In the smaller cities, of course, and in the county almshouses the stimulus to the segregation of children because of the pressure of numbers in the mixed almshouse was not so great. On the contrary, as we have already seen, the Yates Report[46] in New York State, 1824, found the almshouse group of children in the state at large of convenient size to form a school group. Mr. Yates argued that in almshouses the health and schooling of children could be looked after much better than was possible for those children who were being brought up in ignorance and idleness with parents who were merely assisted by unsupervised outdoor relief.[47] Just as county mixed almshouses were established in practically every county in New York as a result of the Yates Report, so also mixed almshouses became the rule in the rapidly growing new states west of the Alleghenies and in the Mississippi Valley.

In spite of all that was being accomplished during the early nineteenth century to separate dependent children from adult dependents by placing them in children's branches of city, county or state almshouses, in orphan asylums, special institutions for the blind, deaf, etc., the adult inmates of mixed almshouses continued for three-fourths of the nineteenth century to play the part of hosts and intimate daily companions and school-teachers to endless processions of destitute children who went "over the hills to the poorhouse" in a majority of the cities and populous counties of our rapidly growing group of states. Furthermore, in New York City, even the almshouse children who had been segregated from adult inmates were still exposed to the contagious influence of pauper and criminal adults who did much of the work of the children's sections of the City Almshouses.

---

[46]Folks, *op. cit.*, pp. 36-37.
[47]It should also be remembered that public schools and compulsory school attendance were then unknown.

By 1875 the tide of official dissatisfaction with care of children in mixed almshouses had risen so high that the Congress of the State Boards of Charities resolved that "the various State Boards of Charities use their influence to bring about such legislation in their respective states, as shall cause dependent children to be removed from county poorhouses, city almshouses and common jails, and from all association with adult paupers and criminals, and placed in families, asylums, reformatories or other appropriate institutions." During the year following this resolution over one thousand children were removed from the poorhouses and almshouses of New York State and were placed in families or in orphan asylums.

Naturally, as children were withdrawn from or refused admission to almshouses, the tendency to build orphan asylums, already strong, was stimulated.[48]

The growth of orphan asylums has kept up until the present day. The census figures of 1923 for children in institutions compared with the number in almshouses, tells the story. On January 1, 1923, there were present in all the almshouses of the United States only 1,992 children under sixteen years of age, and the total number admitted during the year was 4,715.[49] On February 1, of the same year, 1923, there were "in the care of institutions primarily for the care of dependents" 140,312 minors.[50] In spite of the comparatively small number of children remaining in almshouses, as previously observed, the end of almshouse life for little children has not yet fully come. If the reader thinks such a day should come, what is he ready to do about it in his own state? What substitutes for the almshouses should he wish to see established or developed further? We shall have occasion later to il-

---

[48] See William Pryor Letchworth, "Orphan Asylums and Other Institutions for the Care of Children," in *Annual Report of the Board of Charities of New York*, 1876, pp. 95-117.

[49] United States census report, 1923, *Paupers in Almshouses*, pp. 62-63.

[50] United States census report, 1923, *Children under Institutional Care*, p. 18.

lustrate further some of the limitations of orphan asylum care,[51] and we shall also point out some progressive activities among institutions for dependent children.[52] Suffice it to say, in closing this chapter, that enough evidence has been given to show that the escape from the mixed almshouse into the orphan asylum was in general a step forward for dependent and destitute children.

[51]See Chapter VIII. [52]See Chapter X.

Chapter VI

THE FORM OF INDENTURE REJECTED—DEVELOPMENT OF THE FREE FOSTER FAMILY HOME MOVEMENT

I. Emigration from Eastern Cities to Villages and Farms

From the illustrations given in the chapter on indenture, it is clear that indenture is characterized both by a form and by a spirit. In form, as we have said, it is a business contract. In spirit it demands at least enough work from a child to pay for what he costs his master. It is easy for persons who place dependent children in free foster homes to give up using the form of an indenture contract. It is hard to safeguard children from seven to fourteen years old, who are placed in free foster family homes, from overwork and from being treated as employees or drudges—conditions which were almost unavoidable under the old indenture contract.

Charles Loring Brace and The New York Children's Aid Society

Probably Charles Loring Brace[1] and the New York Children's Aid Society which he founded in 1853, were known to more people during the last thirty or forty years of the nineteenth century than any other child welfare worker and agency. Because of their nation-wide influence upon the aims and methods of other child welfare workers and agencies, unusual attention is given to the story of Mr. Brace and of the New York Children's Aid Society.

[1] For biographical data, the writer is primarily indebted to *The Life of Charles Loring Brace, chiefly told in his own letters.* Edited by his daughter, Emma Brace. New York, 1894.

Mr. Brace was a dynamic personality whose spirit is much needed in this day; nevertheless any attempt to keep this spirit shut up within the literal confines of the methods used by him in his day and generation will inevitably result in loss to some of the children of this generation.

Charles Loring Brace, founder of the New York Children's Aid Society in 1853, once for all consciously rejected the form of indenture, but he never completely emancipated himself and many of the thousands of children placed by the New York Children's Aid Society from the influence of its spirit.

Brace's home was in Hartford, Connecticut, and his mother having died when he was very young, he enjoyed a close intimacy with his father, with whom he read history and shared countless rambles in woods and fields and along New England trout brooks. His father was a teacher, and young Charles was fitted for Yale College at fourteen, but did not enter until he was sixteen. These two years were spent, according to his journal, in studying French, German, Spanish, English, Xenophon and Cicero, in writing poetry, and in many forms of recreation, including football, chess, backgammon, fishing, swimming and loafing. At fifteen he heard Bushnell's famous sermon on "Unconscious Influence" and was affected by it for life in his desire for genuineness and personal integrity. Entering college at sixteen, he soon joined the church and was noted while at Yale for his intense earnestness whether in boxing, football, classical studies or religious argument.

Out of college at twenty, he taught school for a year to get money to study theology. Writing that summer of his leisure time, he says: "Imagine me in my trailing, my rambling over mountains and by willow-fringed brooks, all my ecstasies over the fresh green meadows and waving woods and bright flowers and trout streams." A man so steeped in nature could not fail to believe later in the beneficent effect of the country upon boys and girls who had known only the slums of New York City. In the theological seminary at Yale in 1847 he was known as a liberal. Once he wrote to a friend, *"I am determined never for a moment to refuse hearing a truth because it is new, and never afraid to dig under a belief because it is old and dearly loved."*

His second year in theology was spent in New York City where he helped to support himself by teaching forty-six hours a week for six dollars, which he thought good pay. Later he wrote his father that he was surprised that he was not afraid when caught in a street riot, and that although ill himself he had been glad to nurse a man dying of cholera and "to do my little to ease his pain."

During his second year in New York he preached on Sunday in the Almshouse Chapel on Blackwell's Island, talked with prisoners and patients and saw the insane. He wrote his father that this was "one of the most interesting and exciting days 'he' had ever spent. Ghostly faces peering from behind bandages around you, and others all festering with disease, or worn and scarred with passion and some where pure kind expressions must have dwelt once, you felt you were standing among the wrecks of the soul, creatures cast out from everything but God's mercy. Oh! 'twas the saddest, most helpless sight."

To a beloved sister he wrote in 1850: "You can have no idea, Emma, what an immense vat of misery and crime and filth much of this great city is! I realize it more and more. Think of ten thousand children growing up almost sure to be prostitutes and rogues!" And to a friend a little earlier, November, 1849: "And if I can once start, freed from every possible taint of humbug, cant, bigotry, mere custom, true to myself as well as my opinions, and if I can feel to my very heart the love of humanity of which I see a faint spark now within me, why! cannot I do something?"

In the summer of 1850 he was invited by two friends to go with them on a walking trip through England, Ireland and the Rhine country. In Edinburgh and London he studied the "Ragged Schools" and the leading reformatory institutions in the cities of Great Britain. From Germany he wrote, "I have a kind of feeling

FREE FOSTER HOMES

growing on me that my only and great business in the world is man-helping."

He spent the winter of 1850 in Berlin, and in the spring set out through Austria and Hungary. During this European trip he wrote for various American papers in order to pay his expenses.

While in Hungary, in 1851, he was arrested, charged with having revolutionary matter on his person, and with being a friend to revolutionists. Through the efforts of a fellow prisoner, later released, a message was sent to the American chargé d'affaires at Vienna and Mr. Brace was set free after four weeks in prison and thirteen trials by courts martial.

Meanwhile the old desire to be of help to those who needed him in New York City had intensified during his absence, and soon became compelling. He did not at once give up the idea of preaching, but turned in the direction of the work of a city missionary. He first joined in the work of Five Points Mission and occasionally visited Blackwell's Island, the sins and sufferings of whose inmates had made such an indelible impression upon him. During the year 1852 he seems to have become more and more convinced that effort to reform adults was not encouraging. Every day he saw schoolless, churchless, homeless children throng the streets, alleys and wharves of the great city, engaged in paper selling, begging, rag and bone-picking, and thieving. Every day these children fought and jostled with each other, with criminal men and women in prison, and with diseased men and women of the almshouse, for the dominant place in the heart of this young man. Contesting for his life's service were also congregations of well-dressed folk sitting quietly in church waiting to listen to his voice as a preacher.

The issue could not long remain in doubt. From such a youth arrived at such a manhood, there could be but one answer when asked to give his life in service to the children imprisoned by poverty and circumstance in the death-breeding tenements and streets of New York City. In the spring of 1853 he was asked to head what was called "a mission to children" with a salary of one thousand dollars a year. He wrote to his father: "I have hesitated a good deal, as it interrupts my regular study and training, but this is a new and important enterprise. The duties are to organize a system of boys' meetings, vagrant schools, etc., which should reach the whole city; to communicate with press and clergy; to draw in boys, find them homes in the country, get them to schools, help them to help themselves; to write and preach, etc., etc. A new and expanded thing at present, but to become clearer as we go on; mornings in office, afternoons in visiting. It suits my sympathies, has variety and is or can be of infinite use. Can I do more elsewhere for humanity?"

The church had lost a liberal preacher, but the street children of New York City had found a champion who was to fight till death to get for them what he thought they most needed.

Although a pioneer for shelter, religious teaching, recreation, schooling, and remunerative work for the children who must stay in the city, the one road, as he saw it, for the homeless child, and even for the children of poor parents, was that of emigration to foster homes in the villages and on the prosperous farms of the West. So convinced did he become that this way was the one best way to care for all dependent and neglected children away from their own homes that he became at least partially blind to its limitations. By March, 1853, the Mission had been renamed "The Children's Aid Society" and the first circular outlining the scope and method of its work was sent out to the public. Some of the facts relating to the poor, and especially to the children of New York City, during the period immediately preceding the formation of the Children's Aid Society, and which contributed directly to its organization, were these:

Vagrant Children in New York City in the Fifties

In 1852 the number of immigrants who landed at the Port of New York was 300,992, most of whom Mr. Brace thought had settled in the city. "Our poorest streets began to be filled up with a thriftless, beggared, dissolute population. The poor and the idle of a street grew worse for having poor and idle neighbors." The state of the children grew worse and worse. The Chief of Police reported 10,000 vagrant children in the city and that in eleven wards there were 2,955 children engaged in thieving, of whom two-thirds were girls between eight and sixteen. In 1853 the Captain of Police for the eleventh ward reported that out of the 12,000 children of the ward, between the ages of five and sixteen, only 7,000 attended public schools, and 2,500 attended Sabbath schools, leaving 5,000 without the privileges of common schooling, and 9,500 destitute of public religious influence.

Schools of New York City Up to 1853

New York's early schools had been entirely under religious and other private auspices. After 1829 schools run by a "Public School Society" had been free, but were really privately managed. In 1842 the city established a "Board of Education" and in 1843 opened the first real public school under public auspices. In 1853 the "Public School Society" turned its schools and property, to the estimated value of $604,820.46, over to the Board of Education, fifteen of its members becoming members of the City Board. As yet, however, these public schools were woefully inadequate. Even as late as 1870 they had reached an enrollment of only 85,307 pupils out of a total population of school age of 200,000.

In the very nature of the case then, at the time Mr. Brace began his work with the Children's Aid Society of New York, there was no such thing as compulsory school attendance, as we now understand it, and no twentieth century public opinion or law against excessive and unsuitable child labor.

Facilities in 1853 in New York City for Care of Destitute Children

As we have already seen, there was the branch of the city almshouse called the Randall's Island Nurseries, with a capacity for about one thousand destitute children above four years of age. This included children in good health, sick children, and low-grade, mentally defective children. The outlet for those who could not go back to parents or relatives was chiefly by indenture.

Under private auspices there were eight orphan asylums primarily for whole or half-orphans, from which surplus children went out on indenture. Among these there were specializations of care for Negro, Catholic, Episcopalian and other Protestant children.

In addition to the above there were three other agencies for the destitute as follows: The Association for Improving the Condition of the Poor, founded in 1843, was a general family relief agency with district workers in every part of the city and having as an executive a remarkably able man with prophetic social vision, Robert M. Hartley. Like the Brace family, he was from Hartford, Connecticut, and he was associated with Mr. Brace in founding the Children's Aid Society.

The American Female Guardian Society was founded in 1834 to reform females. Its House of Industry for women, and the care of destitute children, brought to notice through these women, had become important parts of the work. The women in charge of the Society had begun to care for destitute children by taking especially needy ones into their own homes. This led to placing children in foster homes for adoption or indenture. Forty-five were thus placed in 1845, and by 1853 the placements of foster children rivalled in importance the work for women. The Society published a paper called "Advocate and Guardian" which circulated in many states and was a medium of appeal for foster homes.

In addition to the above agencies for destitute children, there were two institutions for delinquent children: The House of Refuge, founded in 1824, and the New York Juvenile Asylum, founded in 1851 and having in charge in 1863 only 57 children.

There was also the New York Institute for Deaf and Dumb (1817) and the New York Institution for the Blind (1831).

The first circular of the Children's Aid Society, of March, 1853,

FREE FOSTER HOMES

took into account the needs of children in New York City and the existing agencies and institutions for meeting these needs. It contained in embryo all the kinds of work that the new society afterward developed. It read in part as follows:

In view of these evils,[2] we have formed an Association which shall devote itself entirely to this class of vagrant children. . . . A large multitude of children live in the city who cannot be placed in asylums, and yet who are uncared for and ignorant and vagrant. We propose to give these work, and to bring them under religious influences. . . . As means shall come in, it is designed to district the city, so that hereafter every ward may have its agent, who shall be a friend to the vagrant child. *Boys' Sunday meetings* have already been formed, which we hope to see extended until every quarter has its place of preaching to boys. With these we intend to connect *Industrial Schools* where the great temptations to this class, arising from want of work, may be removed, and where they can learn an honest trade. Arrangements have been made with manufacturers, by which, if we have the requisite funds to begin, *five hundred boys in different localities can be supplied with* paying work. We hope, too, especially to be the means of *draining the city of these children* by communicating with farmers, manufacturers, or families in the country, who may have need of such for employment.

When *homeless boys* are found by our agents, we mean to get them homes *in the families of respectable persons* in the city, and put them in the way of an honest living.[3] [Italics by the present writer.]

In brief, the methods proposed for dealing with vagrant boys and girls were:
1. Boys' Religious Meetings
2. Industrial Schools
3. Workshops
4. Finding places for children to work outside New York
5. Placing children in family homes at work

[2] The status of children in New York City before mentioned.
[3] Reprinted by Charles Loring Brace in *The Dangerous Classes in New York*, 1880, p. 92. Also found (with slight change) in *Life and Letters of Charles Loring Brace*, before cited, p. 491.

The next year, in 1854, another form of work was added, namely, the Boys' Lodging House.

Of these six forms of work, the boys' meetings and the workshops were not kept up permanently; but the industrial schools, the lodging houses, and the removal of boys and girls from New York to live in family homes, whether for work or permanently as foster children (later called the emigration work of the Society) have all been kept up until the present time. Although it is the purpose of this monograph to discuss in detail only the emigration work, it is important for the reader to keep in mind the other activities of the New Children's Aid Society. The relation of all the other forms of work to the emigration department was so close that each, in addition to its own characteristic service to the children remaining in the city, helped to discover homeless and poor children whose parents would consent to their placement in family homes out of the city.

Mr. Brace's first appeal for homes tells by implication its own story as to the variation of his plans from the old indenture:[4]

TO

FARMERS AND MECHANICS

AND

MANUFACTURERS IN THE COUNTRY

FROM

THE CHILDREN'S AID SOCIETY

The greatest charity usually, which can be done to the poor in a city, is to get them into the country. We, as a Society, have devoted ourselves to the aid of the poor children of New York; and we feel it our first duty to put them, wherever possible, in the way of an honest living out of the city. Every occupation here is thronged, and with the poor, nothing so leads to idleness and crime, as this overcrowding of population. We call upon every man in the country who has the opportunities for it, and who would do a Christian charity, to assist us in getting these children

---

[4] A special circular bound between *First and Second Annual Reports*. In possession of present writer.

work. There would be no loss in the charity. These boys are, many of them, handy and active, and would learn soon any common trade or labor. They could be employed on farms, in trades, in manufacturing [italics by the present writer]; and many an intelligent lad might be saved to society from a life of theft or vagrancy.

The *girls* could be used for the *common kinds of housework*. They are the children of parents coarse and very poor, with many bad habits, but kindness has a wonderful effect on the young girl; and of this, the vagrant child in our great city gets little. A charity at this time of life would do what no reform or good influence can do afterwards.

These children are not those whom Asylums or our other Institutions can help. They are not, according to any legal definition, vagrants, though they are growing up often to crime and poverty.

The children whom we shall send on application, will be sent gratuitously. Our enterprise is not one of gain. We want to apply the remedy to the source of these vast evils and sufferings in our city, and bring good influences to bear on *childhood*. If the children are not satisfactory, they can be returned to our hands.

We confidently call on those through the country, who recognize it as a duty never to be avoided, to help the suffering and poor; those who practically believe in Christ's words and teachings, to aid us in this effort; and to aid us in the way most efficient, *by draining the crowded city of these destitute children* [italics by the present writer].

It is hoped that farmers will be found, who will take small numbers of boys on trial, receiving a fair compensation for their board, and then distribute them to those in want of such, through the neighborhood or county.

All communications on this subject, will be addressed to the office of the "Children's Aid Society," No. 683, Broadway; or after the first of May, to the New Bible House.

March, 1853
Secretary,
Charles L. Brace

In form, the appeal of 1853 was for service to a needy child. But it was also made very clear that the child would in personality and work pay for all that was done for him.

In 1859 Mr. Brace expressly stated the principles on which his work was based in these words, which he repeated in substance thereafter on many occasions:[5]

It is based on two principles:
1. The superiority of the Christian family to any and all other institutions for the education and improvement of a poor child, and
2. The necessity, in treating the evils of the poor on a large scale, of following the natural laws and demand for labor.

From the foregoing statements it is clear that the emigration work was the old indenture in a less rigid form. The three parties are the same and the idea of a *quid pro quo* of service by the child is still an essential factor.
1. The child is to get a real home which he is to pay for in work.
2. The family is to get interest in life, and relief from many of the little cares of the farm.
3. The Society is to bear the trouble and expense necessary to deliver the child and to take him away again if a mistake has been made and for any reason the child is not satisfactory.

From responses to the first appeal, and to others which followed, the names of applicants for children were obtained, and many individual children were sent to such persons in nearby states. The following is Mr. Brace's account of one such boy. It illustrates the early method of accepting a boy and of placing him in a home.[6]

In visiting, near the docks at the foot of Twenty-third Street, I found a boy, about twelve years of age, sitting on the wharf, very ragged and wretched-looking. I asked him where he lived and he made the answer one hears so often from these children: "I don't live nowhere!" On further inquiry, it appeared that his parents had died a few years before, that his aunt took him in for a while, but being a drunken woman had at length turned him away, and for some time he had slept in a box in ... street and the boys fed him; he occasionally making a sixpence with holding horses or doing an errand. He had eaten nothing that day,

[5] New York Children's Aid Society, *Sixth Annual Report*, 1859, p. 8.
[6] New York Children's Aid Society, *First Annual Report*, Feb., 1854, pp. 17-19.

though it was afternoon. I gave him something to eat, and he promised to come up the next day to the office.

He came up, and we had a long talk together. He was naturally an intelligent boy, of good organization, but in our Christian city of New York he had never heard of Jesus Christ! His mother, long ago, had taught him a prayer, and occasionally he had said this in the dark nights, lying on the boards. Of schools or churches, of course, he knew nothing. We sent him to a gentleman in Pennsylvania, who had wished to make the experiment of bringing up a vagrant boy of the city. He thus writes at his arrival:

"The boy reached Philadelphia in safety, where I found him a few hours after he arrived. Poor boy! He bears about him, or rather is, the unmistakeable evidence of the life he had led—covered with vermin—almost a leper—ignorant in the extreme, and seeming wonder-struck almost at the voice of kindness and sympathy, and bewildered with the idea of possessing a wardrobe gotten for him.

"So far as I can judge, from so short an observation, I should think him an amiable boy, grateful for kindness shown him, rather timid than energetic, yet by no means deficient in intellectual capacity, and altogether such a one as, by God's help, can be made something of. Such as he is, or may turn out to be, I accept the trust conferred upon me, not insensible of the responsibility I incur, in thus becoming the instructor and trainer of a being, destined to an endless life, of which that which he passes under my care, while but the beginning, may determine all the rest."

In a letter, six months later, he writes:

"It gives me much pleasure to be able to state that Jimmy continues to grow in favor with us all. Having been reclaimed from his vagrant habits, which at first clung pretty close to him, he may now be said to be a steady and industrious boy.

"I have not had occasion, since he has been under my care, to reprove him so often as once, having found gentle and kindly admonition quite sufficient to restrain him. He is affectionate in disposition, very truthful, and remarkably free from the use of profane or rough language. I find less occasion to look after him than is usual with children of his age, in order to ascertain that the animals entrusted to his care are well attended to, etc.

" . . . Jimmy is now a very good speller out of books—reads quite fairly, and will make a superior penman; an apt scholar, and very fond of his books. I have been his teacher thus far. He attends regularly a Sabbath School, of which I have the superintendence, and the religious services which follow."

In addition to placing children one by one in foster homes, as in the case just cited, the plan of taking children in large parties to a single locality was started as early as 1854, when a visitor conveyed 138 children, 66 boys and 72 girls, in one company to families in Pennsylvania. First-hand descriptions of experiences in the first placement of children as far away as Illinois and Michigan in 1856 are vivid and tell their own story as to ideals and methods of "placing-out."[7]

Peoria, Ill.
Jan. 15, '56

Mr. C. L. Brace:
Dear Brother:

Our journey, though slow, seven days from New York to Peoria, was successful. Twenty-four out of the twenty-seven homeless ones are in good homes. A "mother in Israel," (Mrs. R. E. L.) in F——, Indiana, looked at all the children, and fixing her eye upon Elizabeth (the poor girl that nobody would have, because she was so disfigured) said, "This little one needs sympathy more than either of the others, I will take her." I could not ask her to pay for her transportation, and therefore paid it out of my own purse.

John is with Deacon Simms, Tremont, Taswell Co., Ill. Mr. S. is a farmer and a member of the Baptist Church. He is one of the best men in the land. I have long known him. John is happy, and the Deacon delighted. He had one daughter, and now he has a son. He is well off. John has a bright future in prospect.

Charlotte Lord is with Mr. S. S. Stiers, Elgin, Ill., and they are well pleased.

Katherine and James Lord were placed at a good home eight miles

---

[7] New York Children's Aid Society, *Third Annual Report*, 1856, pp. 50-51. Names of persons have been changed.

from here, in the family of an Episcopal minister. *On last Saturday Katherine became dissatisfied, without cause, took James and ran away.*

About six o'clock they came to my house, where they will remain until I procure them another place. He paid their expenses out ($32). I refund.

But the best is yet to be told. You remember Nancy T——, whose mother came to your office the day I was there. O, what a dear little one she is. How I love her. She looked so sad as she *sat between her father and mother* the day I left. *How solemn the trust, when those weeping parents gave me their daughter.* I promised to be a father to her. None seemed so sad after starting, as she. I wrapped her in my shawl, took her in my arms, talked kindly to her, wiped away her tears, and she slept sweetly. She seemed to love me as if I were really her father. She was a dear good girl all the way. I took her to my own home. She sat on one knee and my daughter on the other. All loved her; but we had to lose our treasure. Judge N. R. of this city is one of the noblemen of America. He has one of the finest families I ever knew. They occupy the first place in society. The Judge saw Nancy. His heart melted. He took her on his knee. Soon he pressed her to his bosom. The tear was in his eye. He kissed her and asked if she would be his daughter. She answered "Yes." We all cried for joy when the Judge said "The Lord has given us enough, let us take her to be one of us." All her clothes have been returned to me, which I will send to her parents. She is beautifully dressed. Her name is Jane R. She says "Father, mother, brother, sister." She is addressed as "Daughter, sister."

The Judge has two daughters, Jane sleeps with them, is one of them. She is no longer a servant, but a daughter. She will, with the others, enjoy the advantages of his immense wealth. Yesterday she was placed in the best academy in the city. Soon she will commence taking music lessons. Rejoice, my dear brother, in this, another evidence of the importance and blessedness of your work. Please give to her sad parents this pleasing intelligence. Ask them to let me have *her little sister that is nine years old, and I will find her a good home.* I have not found a place for Mr. S. yet, because it has been too cold to get about. The result of this trip has been glorious. I can only say "my cup runneth over." God bless you and strengthen you for this great work.

I am, your fellow laborer,

W. C. Van Meter

Also in 1856 a party of forty-six boys and girls started, with apparently only one man as caretaker, to make the journey from New York City to Dowagiac, in the southwest corner of Michigan. They left New York via Hudson River by boat, Wednesday night, and spent the next forenoon in Albany, where they recruited another boy from the street. At noon Thursday they took an emigrant train for Buffalo, riding in a freight car with benches but no beds or windows, "crowded to suffocation" with adult emigrants of several nationalities. Friday they spent nine hours in Buffalo and at night took the steerage cabin of a boat for Detroit. "The berths are covered with a coarse mattress, used by a thousand different passengers and never changed till they are filled with stench and vermin." Over their heads were "a hundred horses and sheep, the effluvia of their filth pouring through the open gangway." From Detroit at ten o'clock Saturday night they took a first-class passenger train to Dowagiac where they arrived at three o'clock Sunday morning and slept on the station floor. They attended church in a school where they sang: "Come ye sinners, poor and needy"; and they rolled it out with a relish. "It was a touching sight, and pocket handkerchiefs were used quite freely among the audience in the congregation."

The work of the society was explained and "Monday morning the boys held themselves in readiness to receive applications from farmers. They would watch in all directions, scanning closely every wagon that came in sight, and deciding from the appearance of the driver and the horses, more often the latter, whether they would go in for that farmer." Before Saturday all the children had been "placed," and one had run away from the tinner with whom he was placed, because he wanted to be a farmer.

The account closes at the end of ten days' experience, with this optimistic paragraph:[8]

---

[8]For full account of this trip to Dowagiac, Mich., see letter from the man who conducted the party of forty-six, in *Annual Report* of the Society, 1856, pp. 54-60. Also published as "An Early Experiment in Child Placing," in *Social Service Review,* June 1929, University of Chicago Press.

On the *whole* the *first* experiment of sending children west is a very happy one, and I am sure there are places enough with good families in Michigan, Illinois, Iowa and Wisconsin, to give every poor boy and girl in New York a permanent home. The only difficulty is to bring the children to the home.

[Signed] E. P. Smith

The complete record of this emigration trip throws a flood of light on at least these phases of method in the care of dependent and neglected children of that day:

Intake or acceptance by the Society of children for care

Outfit in clothing

Escort and conditions of travel

Method of application for children and investigation of applicants

Selection of children for particular applicant

Motives for taking children

Assumption as to magnitude of demand for children

Assumption that the needs of all the children were substantially alike

As a further evidence of the effect of the songs of a similar band of young emigrants upon a man who heard them nearly seventy years ago, we have this testimony:[9]

I was a boy living in Hartford, Ohio, about 1861 or 1862, when an agent came to our village with a group of New York City children to be placed in family homes. I think there were six or eight of them. I was then about ten or eleven years old.

I have never forgotten the impression I received from the pathetic singing of these homeless children. They sang several songs. The only one which I can now recall went as follows:

> I have a Father in the promised land,
> I have a Father in the promised land.
> My Father calls me, I must go
> To meet Him in the promised land.

[9]Dr. Hastings H. Hart, in a letter to the present writer in 1929.

The children sang it as follows:

> I hev a Father in the promus lan',
> I hev a Father in the promus lan'.
> My Father calls me—I mus' go-o-o-
> To meet Um in th' pro-o-mus lan'.

Dependent Child Emigration from Boston

New York City was not the only eastern city to send parties of emigrant children west during the third quarter of the nineteenth century. The following is a description of one such child emigrant party from Boston. The trip is described as the ninth to have been made from the New England Home for Little Wanderers, and took place in December, 1867:[10]

Usually one would not select a winter month for such a trip, but because of unusually warm, bright, autumnal weather, Mr. Hughes started in the afternoon with 29 children by boat for New York. The next morning found them in the midst of a terrific snow storm. For four hours the boat struggled to land in New York. When it finally succeeded they found the snow so deep that all street cars, hacks, etc., were blockaded and abandoned. They had to leave the boat, so there was no way but to walk. They headed for the Howard Mission, a mile from the dock. The storm was still raging and it was bitterly cold. How the little folks ever made the journey is a wonder. They fell down into the snow, but they would help each other up and trudge along. One little fellow said, "Never mind, we'll get a good home after a while." They found a warm welcome at the Mission, but the storm continued and they were blocked there for sixty hours. Money began to grow scarce and the first thought was to return to Boston, but the trains were all blocked and derailed in that direction, so they decided to push on. They left about noon on Saturday, but only reached Elmira, New York, at midnight. They were directed to the Delavan House as a good and reasonable place because the landlord was a pious man. He stowed them away three in a bed in an unfurnished room, where they had to spend Sun-

---

[10]From an unpublished manuscript by Rev. Edward C. Winslow, 1929, *How It Came To Be What It Is*.

day, and he fed them as cheaply as decency would allow. They bore it bravely because they were assured that the bill would not be more than $35 or $40. Monday morning when the landlord demanded $75 they felt they had made a mistake in going to such a pious house, but they paid it. They left Monday at midnight, and only reached Buffalo before they stuck again. All had to bunk on the floor of the station house. The next evening found them at Elyria, Ohio, where they intended to make their first stop. Stepping into the Emmons House, Mr. Hughes asked the landlord how many of the company he could keep over night. "Are they paupers?" asked the landlord. "No," said Mr. Hughes, "but they are poor." "Then they are thieves, every one of them," said the landlord, "and I can't sit up all night to watch my property. They can't stay in my house." So out into the dark and cold they went again. It was soon noised abroad that they were in town and one of the ministers found them and secured lodgings for them with his families where it cost nothing. Snow was three feet deep on the level, and drifts were immeasurable. In eight days every child had a good permanent home, and Mr. Hughes said he could have placed as many more if he had had them.

Songs for Publicity and Finance by Children from The New England Home for Little Wanderers in the 90's

From Boston we also have evidence that children not only sang feelingly while en route from the city to free foster family homes, but were also sent out on systematically planned tours when the intention was to gain both money and publicity. The following account describes this practice:[11]

The work for the children became widely known and appreciated throughout New England. The publicity given to it came about largely through services in the churches of all denominations, when some man would explain the work, the children would sing, and by their presence give an object lesson of the work done.

Some people have asked me what the children sang. A variety of

---

[11] From an unpublished manuscript by Rev. E. C. Winslow, *How They Did It*, New England Home for Little Wanderers, 1929.

simple but appropriate songs usually not found in the books of the day—"I know my Heavenly Father knows"; "It is all for the best"; "Count your blessings"; etc. Twenty or more such songs I could call for, and I have never heard children anywhere sing as these children could: taking their own key, speaking the words so plainly as to be heard in the largest churches, giving most delicate expressions, and in a clear, full and natural tone. Sometimes we had good alto as well as soprano singers and their duets were very attractive. The first hour of school each morning was given to teaching these songs. Then a selection was made from the children who could do the best for our Sunday choirs. One was appointed leader, and he or she gave the key and started the song. They were perfectly independent of the man who was with them.

Some people felt there was serious objection to "exploiting the children," as they said, in this way. I watched the effect for years and never felt a child was injured in any way unless he or she was kept too long in the Home for this purpose. Of course there was a tendency to keep a good singer, especially when three of us went out every Sunday and each wanted four good singers. But it was a good training for them, for any misconduct on the street, on the train, or in the family where they stayed, resulted in their staying at home, and that was the worst punishment that could be inflicted. Moreover, the children did not feel they were on exhibition any more than I was. But they made an irresistible appeal to the congregation. I would introduce them something like this: One of the most perplexing problems to a thoughtful mind is the apparent *inequalities* of life. One man is always lucky, we say; everything comes his way, health, wealth, happiness, all that heart can wish. Another man, just as worthy, meets with nothing but disappointment and failure. One family remains intact, all its members spared year after year; another family is wrecked, shattered, scattered. One child has father, mother, home, all that love and care can provide; another child is thrown out of home and never knows a mother's love or a father's care. Why are these things so? We do not know. We only know that in some way "all things work together for good to them that love God"; so I am going to ask these little folks who are with me this morning to come up here and sing their simple song, "It is all for the best." By the time they were through the first verse the handkerchiefs were flying all over the house, and I needed no other text.

Further illustrations of emigration parties from the east might be added, for example, from the records of the New York Juvenile Asylum and the New York Foundling Asylum. The New York Children's Aid Society, however, is the most generally known in connection with westward emigration of dependent children on a large scale, and to a consideration of the later phases of its work we now turn.

For the dependent child in the care of the Children's Aid Society, in the opinion of Mr. Brace, emigration to a foster home was the logical climax to which all previous contacts of that child with the Society were preliminary. This is clearly shown in a circular of "Instructions to Visitors" issued in New York, 1864, which emphasizes the interrelation that existed from the first among the various phases of Mr. Brace's work.

It will be noted that Sabbath Schools in the several districts are mentioned instead of the original Religious Meetings for Boys; also that no mention is made of workshops not connected with Industrial Schools:[12]

INSTRUCTIONS TO VISITORS

1. Your first and especial object is to find in your District, children who are deserted or homeless, or who are in such a state of poverty as to be improved by being taken to good homes in the country. In no case must efforts be made to induce children to leave the city without consulting the parents (if there be any), or their nearest relations. No child, of course, is sent from our office without the written consent, or a consent before witnesses, of its parents or guardians, if such there be. *To the parents of these poor children, representations should be made of the great advantages which a good western home offers over the poverty and ignorance, and temptation, to which they are exposed in the city. The strongest assurances can be given to them that the future welfare of the children will be watched over by the Society. They, themselves, can hear from them if they desire, and in no case is their child indentured* [italics by the present writer].

[12]New York Children's Aid Society, *Eleventh Annual Report*, 1864, pp. 43-44.

2. Your second great duty is to find children for the Industrial School of your District. No child should be expected, or asked, who goes to a Ward School, or to any religious or secular Day School. You should seek out the poorest, the most ragged, and those most exposed to temptation. You should appeal to the conscience of the mother, as to her giving the best education she is able, to her child. You can mention the inducements held out in the School by the meals, the clothes and shoes, and the assistance given—still you should have it understood that these are all given according to marks for good conduct, and that no one has any claim on them. While you never lose sight of an abandoned or very destitute family, you should never appear too urgent, as the favor is to them, not to us. Most parents can be made to understand that the dangers before their children, in the street and uneducated, are very great. Insist especially on punctuality in those who do come to the School.

3. Those who are suitable you can take to the Newsboys' Lodging House or to the Girls' Lodging House, to remain temporarily till better situations can be procured.

4. Seek to get as many truant and vagrant children back to the Public Schools, as possible.

5. Induce them also to enter the Sabbath Schools of the District, while making it understood that the Industrial School is entirely distinct from these.

6. Make yourself the friend of poor children in your quarter by visiting, aiding the families, advising, sympathizing, directing them where they may get work, and helping the children out of any misfortune they may fall into.

You will often be compelled to seek them in the Prison or Stationhouse. For this purpose, make yourself acquainted with the Police Judges in your District, and the Police. They will be a great help to you.

Your work will be very slow and gradual. It takes a long time to secure the confidence of this class of people. But when you have won it, your influence will become immense and lasting for good. Hundreds of unfortunate, and tempted, and outcast children may owe their salvation to your efforts, if the blessing of God be upon them.

You will render a monthly report to the Board, and a weekly one to me.

In all cases, be present at the office every Monday, about twelve o'clock, bringing your Journal with you.

C. L. Brace, Secretary

Some Clues as to Origin of Methods Adopted by Mr. Brace

As to the origin of each of the different kinds of work thus adopted and used by coördination upon a scale city-wide, Mr. Brace himself lays no claim to be the inventor. The workshop idea was in use by Mr. Pease in the Five Points Mission of New York City in 1853 and also by the American Female Guardian Society of New York City in their House of Industry. Boys' meetings had been held in New York City for several years. Placing children in family homes by indenture had been common in the eastern states for generations. The American Female Guardian Society of New York City had also, for some years, been finding foster homes for children in states distant from New York City. Mr. Brace had seen the Ragged Schools of London and Edinburgh and had written about them in 1851 in letters to *The New York Tribune* on "Vagrant Schools." Of his methods as a whole Mr. Brace himself says: "These measures, though imitated in some respects from England, were novel in their combination."

The Geographical Distribution of Children into Family Homes 1853-1923

We may now trace very briefly the main lines of the development of the emigration work of the New York Children's Aid Society from 1853 to 1923. The reader should keep constantly in mind the following basic factors which entered into the plans for the society during its early years. These were:

The overwhelming magnitude of the needs of children in New York City in 1850 and for many years afterward; the unusual personality and the developmental experiences of Mr. Charles Loring Brace up to the time when he was plunged into the midst of the homeless, ragged, hungry armies of neglected children that thronged the streets of New York City; and finally two main interrelated groups of activities started by Mr. Brace during the first decade of the New York Children's Aid Society. First, those activities which were directed toward bettering school, work, and spare-time, conditions for the children remaining in the city; and, second, toward attempting to discover all homeless, dependent and neglected children in the city and to turn them off in many streams of young emigrants into western homes, wherever, to use the early words of Mr. Brace, "a combined appeal to Christian charity and a persistent need for youthful labor" could open for them the doors of family homes. In order to realize the long period of time during which such parties of dependent children as those started by Mr. Brace have been emigrating from New York City, to foster homes in the West, let the reader now imagine that he was born in 1855, just after Mr. Brace had started his first bands of emigrants on the way westward, and let him further imagine himself as having lived through infancy, school days, young manhood, middle life, and now in 1930 to have arrived at the age of three score and ten plus five years. Every year of these seventy-five years, except possibly 1930, has seen parties of children set out from New York for public distribution from a central hall, a church, a court house, or other room, into farm and village homes of the West.

In 1884 Dr. Hastings H. Hart, then secretary of the State Board of Charities in Minnesota, made an investigation of the work of the Society in Minnesota, and made a report in substance as follows.

Dr. Hart found that 340 children in all had been brought to seven counties in Minnesota within three years of his study, which was begun in 1883. Of these 340, he secured information about 264, leaving 76 unaccounted for. The facts he gathered about the 264, summarized from a table which he prepared, are as follows: Out of this total of 264 about whom he secured information, 186

FREE FOSTER HOMES

(70 percent) remained in the vicinity where placed; 78 (30 percent) had gone from the vicinity where first placed; 171 (65 percent) were doing well; no complaint was found about another 33 (12.5 percent); 41 (16 percent) were reported as doing badly; and of 18 he had no report as to conduct.

An extract from Dr. Hart's report is as follows:[13]

> Thirty per cent of the children brought to Minnesota have gone from the vicinities where placed; and, of these, at least forty have drifted off and been lost sight of in less than three years, for lack of adequate supervision. The agents are efficient men but they are not omnipresent.
>
> ... The agents of the Society have revisited the counties where the children are placed—most of them repeatedly. These trips being hurried, have not permitted visits to all the children, special attention being given to urgent cases.
>
> I was a witness of the distribution of forty children in —— County, Minnesota, by my honored friend James Matthews, who is a member of this Conference. The children arrived at about half-past three P.M. and were taken directly from the train to the Court House, where a large crowd was gathered. Mr. Matthews set the children, one by one, before the company, and in his stentorian voice gave a brief account of each. Applicants for children were then admitted in order behind the railing and rapidly made their selection. Then, if the child gave assent, the bargain was concluded on the spot. It was a pathetic sight, not soon to be forgotten, to see those children, tired young people, weary, travel-stained, confused by the excitement and the unwonted surroundings, peering into those strange faces, and trying to choose wisely for themselves. And it was surprising how many happy selections were made under such circumstances. In a little more than three hours nearly all those forty children were disposed of. Some who had not previously applied selected children. There was little time for consultation, and refusal would be embarrassing; and I know that the Committee con-

[13]See National Conference of Charities and Corrections, *Annual Report* for 1884, pp. 143-50. For further published accounts of public distribution of children in 1914 in North Dakota, see Federal Children's Bureau Publication, *Importation of Dependent Children*. Also the writer has newspaper clippings of such distribution in Iowa in 1915 and 1919, and in Missouri in 1929.

sented to some assignments against their better judgment. The Committee usually consists of a minister, an editor, and a doctor, a lawyer or a businessman. The merchant dislikes to offend a customer, or the doctor a patient, and the minister fears to have it thought that his refusal is because the applicant does not belong to his church. Thus unsuitable applications sometimes succeed. Committee men and officers of the Society complain of this difficulty. The evil is proved by the fact that, while the younger children are taken from motives of benevolence and are uniformly well treated, the older ones are, in the majority of cases, taken from motives of profit, and are expected to earn their way from the start. The farmers in these counties are very poor. I speak within bounds, when I say that not one in five of those who have taken these children is what would be called, in Ohio or Illinois, well-to-do. To my personal knowledge, some of them were taken by men who live in shanties and could not clothe their own children decently. A little girl in Roch County was placed in a family living on a dirt floor in filth worthy of our Italian tenement houses. A boy in Nobles County was taken by a family whose children had been clothed by ladies of my church so that they could go to Sunday School. I have seen other similar instances.

In order to give some idea of the experiences and emotions of these emigrant children two brief biographical statements have been secured with permission to publish. They show internal evidence of fairness of mind and of an effort to paint the picture no darker than it actually was. The two biographies are also interesting because each of the boys came to the Children's Aid Society for placement in the West after a previous institutional experience —one in the New York Orphan Asylum Society, and the other in the New York Juvenile Asylum:[14]

The Story of a New York Orphan Asylum Boy Who Was Placed Out by The New York Children's Aid Society

You ask about my experience as a boy placed out through the Children's Aid Society of New York. I shall be glad to tell you about it. I

[14]From a letter to the present writer in 1928. The name has been changed.

was sent at the age of five to the Orphan Asylum Society of the City of New York, both my parents having died before I was old enough to remember them. The Society maintained an orphanage on 73rd Street and Riverside Drive.

I remained in the orphanage until fourteen, being then sent west to Kansas. I was offered the choice of going to work in the offices of a company in New York City at $3.00 per week, or going west, and as I had read a lot about western life, I chose the latter course. The wife of the head of the New York City company was one of the trustees of the orphanage, and quite a number of the older boys had gone to work in her husband's offices. I have often wondered what might have become of me if I had chosen to stay in New York. It seems that the farmer with whom I made my home had had another boy from the same orphanage, this boy having grown up and married his eldest daughter. This man thought he would like to try another boy from the same place and wrote back to New York about it, the result being that I was the one sent out to fill the assignment.

I think I was more fortunate than the average boy going west in those days, in that I had a definite home to go to. I left New York in the spring of 1899. There was a carload of boys being sent west by the Children's Aid Society, three of our boys going with this load. I rode with them a little less than a day, being sent then to a different car of the train, which went direct to St. Louis, while the others went on to Chicago. The man in charge gave me some money when he left me, told me just what to do in order not to get lost, and that was the last I saw of him or the other boys. I remember I was pretty homesick the rest of the trip, but made my destination without difficulty.

I found a farm home awaiting me, about four miles from a small village by name of Brandywine. There were five girls and a small boy in the family, aside from the daughter who had been married and moved away. The people took me in as one of themselves and I made my home with them until I struck out for myself after being grown. In fact, I married one of the girls of the family later on. I think I was fortunate in having such a home, for as I look back I can think of nothing that was not done to make me feel that I really belonged there.

I grew to know the young man who had preceded me there. He told me of his experience. It seems that some ten or twelve years before he, with a lot of other boys, had been sent out to that country. They were taken from town to town, public meetings being called at each place, and the boys being put up for inspection, each farmer picking out any likely looking lad who happened to please him. When his turn came he was selected by a farmer who later mistreated him pretty badly, allowing him to work outdoors in winter until he froze both his feet. In this condition my employer took him away from the farmer and gave him a home, where he stayed.

I know of a number of boys who went out to this section of the west. Some did not turn out so well. Others grew up happily and made something of themselves. It was a country where hard work was the rule, but everyone was subject to the same conditions and as I look back on it, I think it was a pretty good training for me.

I was very well contented there, the worst drawback being a lack of school opportunities. I worked as a boy of the family until eighteen, then striking out for myself, teaching school and earning my way through college. I continued to go back during vacations, and to this day I regard the family with whom I lived as my own people, they being the only real folks I ever knew.

About the system in general, I think it was the best that could be had in those days. In the light of present day knowledge and organization there is, of course, much to criticize, but I think that those who were responsible for the disposition of dependent children in those days, at least those with whom I came in contact, were kindly disposed and really did what they could for the best interests of their wards. Since growing up I have come to realize how serious a loss it is to any child to be deprived of a home and parents. Often any attempted solution of such a problem is only a makeshift at best.

A New York Juvenile Asylum Boy Who Was Placed by The New York Children's Aid Society

The second biography has an added significance because of the writer's great anxiety to find out about his mother and his brother:[15]

---

[15] A letter to the present writer. Names of persons and of western localities changed.

Fertil Valley, Ill.
Jan. 2, 1929

My dear friend:

I will give you a brief outline of my experiences and you may use what you wish.

After being kept in the New York home (N. Y. Juvenile Asylum) for one year, Mr. John Wingate, western agent living at Williamstown, Ill., came in March and took twenty-one boys by boat to, I think Albany, then by rail to Oneida, Ill.; from here the different families came in and looked us over and picked out the one that appealed to them.

I was chosen by a German family here at Fertil Valley, Ill., by Josiah Wood, with whom I stayed until I was twenty-four years old, helping him on his farm or rather his father-in-law's farm, Martin Freeman, who lived with him (his wife being dead). He (Mr. Freeman) was a grand old gentleman and Christian. My boyhood life on this farm was more or less sad because of my foster-father, Josiah Wood, being a very heavy drinking man. As you know, some men when under the influence of liquor want to sleep, some get foolish and some get mean. He was of the latter type. Hitting me with his fist or kicking me so I fell several feet in the mud and would have fared worse if his wife, whom I always called "Mother" quite often interceded for me. She tried to do the best she knew how for me, which I always felt grateful to her for. But for her I surely would have run away a number of times. She would beg me to stay for her sake. She has gone to heaven a little over a year ago. At times like this I long to learn more of my own mother.

When I was nineteen years old I worked for Bolster Brothers in their general store three years, after which I learned the barber trade, running my own shop fifteen years. Then I carried mail in Oneida, Ill., for a short time, when I came back to Fertil Valley and bought this general store I worked in twenty years before. I only had $250 but had good personal credit and borrowed $9000 from a farmer who had faith in me. I had this store a little over eight years, which proved a successful venture as I just sold it, paying off all debts and had about $15,000 left. Just now the state is building a cement road through Fertil Valley and I purchased the old Martin Freeman estate where I spent my boyhood days. It has about seventy fruit trees and I intend to have an up-to-date fruit stand on this highway along with a tourist camp, also a Standard Oil station and a separate little store with soda fountain and lunches, etc. They have just completed the new Statler Hotel at Oneida and the manager selected me for the storekeeper position. When I was twenty-five years of age I used to wonder if I ever would find a girl that would like me well enough to marry me, as I have a pretty fierce-looking map, and whether I would know that I loved her. Well, I met Miss Lydia Sherburn in Packard, Ill., and it was all cleared up then, as I knew I loved her. She has been an exceptional good and talented wife. We have two children, Robert, who is fifteen years old and most of my clothes are too small for him, and Patsy Anne, who looks just like her mother, twelve years old. Which is saying quite a little. A year ago we all drove about four thousand miles through the Black Hills and took pictures of Mr. Coolidge while he was there. Last summer we drove forty-five hundred miles through Canada, New York, Washington, etc. I am very grateful to the New York home for what they done for me and any person contributing money to them is surely doing a good work.

I wish you much happiness this year of 1929. Hoping you will be able to learn something of my parents, I beg to remain.

Respectfully,
Israel Wood

On January 8, 1929, Mr. Wood wrote in answer to some information that had been sent to him:

I am very grateful to you for what information you sent me, part of which I had but not in full detail as you gave it.

Yes, I will write to William Mears or nearest relative at Plainfield, Ill., and see if I can find out any more about my brother. I am hoping that you may find some relative who can tell us about my mother, what she died of, as I am unable to get insurance just because of some of those things. I wish we could find some relative who might have a picture of her or them that I could buy, etc. Just go ahead and see what you can do or have done, and I'll take care of you on the expense. Many thanks.

Israel Wood

FREE FOSTER HOMES

Magnitude of the Emigration Work from 1853 to 1929

The total number of children placed in family homes, including older boys and girls, as given on the books of the Society is given in totals and annual average by decades, as follows:[16]

		Yearly average
1853-1864 (12 years)	4614	384
1865-1874	9456	946
1875-1884	4262	426
1885-1894	2434	243
1895-1904	3118	311
1905-1914	3720	372
1915-1924	2392	239
1925	251	
1926	227	
1927	150	
1928	229	
1929	228	

A Westward and Southward Moving Frontier of Placement

Some general tendencies may be traced in the geographical distribution of these children, by showing the actual number of children placed in each state during each decade. For example, during the first twelve years, 1853-1864 inclusive, placements were practically confined to New England, the North Atlantic states and Eastern North Central states. The largest number placed in any one state was 1,326 in Indiana, New York coming next with 864.

During the next decade, 1865-1874 inclusive, while placements are still made in the same states, there was a decided increase in placements in Michigan, Iowa and Missouri, with a distinct start

---

[16]Figures up to and including 1922 based upon study of the Society's records by Miss Georgia G. Ralph, New York School of Social Work. Later figures taken from annual reports. The trend of the figures is the significant fact.

in Kansas. New York received the largest number, 2,312, with Indiana second with 1,484 and Illinois third with 1,173. A very few were placed in Maryland and Virginia.

The next decade, 1875-1884 inclusive, shows a remarkable shifting of areas and also a remarkable diminution in the total number of children placed, the totals for this decade being only 4,362—less than half of the 9,456 placed the previous decade. Iowa now leads with 1,210 and Virginia comes second with 775. Almost no children were placed in New England, New York, New Jersey, Pennsylvania, Ohio, Indiana and Michigan, and very few in Illinois and Wisconsin. On the other hand, there was a great increase in the numbers placed in Virginia, Minnesota, Iowa, Missouri and Kansas, while a beginning was made in Nebraska. Such a remarkable diminution in number and such a striking shifting of areas in which family homes were found could hardly have been the result of mere accident. Does Mr. Brace himself or do the annual reports of the Society for this period give any clues to possible reasons for these changes which might throw light on the important question of trend in method of care for the dependent child? Attention will be given to this question a little later.

The next decade, 1885-1894 inclusive, shows no challenging changes from the previous decade except that Florida receives 251 children, Kansas takes the lead with 472, Missouri being a close second with 449, and Iowa is now third with 397.

But the next decade, 1895-1904 inclusive, shows some further important changes of area. Minnesota, Iowa, Missouri, Nebraska and Kansas continue to receive considerable numbers, but Texas, a new placing area, outstrips Florida. Delaware for the first time receives a considerable group of 147, and New York again resumes the leading place with 646.

During the next decade, 1905-1914 inclusive, the situation in the West Central states remains relatively little changed, but Oklahoma and Arkansas join Texas as new states. Maryland and Delaware become relatively far more important than before, Delaware receiving 538 children, and New York maintains the leading position with 859; Florida and West Virginia have dropped out.

During the next six years, or until June 30, 1921, Arkansas and Texas gain relatively to Iowa, Missouri, Nebraska, and Kansas, while New York with 592 and Delaware with 173 outrank all other states.

From a study of these facts of distribution, the first impression is that a westward- and southward-moving frontier of homes gave the most hospitable welcome to the youthful immigrants. Was it along such a moving frontier of farm and small village life that just the right combination of what Mr. Brace called "Christian charity and need for youthful labor" was found?

Criticisms from West and East

As early as 1858 Mr. Brace calls attention in his annual report to a criticism from the West that he was sending criminally-minded youth away from New York. This criticism, he said, was unjustified.

In 1868 Mr. Brace protested against the bigoted and ignorant prejudice against his emigration work on the part of certain people in New York City.

In 1876, criticism of New York Aid Society children said to be in penal institutions was expressed in meetings of the National Prison Congress then meeting in New York City.

In 1877, F. B. Sanborn, of the Massachusetts Board of Charities, criticized the Society during a meeting of the National Conference of Charities and Correction for what he called "extraditing" children by sending New York children throughout the western states. He thought that each state should care for its children at home.

In 1879 Mr. Brace reports criticism of his work "from each end of the line."

As an answer to these criticisms, Mr. Brace set on foot a series of investigations of the Society's work, using for this purpose his own agents who had been placing children in the West. Mr. Fry, first resident agent in Chicago (1869) made the first of these investigations in Illinois in 1876. Again in 1883, Messrs. Fry and Schlegel made an investigation in Wisconsin and Messrs. Matthews and Trott in Minnesota and Kansas.

Dr. Hart's investigation in Minnesota, already quoted, came in 1884.

Weaknesses of Child-Placing Methods Stimulate Institutional Care

In this connection, also, the story of the founding of the Catholic Protectory in New York City in 1863, ten years after Mr. Brace began his work with the Children's Aid Society, may well be given briefly for two purposes.

First, to supplement the discussion of motives in founding orphan asylums already given in Chapter V.

Second, to show how certain phases of the philosophy and of the details of wholesale transportation and placement of children in village and farm homes in western states looked to some of the contemporary leaders in child welfare of another religious faith.[17]

The incorporation charter of May 5, 1863, created "The Society for the Protection of Destitute Roman Catholic Children in the City of New York."

Children under fourteen could be entrusted to the Society by written consent of parent or guardian. If this consent was voluntary, the children were deemed to be in the lawful charge and custody of the corporation.

Idle, truant, vicious or homeless children between seven and fourteen years of age could be committed by any legally authorized magistrate in the City of New York.

Children of like age could be transferred to the Protectory by

[17] The data for this story of the founding of the New York Catholic Protectory were furnished by the Rev. Patrick A. O'Boyle, Executive Secretary of the Catholic Guardian Society of New York City.

the Commissioner of Public Charities and Correction of the City of New York.

The Society had power to return children to parents or "at discretion to bind out the said children, with their (the parents') consent, as apprentices or servants during minority or for any less period."

Regarding the supervision of such children it was stated in the act of incorporation: "This Corporation shall be the guardian of every child, bound or held for service, by virtue and in pursuance of the provisions of this act. It shall take care that the terms of the contract be faithfully fulfilled, and that such person be properly treated; and it is hereby made its special duty to inquire into the treatment of every such child, and redress any grievance in manner prescribed by law. And it shall be the duty of the master or his assignee, to whom any such child shall be bound to service, and he shall, by the terms of the indenture, be required, as often as once every six months, to report to the said corporation, the conduct and behavior of the said apprentice or child so bound to service, and whether such apprentice is still living under the care of the person to whom he was originally bound, and, if not, where else he or she may be."

In the *First Annual Report,* December 31, 1863, we find several principles of procedure that were different from those practiced in the migration work of Mr. Brace through the Children's Aid Society. For example, "it has therefore been a matter of deep solicitude with the managers so to discharge their duty, as that children may not be alienated from their parents, or let to forget or disregard their obligations to them." After short periods of training, therefore, many children who had been received for some delinquency and whose parents were able to support them had been returned to their parents for a double purpose: "to strengthen the family bond, and to promote the essential virtues of industry and economy. For we have not only the serious evil of weakening the family tie by unnecessarily separating children from their parents, but also to guard against what is hardly less pernicious, the mischief of taking away from these parents that main stimulus to exertion . . . the necessity of providing for their own households."

The *Third Annual Report* pronounces the apprenticeship system, as then practiced, a "great evil," and for two reasons:

1. Because the children were not prepared by previous discipline and education to ensure contentment, obedience and fidelity.

2. That the avarice of the persons to whom they were apprenticed caused most of them to be overworked, their education neglected, and the necessary supplies of food and clothing withheld. *Three-fourths* of those apprenticed up to that time, it was stated, had "become perfectly worthless."[18]

A lecture in Cooper Institute on November 23, 1864, delivered by L. Silliman Ives, LL.D., illustrates the attitude of the lecturer, who was speaking in behalf of the newly-established Catholic Protectory, and against the methods and philosophy of Mr. Brace. In turn, it was, at least in part, to criticisms such as these that Mr. Brace undoubtedly referred, in his *Annual Report* for 1868, when he protested against the "bigoted and ignorant prejudice against his emigration work on the part of certain people in New York City."

Among the things said by Dr. Ives, a few may be quoted:

Never in the history of that city has infant wretchedness stalked forth in such multiplied and humiliating forms. . . .

You will say, perhaps, that under the promptings of charity much has been done to check this evil. I reply that, in addition, much under the name of charity, has been done to foster and increase this evil. Efforts well meant, efforts flaming from a desire to do good, often actually do harm, sometimes from ignorance, sometimes from false zeal,

---

[18] This and other statements are given here with no responsibility assumed by the present writer for their statistical accuracy, but to show truthfully how the situation looked to those who were in charge of the Catholic Protectory. The writer of this historical sketch understands the statement in *The Third Annual Report* as to apprenticed children to refer specifically to those already apprenticed from the Protectory.

sometimes from false principles. An impulse of true charity may sometimes be perverted or misdirected by some other predominating impulse. Let us illustrate: A number of destitute families land upon our shores, seeking protection and subsistence in our city; they are strangers, and know little of the hardships and difficulties to be encountered in their new situation. Their extravagant expectations are not realized. Where they had been assured of ready employment, high wages, and encouraging sympathy, they experience only cold looks, hard labor, and scanty remuneration. Sickness overtakes them, debt turns them out of doors, or intemperance, perhaps, brings upon them its deadly swarm of miseries. Their children cry for bread, and are turned as beggars into the streets. They rehearse from door to door their piteous tale. Frequent repulse hardens them, drives them to exaggeration, to falsehood, to theft, sometimes to the most wretched haunts of vice, to save them from starvation. Public sympathy is excited. Measures are adopted to rescue these unfortunates from their deplorable condition. Here, then, may be the promptings of charity, the enlistment of the heart in a good and praiseworthy enterprise, but suppose these children differ from their benefactors in religion? Here a temptation prevails, steps are taken, in effecting this purpose, to place a bar between these children and their parents, to sever the precious tie which binds them to the parental heart and the parental influence. The yearnings of the mother are stilled by tales of wonderful advantages for her children, and promises of their speedy restoration to her arms. Yet all this while they are undergoing a secret process by which, it is hoped, that every trace of their early faith and filial attachment will be rooted out, and, finally, that their transportation to that indefinite region, "the far West," with changed names and lost parentage, will effectually destroy every association which might revive in their hearts of love for religion of which they have been robbed—the religion of their parents. Here, then, a new principle has been at work; what charity commenced, fanaticism has grossly perverted; or what we had supposed charity turns out to be only sectarian zeal.

Criticism again came to the surface in the National Conference of Charities and Corrections in 1887, when Mr. Elmer of Wisconsin attacked the investigation of Mr. Fry as made in that state.

The thoroughness of Mr. Fry's investigation in 1876 was also discredited at the time it was made.

Mr. Brace's Reaction to Criticism

The attitude of Mr. Brace toward all this criticism was not thoroughly scientific. He sent his own agents to investigate the results of their own work and when they found that the statements as to the numbers of their children actually in almshouses, jails or prisons were exaggerated, Mr. Brace seemed to accept their reports as justifications of his work as a whole. His position seems to have been that, short of definite knowledge that the boys and girls he had sent West were paupers or criminals in the clutches of the law, their lot was certainly better than it would have been had they remained in New York City. Although criticism of his work was openly resented by Mr. Brace, some influences suddenly reduced the volume of his emigration work between 1873 and 1876. The reduction began before the criticism expressed at the meeting of the National Prison Congress in 1876. The peak of emigration was reached in 1873 and has never in any year since 1875 attained even half the magnitude of that year. An improvement in methods of work seems to have been inaugurated in 1869 by the appointment of an agent, who was to have his residence in Chicago, rather than in New York. This was later followed by the appointment of agents resident in other western towns and confining their work to fairly definite districts, with the people and children of which they could be more often in touch. Up to this time, and afterward, to a less degree, supervision of children was left to a voluminous correspondence from the New York office and to the volunteer efforts of local committees that had taken part in the various distributions. The correspondence from the New York office was apparently faithfully persisted in for every child until repeated letters failed to bring any reply, or until the child was well established in the new home. The magnitude of the work of a single agent in the pioneer days is convincing evidence of the impossibility of anything like his attention to many individual children after the initial placement. For example, in the report for 1863 (page 50), we find the statement by one of the western agents that during the seven years since he had begun to work for the Society, he had "taken West fifty companies, averaging twenty-eight children each, and placed them in homes." This would be two hundred children a year, or a total of fourteen hundred. In addition he reports three trips "for prospecting, visiting, etc."

Another agent (Mr. Friedgen) was reported to have travelled over 102,000 miles in making thirty-four trips, with an average of fifty children, or a total of 1,700 children taken to western homes.

In the report for 1863 (page 6), Mr. Brace shows that he was becoming aware of some inadequacies in his procedure and argues for closer supervision. He says, "Letters are not enough. We endeavor to take the closest precautions in regard to the character of persons applying, but references are often given by clergymen or magistrates with too little care. It is our hope now to have a permanent agent to travel through many portions of the country and personally satisfy himself of the condition of the children." The considerations which led to the appointment of a Chicago agent in 1869 and the demands upon this agent's time, preventing the majority of the children from receiving much, if any, attention, are further evident from the following:

The plan, which had prevailed up to 1869, of arranging for the distribution of parties of children by correspondence with resident clergymen had proved unsatisfactory to the Society. In the first place, it had sometimes been found "impossible to obtain such information regarding localities as was desirable" with the result that "companies were not always located in the places best adapted for them." Also, where large companies were taken out without definite arrangements for their disposal, serious delays sometimes resulted, "accompanied by heavy and unavoidable expense."[19]

[19] *Annual Report*, 1870, pp. 12-13.

Another important fact which had been made clear to the Society by the experience of the pioneer period, was that absentee supervision, by letter and by proxy, was not in itself adequate to meet the many problems of maladjustment which arose among the rapidly expanding numbers of placed-out children. "There were continual cases to be looked after, defective children to be returned, refractory children to be visited, changes to be made, employers to be satisfied, and the interests of the little ones to be guarded, as well as preparations to be made for the parties now going out every fortnight."[20]

The chief work of the first Chicago agent during the first year was to prospect for suitable localities in which to place children, and from the many towns visited he selected and recommended those which seemed best adapted to the Society's needs.

In each town selected he made the acquaintance of "the people generally" as well as of "the leading persons" and from them a local committee was chosen whose duty it was "to distribute bills advertising the arrival of the company, to meet and assist the agent" and to pass upon the fitness of applicants for children, who were expected to apply in advance to some member of the local committee.

As one result of this change we are told that the work of placing was much more expeditiously handled, saving "serious labor and anxiety on the part of the agent in charge—a whole company sometimes passing out of his hands in half an hour after his arrival at his destination." Another result was the "saving of large hotel bills by the saving of time."

Once the ground was broken in a community and a local committee established, practically the entire responsibility for the placement and supervision of the children in that locality rested with the committee, except in the case of children who did not "give satisfaction." The entire work of transferring such children, we are told, was imposed upon and performed by the western agent,

---

[20] *Annual Report*, 1870, p. 11.

who reports, however, that from this source his "labors have not been seriously increased."[21]

From the remark of the western agent it may be pretty clearly inferred that as yet nothing approaching a positive personal supervision of each placed-out child could have been attempted. His supervision and transfer activities were still largely confined to children about whom complaints from other sources reached his ears.

Brace Succeeded by His Son

In 1890 Charles Loring Brace died, and his son, Charles Loring Brace, Jr., succeeded him in the work of the Children's Aid Society. The son had been trained as a civil engineer but, during the year before his father's death, had given up his position, and came to the Society to carry on, with steadfast loyalty to his father's methods, the many-sided work his pioneer father had started.

In 1898 the new leader made a personal study of the welfare of 151 children who in fifteen different parties had been placed in Iowa, northern Missouri, eastern Nebraska and Kansas. His conclusions were as follows:[22]

Doing well	90 percent
Dead	3 "
Brought back to New York	3 "
Sent to institutions	2 "
Lost track of	2 "

Likewise, in 1900 the Society made an attempt to estimate its success with the whole 22,121 children they had placed in free foster family homes up to that time. Their figures have a marvellously accurate appearance when the kind of information that was available for a period of forty-seven years is taken into consideration. As quoted first in the *Annual Report* for 1900 and thereafter repeatedly without change in the *Annual Reports* for 1905-1914 inclusive, the percentages arrived at are:[23]

[21]*Ibid.*, p. 13.   [22]*Forty-sixth Annual Report*, 1898, p. 32.
[23]*Forty-eighth Annual Report*, 1900, p. 5.

Doing well	87 percent
Returned to New York	8 "
Dead	2 "
Committed petty crimes	0.25 "
Left their homes	2.75 "

These percentages were a challenge to the accuracy of Dr. Hart's conclusions[24] as to the percentage of success among the children who had been placed by the Society in Minnesota previous to 1883. Because of the discrepancy between these findings, and on account of the magnitude and prominence of the Children's Aid Society, it seemed wise to make an independent effort to estimate the work of the Society, at least in so far as the records of the Society would permit.

This effort was made in 1922 by Miss Georgia G. Ralph, of the New York School of Social Work, with the coöperation of Mr. Brace, who gave full permission to consult all the Society's records.

The method used was to trace certain developments in the work of the New York Children's Aid Society, by summarizing the general status of all the children under sixteen placed out during one year in each of five decades, as shown by the latest information on the books of the Society. The years 1865, 1875, 1885, 1895 and 1905 were taken. 1855 was omitted because the methods of work of that year were of the same general character as those of 1865, changes in methods of placing and supervision not having begun until 1869. 1915 was omitted because the children placed then had at the time of the study been in care too short a time to be comparable to those placed in earlier decades. This summary disclosed five well-defined groups, as follows:

1. Children about whom no information is recorded after placement.

2. Children who left the homes in which they were placed without the knowledge or intervention of the Society.

---

[24]See this chapter, pp. 114-16.

FREE FOSTER HOMES

3. Children who returned, or who were returned to New York, or to relatives there or elsewhere.

4. Children who were in reformatories or other institutions at the time of the latest report.

5. Children not included in the preceding groups. These remained for longer or shorter periods in the homes found for them and were supervised by the Society through correspondence or visitation.

Under these headings the information was summarized in the following table. The last two columns show a decreasing percentage of unfavorable facts and a correspondingly increasing percentage of favorable facts, over a period of forty years.

Year Placed	Total No.	Group 1 No Information	Group 2 Left Foster Home	Group 3 Returned to Rel. in N.Y.	Group 4 In Institution or other Information about Child Unfavorable	Group 5 Total Unfavorable	Group 5 Total in Home Favorable	Total Unfavorable, percentage	Total Favorable, percentage
Boys									
1865	318	80	70	27	16	193	125	57	43
1875	222	62	18	21	5	106	116	48	52
1885	182	5	36	25	8	74	108	40	60
1895	127	0	12	23	11	46	81	38	62
1905	273	1	19	69	14	103	170	38	62
Girls									
1865	71	7	4	6	5	22	49	31	69
1875	32	2	0	4	4	10	22	31	69
1885	29	3	0	1	3	7	22	24	66
1895	42	0	0	5	1	6	36	14	86
1905	92	0	2	10	6	18	64	22	78

Although the above table shows progress, a careful study justifies at least an honest doubt as to unqualified success with boys, the figures varying from 57 percent doubtful in 1865 to 38 percent in 1905; and with girls from 31 percent doubtful in 1865 to 20 percent in 1905. In short, the above study of all the facts available suggested the need for a genuinely critical attitude of the Society toward the validity of some of its methods. This attitude was long in coming.

Although with the smaller numbers sent West after 1880,[25] more attention could be given to the individual child with correspondingly lower percentages of children showing signs of unfavorable experiences on the records, still the distribution of children in public was kept up as previously described. Also, as late as the 1918-1919 *Report,* there was evidence of undivided faith in a substantially unchanged philosophy of permanent separation of children from their own relatives, and of the importance of the Society's emigration work. The cost of the emigration service for the current year was $51,469.30, in comparison with total current expense of the Society of $539,740.79.[26]

The crowning work of the Children's Aid Society is in rescuing orphan and deserted children, as well as children of dissolute parents who are unfit guardians, and placing them in carefully selected homes in various parts of the country, where they will have the benefit of good family influence as well as proper schooling and training.[27]

The sources from which the 252 children of 1919 came are given as follows:

From social workers	5
From orphanages and institutions	150
Surrendered by relatives in order to remove the children from dangerous influences	63
From our lodging houses for homeless boys	34
	252

[25] See summaries by Miss Ralph, given on p. 121.
[26] Expenditures other than for emigration work included support of schools, boys' clubs, lodging houses, farm school, medical work, shelters for mothers and babies, and fresh air work.
[27] New York Children's Aid Society, *Annual Report,* 1919, p. 33.

In principle, therefore, at the end of sixty-seven years of continuous service by father and son, the emigration work in 1919 was the same as it had been at the beginning—namely, to provide permanent free homes in the country for those whose homes were unfit, and for the homeless children of the city. Although the terrible pressure of numbers has not been felt of late years as it was by the elder Brace in 1853, the free foster country home is still offered, not only to the whole orphan and to the child who has been taken from his unfit parents by the courts, but also to the child whom parents and relatives are willing to surrender to the care of the Society. The readiness to take children surrendered voluntarily by parents or relatives, and to place such children in permanent free homes in other families, raises a serious question as to the general soundness of the policy as such and as to the Society's standards in the matter of intake, at so late a date as 1919. The percentage of boys returned to relatives, based on the records of all the boys placed out in 1865, 1875, 1885, 1895 and 1905, shows a steady rise for total numbers of boys under sixteen placed out in those years, from less than 10 percent in 1865 to over 25 percent in 1905. This increase in returns to relatives may be due to harder treatment of boys in foster homes and to greater ease of travel back home; or to the fact that boys taken from relatives have been in a less and less desperate condition compared with earlier years; or to still other causes. Whatever the cause, the facts of acceptance of surrendered children for permanent free placement in foster homes, taken together with the fact of an increasing number of returns of such children to their relatives, raises these questions: Is it fair to the foster parent, to the boy, or to his relatives, to place such a boy in a free foster home and try to keep him there during his minority?

It does not seem fair to the relatives that they be compelled to surrender a child permanently in order to get whatever care he may need temporarily.

It does not seem fair to the boy, because it implies failure to recognize his individuality, and because blood ties that are too strong to permit him to forget them are a constant stimulus to him to try to reëstablish his own family relationships whenever possible.

It does not seem fair to the foster parents, who undertake to give a child a free home during his minority, only to find that no matter how much they do for him, his heart and his allegiance belong, not to them, but to his own kin.

Philosophy of a Society Placing Children in Free Homes Only

In short, after seventy years of work in placing destitute and neglected children in foster family homes, the Society still failed adequately to recognize the individuality of some children; it forced them into free foster homes where the relationship could not always be permanent and where they could not be loved as own children are loved; and yet were too young and too much in need of education to pay the whole of their keep by their own work. The Society still stopped short of full success because it did not consistently refuse to put any child into a free family home unless it was clearly for the good of that individual child to go there. The philosophy of placement of a child during the compulsory school age and under the legal working age in a free home which needs his work more than it desires to see his potential capacities developed is a false philosophy. It is the wolf of the old indenture philosophy of child labor in the sheepskin disguise of a so-called good or Christian family home.

In actual practice, the only way to safeguard the individuality of a child is to recognize that an immature boy or girl is a money liability and not an immediate money asset. If a foster family will not pay the bill because it loves the child as its own, a child-placing agency ought to help pay the bill or refuse to accept such a child for care. Slowly the Society began to recognize something of the force of this truth.

Signs of Self-Criticism and Change within the Society

In 1915 changes were made by the Society in its methods of studying children prior to placement.

All children were examined by a physician and suggestions made by him as to treatment. Where this examination or the previous history suggested the possibility of mental abnormality, children were examined at some clinic for atypical children and the advice of the clinic was considered in disposing of the child.

Blanks for reporting by the foster home and the school teacher were introduced and used for children placed in localities where school advantages were not of the best and where there was likelihood of children being kept out of school to work. These blanks asked for a report on length of school term (in days), number of days attended, etc.

When Miss Ralph made her study in 1922, the quality of the homes in the south seemed, from the records, to be distinctly inferior on the whole to that of homes in the east and west. The labor motive was plainly visible. The legal requirements as to education were low and the chances of children securing adequate education, as a rule, were not good. The Society placed its dull and less promising children in southern homes.

But investigations of the families of children received were becoming much more comprehensive, and all the records were fuller and more explicit. There seemed to be closer coöperation with other organizations.

Still the disposition of difficult cases which are not absorbed under the system of placing in free family homes was not fully met. It began to seem distinctly advantageous, if money could be had with which to pay board of children, that some should be so boarded. Especially was this true of those children who were too great a tax on the average free home and in consequence had to be shifted too often for their own good. Also some provision was necessary for the longer training of older boys who proved to be seriously unstable and in danger of becoming chronic drifters.

This need for temporary family care of children, in addition to the free home placement of permanently destitute and orphaned children, was further emphasized by the work of the new Medical Bureau started by the Society during the year ending June 30, 1919. The report of this Medical Bureau for its first year stated its needs as follows:[28]

There are many children referred to us whose mothers have suddenly been taken ill or placed in a hospital. The children must be cared for at once and our places are already crowded. These children are of all ages, but the greatest need is for infants.

Again, in the *Report* for 1923, Mr. William F. Johnson comments on the work of the Society, after a survey of all its phases. He personally accompanied a party of twelve children and helped to place them in homes in Iowa. Mr. Johnson emphasizes points in child welfare procedure which have already been emphasized in these pages and which for seventy years had not been sufficiently regarded by the emigration work of the Society:[29]

There is a well-established conviction on the part of social workers that no child should be taken from his natural parents until everything possible has been done to build up the home into what an American home should be. Even after a child has been removed, every effort should be continued to rehabilitate the home and when success crowns one's efforts, the child should be returned. In other words, every social agency should be a "home builder" and not a "home breaker."

There is a large field of child welfare work being met so well by cities like Boston, Chicago and Philadelphia (but practically untouched in New York City), through a scheme of boarding homes, which care for children from homes temporarily broken down by illness and temporary economic disaster.[30]

Every department of every child-caring organization shares the responsibility for the continuation of this distressing situation. Why should not the Home-Finding Department of the Children's Aid So-

---

[28] *Annual Report*, 1919, pp. 19-20.   [29] *Annual Report*, 1923, p. 14.
[30] The story of this development in Boston will be told in Chapter VII.

FREE FOSTER HOMES

ciety, the pioneer in bringing together the child without a home and the home without a child, also be the pioneer in meeting the need of the suspended home?[31]

Charles Loring Brace, son of a pioneer father, heard these words and acted by establishing in 1923, within the New York Children's Aid Society, a new department of Boarding in Foster Family Homes. In so doing the son was not disloyal to the method of his father. The free foster family home remains for those young children who, because of the death of their parents, or from some other impossible home situation, need a permanent substitute for their own homes. He was not denying the truth of the father's vision of the worth of the family home for a child, but he enlarged it by opening boarding family homes under careful supervision as temporary substitutes for their own homes to those children who should not be permanently separated from their kin. In so doing he was making it possible to use what Lincoln once called "the mystic chords of memory," and, we might add, of affection, as means to draw the hearts and minds of unfortunate children toward a larger life and stronger character. Already, after six years, the number of new children placed during 1929 in boarding foster family homes by the New York Children's Aid Society's new department is 1623[1] as compared with 228[32] new children placed during 1929 by the same society in free foster family homes. Truly, with all reverence, the son can say, "I have come not to destroy but to fulfill my father's work."

Henceforth it should be impossible for the New York Children's Aid Society, or any of its followers, to urge loving, but poor or ill, parents to seek their child's welfare by permanent surrender for placement in a free foster home. During seventy years an exclusive zeal for the free foster home, as the only method of relief for the destitute child away from his own home, had led Mr. Brace,

---

[31] New York Children's Aid Society, *Annual Report*, 1923, pp. 18-19.
[32] Figures reported to writer by New York Children's Aid Society office, April 16, 1930.

and at least one other pioneer, as well as scores of followers, to offer sorrowing parents the solution described by one of Mr. Brace's agents. The reader will recall the passage:[33]

> You remember Nancy T. whose mother came to your office the day I was there. Oh, what a dear little one she is! How I love her! She looked so sad as she sat between her father and mother the day I left. How solemn the trust, when these weeping parents gave me their daughter. I promised to be a father to her. None seemed so sad after starting as she. . . . Please give to her sad parents this pleasing intelligence. Ask them to let me have her little sister that is nine years old, and I will find her a good home.

In a later chapter, a family situation will be described in which the recently organized Boarding-Out Department of the Children's Aid Society has been of service. The contrast between the philosophy of family relationship, on which the Society acted in caring for Nancy T., and the philosophy that recognizes the importance of maintaining every possible asset available in kinship ties, exemplified by the same society in the help given the Kimbark children, is one of the most striking evidences of fundamental change known to the writer in all the long history of the care of dependent children.

II. Origin and Development of the State Children's Home Societies

Another influence that for over forty years has tended in many states to modify both the form and the spirit of the old indenture system, came through the personality of a man from the Middle West, Martin Van Buren Van Arsdale. He founded the first State Children's Home Society, of which afterward there were many, so-called, not because administered by the state, but because their activities were state-wide. These "state" societies later became federated in the National Children's Home and Welfare

---

[33]Page 105, this book.

FREE FOSTER HOMES

Association, an organization still kept up for reasons of historical sentiment and social fellowship, although for some years its professional activities have been affiliated somewhat with the National Conference of Social Work. Some of the individual societies have become members of the Child Welfare League of America.

This movement did not start until 1883, thirty years after Mr. Brace founded the New York Children's Aid Society, and seems ot to have been directly inspired by the New York movement. This apparent fact of independent origin is of some interest, because the new movement started in Illinois, which state, with Indiana, Michigan and Wisconsin, had received the largest share of the flood of immigrant children from New York during the decade from 1865-1875. During the next decade, 1875-1885, the crest of the wave from New York had swept westward, leaving Illinois almost dry of further influx from the New York Children's Aid Society. In brief, the rise and development of the free foster home movement of the State Children's Home Societies is as follows.

Martin Van Buren Van Arsdale[34] was born in 1841 near Vincennes, Indiana, and was graduated from Hanover College in the same state. He served honorably in the Civil War and graduated from the McCormick Theological Seminary in Chicago, entering upon his first pastorate in Princeton, Indiana, in 1868. He married in 1869 and was successively pastor of five more churches, two in Indiana and three in Illinois, holding the last in Green Valley, Illinois, from 1877 to 1882. He gave up this charge to make preparations for his permanent work of placing children in free foster homes, which he began in 1883. The next paragraph, taken from Mrs. Van Arsdale's account, tells how the idea of his life's work came to him.

[34] The early part of Mr. Van Arsdale's story is based on a narrative given to the writer in April, 1925. The account of later development of the movement has been prepared in part from the testimony of the founder, in part from the testimony of associates in the work, and in part from other records and statements of first-hand observers and students.

In my early acquaintance with my husband I found him to have a great desire to be of service to humanity. . . . He said that the world needs love, and of course suggested that he needed me to help him in his work. He wondered if I could love everybody. I was not so sure but said I would try. This may sound very personal to you, but it tends to show you that he was determined to do a work, and for this he lived. . . . I will give you some experiences which show that Mr. Van Arsdale was imbued with the idea of child saving work as far back as when he attended college. The first year of our pastorate work we attended an alumni meeting. There we took a walk through a wooded grove and came to a large log. He said, "This is where I promised God with his help I would deliver all children from the poorhouses." He pointed to the poorhouse in the distance and said "There is where I spent my Sunday afternoons conducting a Sunday School among the paupers. There I saw the innocent children mingling with the degraded grown-up men and women." There was one child—a fair little girl—who always went with him to the top of the hill and begged him not to leave her—so this touched his heart to make the promise.

When attending the Theological Seminary his work was among the newsboys of Chicago, and the result was, he organized the Newsboys' Home. He said "these boys have sisters, and something should be done for them some day. I am going to start a work for them." One day, this was in 1882 in Green Valley, Illinois, while working in his garden he came in, hoe in hand, and said, "I have found the way I am going to do my work. The Bible tells us God setteth the solitary in families." I think my statements will show you the idea was original, not copied from Mr. Brace or any other work of the kind. I never heard him mention Mr. Brace's work, but after we had the work started, children were sent out by Mr. Brace.

The first child taken by Mr. Van Arsdale was from Vandalia, Illinois. Children were cared for one year in our home in Bloomington. We started without an organization, but soon headquarters were at Chicago with a strong Board of Directors. A home for children was provided and the work became prosperous.

The reader of this account of Mr. Van Arsdale's contact with children in the almshouse near Hanover College, Indiana, has doubtless recalled the story of Mr. Brace in the almshouse of New York City on Blackwell's Island in 1849. The stimulus to service seems to have come to both men directly from the sight of actual human beings in need—not from any secondhand academic accounts of such need.

The vow made by this undergraduate student some time in the 60's was not fulfilled until after a lapse of fifteen years. Apparently the first and persistent idea in this young man's mind of the way to get children out of mixed almshouses was to build institutions into which children only were to be gathered. The need for large buildings as a means to help needy children may easily have been kept in his mind by the Newsboy's Home in Chicago, which he was partly instrumental in founding while a theological student at McCormick Seminary in the late 60's. It would seem that the idea of institutional care as the only means of keeping his vow to get children out of almshouses, persisted in Van Arsdale's mind until the memorable day in 1882 when the thought of the one-by-one method of foster family home care came to him in his Green Valley garden. Thus it becomes easy to see why the fulfillment of his vow was so long postponed.

Now that the revelation as to the method of caring for dependent children had come to him, how was he, a young minister, still poor in spite of his "call," to put this method into actual practice?

Again in the words of Mrs. Van Arsdale:

For about one year after he resigned his pastorate, Mr. Van Arsdale did not commence his child-saving work. He moved to Bloomington, Illinois, and accepted a position as financial secretary (which had been previously arranged) with the Industrial School for girls at Evanston. He was successful in raising money, but could not take children, only girls committed by the courts. Mr. Van Arsdale soon found that this was not his work. His resignation was handed in before the year expired. He said when taking the position that it would be a stepping-stone to his child-saving work; he thought he might learn something about how to help girls.

The story of the first child taken on Van Arsdale's own initiative is told as follows by one of Mr. Van Arsdale's early and trusted colleagues:[35]

He went in May 1882 (Mrs. Van Arsdale says 1883) to Vandalia with the thought that he would obtain an opportunity to lecture and take up a collection in behalf of homeless children. With his own heart all aglow in their behalf he thought everybody would be interested in their welfare. His reception by the deacon, however, was so cold that he says, "I began to wonder if there was any train out of town that night, but I proposed to call to see the pastor, Brother Todd, next morning. Brother Todd was kind and considerate. He asked me to take dinner with him after morning service, but I preferred the hotel. He asked me to go to church with him, and I said yes."

"He preached from the text, 'If the righteous scarcely be saved, where shall the ungodly and sinner appear?' I listened for the application of the sermon, as I knew that he being a Scotchman would make an application at the close, and expected to hear him say 'Thou art the man!' But he closed more tenderly, addressing the unconverted and pleading with them to come with the righteous, though the righteous were 'scarcely,' yet they were 'saved,' and this after all was the end and aim of Christ's coming. I felt pretty good and walked up to him just before he said the benediction, while the people were standing, and asked him if I could make an announcement. I began by saying, 'If you have any homeless, neglected children in Vandalia, I have come to see them, and if possible to provide homes for them.' I sat down and the people all went home without speaking to me. I then went to the hotel sorry that I had said anything about homeless children, almost sorry that I had been born. I craved sympathy, wanted to talk to someone, wanted to see my wife, but I could not till next day, so I thought I would talk with the landlady, and I did. To my surprise she said, 'I am so glad to see you. We have a child here whose mother works for me.' I said that I would like to see the mother. After a little time the mother came into the room. I went to Greasy Row where the child had been sent to board. I saw her sitting on the floor picking the bones from the hotel. The mother said I could have

[35]Rev. E. P. Savage, *Home Finder of Minnesota*, November 1904.

her. Well, this was not what I wanted. I wanted to lecture and take up a collection, but since I could not get this, I said, 'All right, I will take her.' By this time the church bell began to ring. I went to church, determined that I would speak to the people. After the sermon I rose and asked the friends to patiently hear me from three to five minutes. Well, I told them all I knew, and had a few moments to spare. After the benediction the brethren and sisters came and asked me who the little girl was. Deacon McCord came too, and when I said, 'Brother McCord, you must be guardian of the child,' 'Not for this town,' said the Deacon, 'that child no one in the country would have.' I walked on with the Deacon. I found something now to say about the righteous who are scarcely saved, and the sinner too. I succeeded in wiring the wife, and then I got the Deacon to consent to be appointed the guardian of the little girl. Next morning the County Judge made the appointment, and I soon took the child and was on the train bound for home. I now felt that I had someone else's child and had become responsible for it. I did not know what to do. I was like an elephant with the care of a little chicken. The best thing I could think of doing was to hire a berth on a sleeper, which I did, and was sorry when morning came, as the Lord only knew what I would do with the child when she woke up. I wished for my wife now as I had never done before. About eight o'clock the next day I arrived home. The little girl, the same week, was placed in her home, where she is today, a bright, promising girl of twelve years. I have been to Vandalia since and Brother Todd and all his people and all the ministers and all the churches welcome us, and not a year passes without contributions from Vandalia to our Society, and we have taken many children from among them."

Of this first experience in child-helping on his own plans, Mrs. Van Arsdale gives this account:

Mr. Van Arsdale resigned (as financial secretary of the Evanston School) and started his work at Vandalia without my knowledge. He telegraphed that he was bringing with him a child, so from that time I had the care of the children until we moved to Chicago. I did all my own work, washed and cared for the children. When I heard a carriage drive up at night I knew there were children coming. Then they would be washed and put to bed even if it was two o'clock at night.

At first the independent work of Mr. Van Arsdale seems to have been a combination of placing children in family homes and helping girls to get an education. He called his work at the outset, in 1883, "The American Educational Aid Society" whose objects, according to its first annual report were "to coöperate with young women and homeless and dependent girls of special promise in fitting them for the requirements of life."

Of this name and this educational part of the work, Mrs. Van Arsdale further says:

I want to explain to you that the name for our work was Educational Aid Society because at that time there was a need for a work for girls. This was decided on by Mr. Van Arsdale after his experience in the Industrial School for Girls. The class of girls he wanted to reach was mostly girls who needed a little help to fit themselves to be self-supporting. However, he did not start out at Vandalia with this idea in mind and did not represent his work as such, but only the work for children. In travelling in the children's work, many times his attention would be called to a case of some worthy girl who, if she could only have a little help, would be saved to a successful life. This need seemed to impress him to add this department to the child-saving work. This part of the educational work was not expensive as schools and colleges coöperated by giving free tuition in many cases. Dr. Green's school at Poynette, Wisconsin, was one, also Oberlin College of Ohio, and the normal school at Normal, Illinois. I was in love with this part of the work as well as the work for children. There were twenty-eight assisted at different times in our home while they were preparing and getting ready to go to school. The Board ladies of Bloomington and Englewood helped me in this work. The girls made good records that would be interesting to write.

This total number of girls helped toward an education may be compared with the number of children taken during the first years for placement in foster homes—40[36] the first year, 71 the

[36] Figures given in a letter written in 1917 by Mrs. Eva L. Evans, a Bloomington woman who was closely associated with the work of the Van Arsdales from 1883 on.

second, 114 the third, and 140 the fourth. These numbers indicate that in spite of the name of the new society, the chief activity of Mr. Van Arsdale was, from the first, the placement of dependent children in free family homes.

Of this home-finding work, Mr. Savage says:[37]

When Brother Van Arsdale began he had to blaze his way through an almost untrodden wilderness. So far as we know no one ever started out with the one great thought burning in his soul, "There is a home in a good family for every homeless child and woe be to me if I do not find it." He laid his plans and toiled laboriously to reach the ideal of covering the land with a network of kind-hearted and efficient helpers who should make this great idea a blessed fact. "It is the solemn obligation resting upon God's people everywhere to help, and I will organize them in every town into coöperating committees who will feel as I do, their obligation to God for the welfare of needy children within their reach. I will cast myself and my work upon the sympathy of the people for the means to do it with."

He has told me of the early days of struggle, going to towns in Illinois where he was not received with any favor and not a penny could be obtained, so that he was accustomed to carry a patent window fastener which he would go from house to house to sell in order to obtain enough to pay his bills and get out of town.

From the very first, Brother Van Arsdale seemed to be imbued with the belief that his society was destined to be national in its scope. The first name he adopted was the American Educational Aid Association. It was the American, not the Illinois, Aid Association; it was for America, the whole land, not for Chicago or Illinois alone.

In 1885, two years after Van Arsdale began his independent work and gave his society a name, he took out a charter in Illinois. Before his death in 1893, he had changed the name to "The National Children's Home Society." There was a General Board of Directors and Mr. Van Arsdale was the superintendent.

Apparently he had worked for at least two years without either a legal charter or formal backing. His actual procedure, from the

[37]Savage, *op. cit.*

first, in the care of dependent children, seems to have been as follows. He went from town to town, literally from door to door, explaining his method, collecting money, taking destitute children, and seeking for homes in which to place these children. He also took every opportunity to tell of his work and ask for support in churches. In each town where he placed one or more foster children he created a local advisory board among people who had helped him in finding foster homes and who were willing to subscribe from one to ten dollars a year for the support of his work, and also to help him in the supervision of children.

The poverty of those first days is shown by the fact, already mentioned by Mr. Savage, that he sold small articles to housewives to supplement church collections and individual subscriptions, and also by the fact that his own home was used as a temporary shelter for the children taken but not yet placed.

Mrs. Evans, in the letter before quoted, further says:

At the very first, so far as he could not find foster homes at once for destitute children taken under his care, Mrs. Van Arsdale took care of the children in her own home. Her statement is "Before the Society was organized and for years thereafter, when it had no friends, no following, no money, nothing but a few children and but three workers, when discouragements were more plentiful than dollars, Mr. Van Arsdale never faltered in his confidence of the ultimate success of his undertaking."

He was most ably seconded by Mrs. Van Arsdale, who carried the heaviest end of the load by staying at home and caring for the children[38] until homes were found for them.

Equally with her husband should Mrs. Van Arsdale be honored of the Society, for without her help Mr. Van Arsdale could not have established the foundation of the work which has become so far-reaching.

[38] A small receiving home for this purpose had been started in Aurora, Ill., by 1885, after which time the Illinois Society developed such homes in a succession of places: Englewood, Evanston, DuQuoin, Rantoul, Shelbyville and Potomac. At present all but DuQuoin and Evanston have been given up as receiving homes; and Potomac Industrial School for Girls has taken the place of the old receiving homes at Rantoul and Shelbyville.

Extension and Philosophy of the State Children's Home Society Movement

For the first few years the actual acceptance and placement of children by Mr. Van Arsdale seems to have been confined to the state of Illinois; but at least from the date of his charter, in 1885, he had plans for extending the same kind of work to other states. In 1888, the Board of the National Children's Home Society gave a charter to a State Board of Directors in Iowa. An Iowa superintendent was chosen who began child-placing in that state with the aid of local advisory boards, as in Illinois. Minnesota, as the third state, was organized in the same way in 1889. Men of state prominence have been willing to serve upon the Boards of these State Children's Home Societies. For example, the first president of the Minnesota State Board was Dr. Cyrus Northrup of the State University.

In addition to the State Board of Directors, the superintendent and staff, it was planned to have a local advisory board in each community where children were placed in foster homes, and also in each state a receiving home for the temporary care of children. By 1892, state societies had been organized as above in ten states, with ten receiving homes and 1,500 local advisory boards. A monthly paper was published to the number of 16,000 copies, each contributor of a dollar or more per year being entitled to receive a copy. The first ten states to be organized were: Illinois, Iowa, Minnesota, Michigan, Missouri, Indiana, California, Wisconsin, Tennessee, North Dakota and South Dakota. In 1892, in the National Conference of Charities,[39] Rev. F. M. Gregg, an associate of Mr. Van Arsdale's in the extension of his work, who had become the assistant superintendent, stated, as follows, the purposes of the National Society, during these formative years under Mr. Van Arsdale:

To seek the homeless, neglected, and destitute children and to become

[39] *Report*, 1892, p. 415.

their friend and protector, to find homes for them in well-to-do families and to place them wisely; to look occasionally with discretion into the homes, and thus prevent abuse and neglect, and to replace children, when necessary; to make it possible for persons (without children of their own) to adopt a child; to minister in comforting assurance to parents in fear of leaving their children penniless and homeless; to protect society by guaranteeing proper home training and education to the unfortunate little ones against its greatest enemies, ignorance and vice; to extend our organization into sister states.

By 1903, the number of states in which there were Children's Home Societies organized on substantially the above lines for the placement of children in free foster homes, was twenty-five, these having under their supervision about 12,000 children, and receiving within the year about 2,229 new children. A movement had set in, however, to break loose from any administrational dependence upon the National Society. In 1897, Wisconsin took out a separate charter, and in the same year Illinois itself also took out a new state charter as the Illinois Children's Home and Aid Society. Hereafter, the National Children's Home Society became more and more a federation of the administratively independent state societies for the purpose of conference, education, and exchange of ideas and service.

By 1916, there were thirty-six state societies in the national organization, its name being changed to the National Children's Home and Welfare Association.

To show clearly how these early efforts influenced the development of methods and ideals of work for the dependent child, the first-hand record of a pioneer worker in the southern part of Illinois is now presented. This part of the state used to be known as "Egypt," and the record is illuminating because of the variety of functions which a worker in those days was expected to assume, as well as for the precariousness of her compensation.

Pioneer Case-Work in Foster Home Care in "Egypt," Southern Illinois

On a cloudy November morning in 1894, two women left Chicago to become district superintendents for the Illinois Society in "Egypt." They were the first women workers in this area, although for the three previous years a civil war veteran, Mr. J. E. Field, had been laying the foundations for the work. His pay was fifty percent of his collections, and his early experiences and methods were similar to Mr. Van Arsdale's. These two women worked together for the first few days and then separated, each to her own district, the western and the eastern parts of southern Illinois. Mrs. Arvilla Haines was to take charge of the territory lying west of the Illinois Central Railroad, and Mrs. A. M. Wilcox that on the eastern side. The statement gives a vivid account of the question of wages; of the day by day contacts with people, churches, county boards of supervisors, and with dependent children and, finally, of the acquisition of a receiving home at Du Quoin:[40]

My little notebook gives brief record of those first experiences in the town of Kinmundy. Being strangers, we were, of course, obliged to go to a hotel, finding a good one. Mr. Lingenfelter, editor of the *Gazette*, and J. F. Donovan, mayor of the town, called on us, helping us much by suggestions and information. We found both Northern and Southern M. E. churches, also a Presbyterian church. Making as busy a day as possible, we attended a prayer meeting in the evening, being invited to speak on the work of the Children's Home Society as freely as we wished. A meeting was arranged for the next evening which was not large, but those present were attentive and interested enough to ask questions and promise help for the future, though seeming to feel unable to help financially at that time. South Illinois was not rich, but her people were warm-hearted and kind to the stranger. We had both started out on our own finances; received fifty-five cents in collections; stayed from Wednesday evening until Saturday morning, hotel bills being $2.50 each. Not encouraging!

[40] Letter of Mrs. A. M. Wilcox in 1917.

Odin was our next point. Saturday, November 10th. Weather cold, windy with snow, and the mental mercury at as low an ebb. Made several calls and arrangements to speak at three churches tomorrow. Even at this late day a delightful interview with several ladies and gentlemen comes back to my mind, telling again of the restful effect of their genial understanding and wise suggestions. How helpful, when everything was so new and hard to get hold of. Spoke at three churches during the day, having the entire evening to myself at the fourth church. Receipts $4.00.

A letter from Mr. Hoover[41] to Mrs. Haines put us right as to our financial gains. It is here, verbatim: "Divide your income by two, then the expenses incurred by you in performing the district work is to be deducted from your half, and the balance of your half to be kept on your salary. The other half is to be sent to this place, unless you have incurred special expenses for the Association as a result of directions from me." I recall that we caught ourselves staring at each other rather stupidly, as we strove to reckon where a salary was to be pinched out. Our combined receipts thus far did not exceed $10.00, and expenses more than covered that amount. What was there so far, for the man at the head of the work as state superintendent? What, indeed, for our two selves, while we had paid our own expenses so far? Well, time will tell, and we must still push on and see what progress we can make on the funds we started with of our own. If at the end of this month we cannot see how to solve the financial problem we can quit and go home.

From Odin, Mrs. Haines took the train for her own district, Sandoval being her first stopping-place.

Mt. Vernon is my next stopping-place. An apparent mistake in choosing my hotel proved to be providential, as it led to finding a boy who

[41]About a year after the death of Mr. Van Arsdale in 1893, Mr. George K. Hoover succeeded him as Superintendent of the National Children's Home Society. There was dissatisfaction with his method. During his régime, the Hon. Harry B. Hurd (later drafter of the Illinois juvenile court law of 1899) had with others formed the Chicago Children's Aid Society. After Hoover's removal from office in 1897, a new charter was taken out in Illinois for a union of the National Children's Home Society and the Chicago Children's Aid Society, under the name of the Illinois Children's Home and Aid Society. Dr. Hastings H. Hart then became Superintendent of the new Society.

was to be sent to the Reform School. This motherless lad, gone astray because of lack of proper care, did come into our care after a trial, and was sheltered in the Christian home of our dear Mr. Field; his father paying the magnificent sum of $10.00 a year for the term of five years. Thus the work was begun. Here I found my most efficient helper, Mrs. Joel Watson, who was president of our local board in this county seat of Jefferson County. Here I decided to make my headquarters if it became possible for me to remain in this work in "Egypt." Mrs. W. went with me to call on all the ministers, to make arrangements for presenting the work in the different churches on Sunday. Four talks in churches; two disappointments; and $3.75 in collections. $1.50 out of many calls on Saturday; a most genial place to rest in. But I repeat, I have an assurance that the work is practically begun.

With the New Year I was domiciled in rented rooms in Mt. Vernon.

Surely angels must have recorded the things done by the family of Joel Watson, who gave me, the following summer, the free use of a lovely old homestead, finely situated for such a child-saving shelter, near to the oftenest-used railroad station, with plenty of room inside and out. We here gathered our forlorn little charges, making it not only a food and lodging shelter, but a place where most of them received Christian teaching for the first time in their lives. Some of the sidelights of this period are a comfort to me now, when memory recalls the many results arising therefrom.

Miss C—— K—— as matron, and Miss M—— B—— as our cook and housekeeper, proved efficient as such, and were agreeable to all friends, as well as to the children. Bible study and Scripture reading at night, and the singing of many of the religious hymns, sent the children to bed with many good thoughts and impressions which were quite new to the majority, many of whom had never seen or heard of the Bible before.

Two years thus. . . . The work had strangely outgrown itself. Something just had to be done. Mrs. Watson had hoped to prevail upon the owner of this most homelike home to donate it to the Society, so she could secure promised help for enlarging and bettering the buildings. Almost the entire district had become proud of its good name, and the saving work that had resulted. Mr. Watson seemed quite in favor of the plan, but members of his family opposed it strongly; nobody could blame them, as it surely was a beautiful home. Meantime, in my district work I had found in DuQuoin an old Presbyterian Academy; four stories of well-built brick walls, and a sufficiently sound, well-divided arrangement of rooms. During my regular visit I had gone with some members of our local advisory board to look at this property, the Du Quoin people being greatly in favor of its purchase for our purpose if it could be done. The house stood on a low hill, overlooking its forty acres of tillable and pasture land, the beautiful cedar and other kinds of trees scattered over them making a beautiful picture. And all this for $2,500. Could any woman carrying the already sleep-defying task of that district, dare to hope to also compass this? Then there came like an answer straight from the Infinite, the call at the home of Mr. Charles Stinson (of the mercantile firm of Stinson Brothers) who urged the trial of it, and promised to give $500 if the rest of the price was raised. Before the transaction was completed, he doubled his offer, putting the full amount in the bank to await the final outcome. Well, the superintendent stepped right off the thin ice, and walked on solid ground clear to the "Great Day" besides losing no time for the general work for the children. She carried a $1,000 staff, and knew the hand which proffered it. When the plea of homeless children once became fully comprehended through that warm-hearted "Egypt," there would be no delay in securing the right hand of fellowship of one and all. Well—it was done! Whoever has gone through an effort of this kind can understand. No others can begin to realize it. At last it was done, and when the worn-out field laborers sent word to the local secretary of a date for a meeting, they were all there. The purchase was completed, the Home secured.

From this account by Mrs. Wilcox and from other sources it is clear that the district superintendent in Illinois was expected to find destitute children who apparently needed care; to make such personal, family and economic investigation as was made; to accept children for care either with or without advice from the state superintendent in Chicago; to take physical care and custody of these children from the county commissioners, who in Illinois were responsible for dependents; to provide temporary shelter for these children when there were no receiving homes available in their own or other districts; to find foster homes that would take the children free; to place children in these homes and supervise them while there, assisted in this by the volunteer service of members of advisory boards; and to collect money, not only for their own wages and expenses, but to help pay the salaries and expenses of the superintendent and workers in the state office and the detention homes.

Innovations by Dr. Hastings H. Hart

One of the first things done by Dr. Hart, who succeeded Mr. Hoover as superintendent, was to put an end to the payment of district workers on a commission basis and to substitute therefor a definite salary. This did not lessen the variety of the tasks which the district superintendent had to perform, but it removed the desperate necessity of making receipts cover expenses every week. He also took from the superintendent and members of the staff the power of electing their own board of directors directly through their own votes and by proxies from other contributors (each contributor of one dollar being entitled to a vote). Another important step taken by him was gradually to discontinue receiving small appropriations from county boards of supervisors for each child taken from their county. This removed any temptation there might have been to take a child for money, and left the Society free to accept or reject a child solely on the basis of the Society's understanding of his need for foster home care. A fourth step in the direction of better and more responsible care of dependent children received by the Society, was taken after the Juvenile Court law went into effect in July 1899, namely, that children accepted for permanent placement in free foster homes must be committed to the guardianship of the Society by the Juvenile Court of the county legally responsible for his care as a dependent child.

In addition to the progressive steps already mentioned, Dr. Hart built up, during his ten years as superintendent, a very large and steady list of contributors all over the state; he installed a modern system of bookkeeping and accounts; he built a new receiving home for southern Illinois in the village of Du Quoin. He also built a receiving home for northern Illinois in Evanston, which had facilities for segregation of older boys, quarantine of newcomers, the best medical examination and treatment then known, and which made possible later the introduction of better psychological and psychiatric methods of studying children. He had also acquired four hundred acres of the best Illinois corn land to help endow a small industrial school for some of the older girls who did not make good progress in free foster homes. This school is in Potomac, Illinois, and is called the Mary A. Judy Industrial School, after the mother of the donor. The building of this small school for girls who were not doing well in free foster homes, and the payment of board for foster home care of children, which was now begun by the Aid Department of the Society, have great professional significance. Both undertakings were started as necessary supplements to the work of placement of dependent children in free foster homes. Except by a few of the leading State Children's Home Societies, the necessity of adequate boarding foster care in every state had not yet been recognized.

Further Steps Ahead in the Illinois Society

The writer of these pages succeeded Dr. Hart as superintendent from 1909 to 1912. It fell to his lot to secure plans and to build the two buildings used for the Mary A. Judy Industrial School. In certain experimental districts he began to free the district superintendents, who still had the diversified job of receiving, placing and supervising children, from the obligation of raising funds. He also strove for more care in social investigation, and for greater legal accuracy in the commitment of children to the Society for permanent placement in free foster homes.

FREE FOSTER HOMES

Mr. Wilfred S. Reynolds, the next superintendent, continued to improve intake methods and to raise standards of placement and supervision. He expanded the work the Aid Department was doing in the matter of temporarily boarding children in order ultimately to preserve the natural family relationship. The following statement of progress under Mr. Reynolds from 1912 to 1921, is given by Mr. Reynolds himself in a letter addressed to the present writer, under date of February 16, 1921:

I have tried to think earnestly about this matter in light of our own work, and what comes to my mind is that we are increasingly applying the principles of good case work to every child's problem that is presented for our consideration. It has been, I think, a rather continuing but very slow process, step by step, of more thoroughly diagnosing and deciding upon treatment regarding these cases of children who supposedly need care away from their own families. In the past ten years the application of these principles, of course, has brought about changes in the organization of our departments of service and has tended to change the character of treatment of our cases.

It has meant with us in the last ten years the handling of a much smaller number of children for permanent foster home adoptive care, and a tremendous increase in the number of cases under the more temporary plan of boarding home care. About eight years ago the Society accepted for care during the year approximately 300 children for permanent adoptive care. In 1920 we accepted only 140 for this type of care. It has meant further the increase in personnel from about 30 workers ten years ago to 60 at the present time. It has meant the provision of funds for temporary boarding work of $28,000 in 1920; it has meant the specialization in departments of service, providing specialized interviewers for first contact with cases; a department of investigation for the investigation and diagnostic period of the treatment; a department of visitation and supervision for the supervision of children after the plan of care is adopted and the child is established in its family at board or free; it has meant further the assignment of special problem cases to special workers adapted to the supervision and needs of these special cases.

FREE FOSTER HOMES

Some Questions for Children's Home Societies in Other States

It is a good professional question for any Children's Home Society to ask itself how its work compared with that of Illinois during the period noted above and how it compares today with that of Michigan. The census of 1923 shows that the reliance of these societies was still mainly upon the placement of dependent children in permanent free homes without indenture.

As listed in the Report of the National Children's Home and Welfare Association for 1917-1918, there were then the following thirty-two member state societies:

1. Alabama Children's Home Society
2. California
3. Florida
4. Georgia
5. Idaho
6. Illinois
7. Iowa
8. Kansas
9. Kentucky
10. Michigan
11. Minnesota
12. Mississippi
13. Missouri
14. Montana
15. Nebraska
16. New Jersey
17. New Mexico
18. New York Children's Aid Society
19. North Dakota
20. Ohio
21. Oklahoma
22. Oregon
23. Pennsylvania Children's Home Society
24. South Carolina
25. South Dakota
26. Tennessee
27. Texas
28. Virginia
29. Washington
30. West Virginia
31. Wisconsin
32. Wyoming

Adding Arkansas and North Carolina to this list, as their societies also were founded by the National Society, the United States census for February 1, 1923, shows that these 34 societies, most of them operating over a whole state, had children under care distributed as follows:

In receiving homes	1,528	children
In free foster family homes	12,379	"
In boarding family homes	685	"
Elsewhere under supervision	200	"
Total	14,792	"

Twenty-two out of the 34 reported no boarding family care at all. Seven others reported a total of 29, an average of only 4 plus each, and 5 reported 656 distributed as follows: Alabama, 46; Florida, 42; Illinois, 141; Kansas, 34; and Michigan, 393. In short, one society—that of Michigan, was boarding more than half of the children so cared for by the whole 34 State Children's Home Societies, while 27 states had made no serious beginning of this form of care of dependent and neglected children to supplement the care that can be given in institutions and in free foster family homes. Another good professional question for those agencies to ask themselves persistently during the next decade is this: To what extent is the lack of temporary care of children in boarding family homes resulting in permanent separation of children from surviving parent or adult relatives, or each other, when such permanent separations should not occur? And still other questions follow: What is the reason for the care of such a large number (1,528) and percentage (10 plus) of the total of 14,792 children in receiving homes? Does the extreme reliance of these agencies upon the free foster home method of care result in the gradual accumulation in receiving homes of children who, because of physical or mental defect or personality, are practically unplaceable in free homes? If so, how should these children be cared for? Should the community neglect them, giving no help? Should they be forced into institutions irrespective of the kind of care they need, and in spite of limitations upon the kind of care that institutions can give them? Should a system of boarding foster home family care be developed to supplement institutional and free home care?

In short, if Mr. Van Arsdale were alive today, what modifications of, and additions to, his free foster home method of caring for dependent and neglected children would his pioneering spirit now force him to make? If his followers would be true to his spirit, and not merely to the letter of his method, what modifications in their child welfare program should they now make?

CHAPTER VII

SYMPATHY AND SENTIMENT BEGIN TO INVOKE
THE AID OF SCIENCE: "WHAT DOES THE
CHILD REALLY NEED?"

The man who began to ask these questions so persistently as to make himself heard by the leaders in work for the dependent child, whether or not he was the first to frame the questions, was Charles W. Birtwell, who began work with the Boston Children's Aid Society in 1886—twenty-three years after it was founded. He was not, therefore, like Charles Loring Brace, in New York, in 1853, and Martin Van Buren Van Arsdale, in Illinois, in 1883, a pioneer founder of a great new agency to care for dependent children. No, Mr. Birtwell's contribution was to consist in the formulation and enunciation of a basic philosophy that would increasingly introduce harmony, meaning and efficiency into the persistent chaos of self-assertive and often conflicting methods and systems of care for dependent children. Just because Mr. Birtwell was not a pioneer founder, but a philosopher with a scientific bent who had to find out the *why* before he could see the *what*, we must forget him for several pages in order that the reader may see more clearly what the state of Massachusetts and the Boston Children's Aid Society situation regarding the care of dependent children needed when Mr. Birtwell came upon the scene in 1886.

ALMSHOUSE AND INDENTURED CHILDREN AS SEEN BY
THE FIRST STATE BOARD OF CHARITIES IN MASSACHUSETTS

Massachusetts was the first state to establish, in 1863, a State Board of Charities. This first Board consisted of seven men with Franklin B. Sanborn as executive secretary. At the time the Board began to function, it found that, in addition to local town and city almshouses with their unclassified population of adults and children, Massachusetts some ten years before had also established three state almshouses to care for great numbers of unclassified destitute adults and children who had lived in various towns in the state and had therefore not acquired a settlement in any one locality. These state almshouses were located in Bridgewater, Tewksbury and Monson. During the first year of the activities of the State Board of Charities in 1864, a beginning was made toward removing the children from two of the three mixed, or unclassified, state almshouses and bringing them together in the third almshouse at Monson. The reasons for this transfer as given by the Board were these:

Thus the almshouse, as far as it relates to these unfortunate children, is changed into an educational establishment. The effect of this change on the lives and character of these children cannot be estimated. The location of Monson affords excellent chances for indenturing children in good families in country towns. The demand for boys and girls from twelve to fourteen years of age has frequently been greater than the supply[1]. . . . The State has already indentured from each of the Reform and Industrial Schools an average of one hundred annually; and the State almshouses have sent out over fifteen hundred more. In this way, nearly four thousand persons have already been transferred from a state of public dependence to homes in families. The by-laws of these institutions make it obligatory upon their officers to see that the parties applying for boys and girls to indenture, sustain a good moral character; and they are also required to exercise a watchful care over those indentured. But these requirements are very imperfectly carried out. The officers of these institutions find their time so occupied with special duties assigned them, that *they cannot give much attention to incidental matters* [italics by the present writer]. In some cases this watchfulness is continued with some degree of fidelity for months or years, while in others, little or no information is obtained respecting the situation and treatment of the indentured. Besides, this oversight cannot be maintained as it should be, by correspondence; it needs personal inquiry and

---

[1] *First Annual Report*, 1865, p. xxv.

THE AID OF SCIENCE

acquaintance. There are instances, moreover, where the indentured boys and girls are badly treated, and not unfrequently returned to the institution, without any fault on their part. If the state takes the place of a parent or guardian, is it not her duty to follow up that parental relation and see that the compact is faithfully adhered to, and that no harm befall the party dependent upon the state? To do justice to this class of boys and girls, there should be a person, possessing the right qualifications, charged with this particular duty. He should visit all these indentured children, ascertain from different sources the character of their masters, and how they are treated, hear and dispose of any complaints on either side, and advise and counsel as a parent would, with these indentured boys and girls. While doing this work, such an agent might readily find homes for others. Thus the number of those indentured from the State Institutions might be greatly increased, thereby saving to the state every year a sum far greater than the whole expenses of such an agency. We would therefore recommend to the Legislature that an agent of the kind be appointed.[2]

Abuses of Indentured Children Found by the First State Agent

The agent above referred to began work during the last three months of 1866[3] and visited during that time 160 children who had been indentured. Among the abuses cited by this agent were:

1. A girl who lived within a stone's throw of a schoolhouse had never been to school during the four years she had been in the home. She had once run away and had been brought back and beaten till the blood ran from her arms.

2. A girl had borne a child by the son of the master to whom she was indentured. This young man had taken her and her child, on pretext of marrying the mother, from Massachusetts to Utica, New York, and deserted them at night in the railroad station. The mother worked her way back, suffering from ill health and poorly clad. The master had failed to pay the girl the fifty dollars he had promised to pay when she was eighteen. The agent settled this case by having the father of the child arrested, "who on

[2]*Ibid.*, 1865, pp. xxi-xxii.   [3]Report of State Board dated 1867, pp. xlv-xlvi.

seeing the formidable preparations made for him, settled the matter by marrying the girl and taking her and his child to his father's home." Apparently the agent expected the girl to live happily ever after this marriage ceremony.

3. A third girl had been whipped in a cellar with a horse-whip because she did not recall what had become of a Testament that was missing. She was then told she would be whipped again the next day if she did not tell where the Testament was. She ran away:[4]

> Barefooted, barearmed and bareheaded, the girl had fled to the woods to escape the threatened punishment. She sought refuge in a cluster of hemlock bushes, and there remained through the night. (It was the twentieth of November, 1866.) I asked her if she was frightened in the woods. She said she was not at first, but when it grew dark and cold she was afraid and began to cry. Then she covered her bare feet and limbs with leaves, and her shoulders and face with hemlock boughs, and lying down among the leaves she repeated to herself the verse she learned to say in the almshouse commencing "Now I lay me down to sleep" and cried herself to sleep. She said she was startled several times in the night by the hooting of owls and the bark of foxes, but she slept pretty well till morning. The whole neighborhood was aroused early the next morning, and the girl found about nine o'clock, benumbed and almost speechless. . . . The Testament, which was the cause of all the trouble, was found by a son of Mr. F. where he had left it and forgotten it.

In the same report the Board also records the following opinion as to the frequency of the profit motive in taking children on indenture and makes the prophetic suggestion that a payment for board of children might do much to secure better homes and better treatment for destitute children:[5]

> It is a matter for consideration whether the inducements offered to worthy families to take charge of children from the Primary School, the Reform School, and similar establishments cannot be increased. At present these children are generally taken because the head of the *family*

[4] *Ibid.*, p. xlvii.   [5] Report of State Board, 1867, p. lxix.

THE AID OF SCIENCE 165

desires their labor, and thinks he can get it *cheap in that way.* Hence such abuses as our visiting agent reports, most of which might be prevented by making it worth the while of better families to receive the children. A small sum paid for the board of a child for a short time would cost the state less than his support in the institution, and would often secure good treatment in a good family.

On October 1, 1867, after a full year of work as visiting agent to the indentured children of the state primary school at Monson, the agent made a report of great interest. The following items have been selected from this report. Of 977 children indentured from this institution since 1854, 218 were reported to have served their legal time, returned to their friends, or as having run away, leaving 759 who were supposed to be in their places. Of these the agent had ascertained the condition of 217 girls and 278 boys, having seen in person 194 girls and 187 boys. Of their experiences in general the agent says:[6]

These children have been scattered over the states of Massachusetts, Connecticut, New Hampshire and New York, with here and there one in the western states. A large number have not been heard from since leaving the institution, and it was not known how they were faring, or what had become of them. The authorities of the almshouse had placed them out, requiring a yearly report of their condition, but these reports were seldom made. Masters moved from one town or state to another, without giving information to the superintendent of the institution. Children were transferred from family to family, without authority, and became lost to the knowledge and care of the state. That neglect and abuses were frequent is not surprising. The State has for twelve years been providing homes for its orphans and friendless children, without causing them to be looked after, or correcting the wrongs that had grown up among them.

Of specific abuses, the agent says:[7]

The common neglects from which these children suffer are insufficient schooling, non-attendance at church upon the Sabbath, and inade-

[6] *Report,* 1867, p. 145.   [7] *Report,* 1867, p. 153

quate clothing. Occasionally a child is overworked and maltreated, but such instances will diminish now that the children are visited and more carefully looked after.

And again:[8]

In the settlement of twenty-five of these cases of injustice and abuse, three thousand four hundred and seventy-eight dollars and twenty-three cents ($3,478.23) have been recovered.

It may be asked why these children have not appealed to the authorities at the almshouse for protection and justice, and the reply comes back that they have usually shunned the almshouse as if it were a hideous monster, revolting to their pride and finer feelings, and suffered hardship and wrongs rather than ask assistance from that quarter. With the state primary school pupils it will no doubt be different.

But these cases of injustice and abuse are the exception, not the general rule. Aside from slight neglects, which are now being corrected, the majority of the children are doing well, and have pretty good homes. Some of them take the names of the families in which they live, and are treated in all respects as children of those families.

How the State Agent Began to Help Individual Children

In visiting the children your agent has endeavored to make them feel that he is their friend—that he has their interest at heart and desires to benefit them. He has been happily surprised to find how readily they have confided in him and made known their various wants. They have been anxious to learn about their brothers, sisters and other friends, information of whom has been communicated by letter as soon as it could be ascertained. To each of the children visited a book has been presented, at an expense to the agent of about one hundred dollars. These little gifts have been kindly received by the children and have aided materially in obtaining their good will.

Another practice of the agency which is calculated to interest children is correspondence. During the year your agent has written to them over three hundred letters, and received nearly as many.

[8]*Loc., cit.*

THE AID OF SCIENCE

The Beginning of Case Records

As an illustration of his method in looking after the welfare of indentured children, the agent gives this list of the inquiries made about each child:[9]

After a careful examination into the condition of each child, the following blank, provided by your Board, has been filled out, with such additional facts as could be ascertained:

The condition of ...., placed in the family of ...., in the town of ...., 18.., at the age .... post office address ....
Nativity of the child's parents?
Their habits of life?
Are they still living?
Has the child any brothers and sisters?
Does the child retain its original name?
Present age?
Is the child in the family where first placed?
Has the child ever left its present place?
Has the family any children of its own?
If so, how many?
Physical condition?
General temperament? Scrofulous, or not?
Habits and inclinations?
Attendance at school?
Studies pursued?
Progress in studies?
Does the child attend church? Denomination?
Does the child attend Sabbath School?
Is the child obedient?
Is the child truthful?
Is the child industrious?
Is the child studious?
Is the child fond of reading?
Is the child accustomed to hearing good language?
Are the child's associates good?

[9] *Report of Massachusetts State Board of Charities*, 1867, pp. 150-51.

Evenings how spent?
What is the child's occupation?
Is the occupation suitable?
What has been the child's general treatment?
Does the child sleep alone?
Is the bed suitable?
Is the child's clothing suitable and proper?
Does the child take its meals with the family?
Is the food sufficient and proper?
Are ardent spirits used in the family?
Does the child complain of anything?
Date of visit?

Four hundred and ninety-five of these blanks have been filled, showing that so many of the children have been visited or their condition ascertained by visiting the families where they were placed. This number includes twenty-three who had left their places or had run away from the almshouse and found places for themselves. The condition of the latter was generally found to be deplorable—they were penniless, ragged, running from place to place, and fast sinking into vicious habits. To improve their condition by establishing them in permanent homes, or hiring them out and looking after their wages, has been one of the cares of the agency.

The next year, the agent says:[10]

I am satisfied, however, that the only sure way of ascertaining the condition of a child is by a personal visit. If the child has been out only a short time, the first visit will not answer all purposes. A child "must be summered and wintered" before it can be ascertained how he is to be treated—whether he is to be properly fed, clothed, schooled and worked, and quite as much may be learned from a second visit as from the first. The child in its growth often develops qualities in striking contrast to those exhibited when first taken, and the family quite as often changes its treatment of a child; hence the need of constant watchfulness over these wards of the commonwealth.

[10] *Report for 1868*, p. 178.

THE AID OF SCIENCE 169

In closing the report of his second full year of service, October 1, 1868, the agent also says:[11]

Your agent has given nearly his whole time and his entire heart and thought to the interests of these wards of the state. It has been his privilege to bring together brothers and sisters long separated, and in some instances forgotten by each other; to restore to parents their long-lost children; to be as a father to the fatherless and a friend to the friendless; to rejoice with them in their joy, to sympathize with them in their sorrows; to be their counsellor and help in misfortune; to visit them when sick or in prison, and to follow some of them to the portals of the tomb. The more he has done for them, the more there has seemed for him to do. Every mail brings the request of some child or master.

Beginnings of Boarding-Out by the State of Massachusetts

The Board of Charities, in July, 1869, extended its program to include the visiting of all children indentured from all the state institutions, including industrial schools and reformatories, instead of only the state primary school at Monson and the two other state almshouses. An agent was commissioned to do this work. As a result of such supervision, the state began to pay board, not only for infants, but for older children, as will be seen from this extract:[12]

The establishment of the visiting agency, in 1866, and subsequent years, led to the placing of thousands of children above the age of ten, who would otherwise have remained for years in the state establishments. The opening of the Massachusetts Infant Asylum in 1868 was soon followed by boarding out of infants in families; and this has now become so important that 135 children under three years old are now supported by the state in such families. In 1879 the legislature forbade the return of children in city and town almshouses, and in 1881 made appropriations to pay the board of children under ten years old instead of allowing them to remain in the state Primary School. Under the legis-

[11]*Report*, 1868, p. 198.
[12]*Report of Massachusetts State Board of Charities*, 1885, p. cxl.

lation last named about 130 children are now at board in different parts of the state, making a total of 250 children, including motherless infants, whose board the state now pays in families rather than in almshouses, asylums and large institutions.

Thus in 1881, the prophetic suggestion made by the State Board in 1866 that the state ought to pay board for children in family homes instead of expecting them all to pay their own way on indenture, began to be realized in Massachusetts by the State Board itself.

Beginnings of The Boston Children's Aid Society

With the foregoing brief account of the public care of destitute children in the local and state almshouses of Massachusetts and in family homes, we may now turn to the story of the private organization called the Boston Children's Aid Society, founded the same year, 1863, in which the Massachusetts State Board of Charities was organized. This was ten years after Mr. Charles Loring Brace began his work with children in New York, and twenty years before Martin Van Buren Van Arsdale began his work in Illinois. It was not the sight of homeless children in the streets, as with Mr. Brace of New York in 1853; not the memory of little children seen in almshouses in college days, as with Mr. Van Arsdale of Illinois in 1883; not even the story of cold, hungry and beaten children indentured in family homes, as with the members of the first State Board of Charities in Massachusetts in 1863-1864; but the sight of little children in solitary confinement in jail that stirred Boston women to action in 1863. What they saw is told in these words:[13]

Some ladies interested in the Newsboys' School, having occasion to visit certain boys confined in Boston Jail for petty larceny, found that the jail always contained a number of children, from ten to fifteen years

---

[13]From a leaflet entitled *Children's Aid Society: Its Origin and Objects*, 1864. Apparently this was in the nature of a financial appeal.

THE AID OF SCIENCE

of age, who were kept in solitary confinement. The cell in which the child is confined is large, clean, dry, well lighted, and warmed, and comfortable. His food is good, and ample provision is made for his bodily wants; but he is alone from morning till night, except when by accident he sees a passing face, or receives a visit. Little children, ten or twelve years old, accused of crime, but not convicted, unable to find bail, are here shut up by themselves, without society or occupation. They stand by their grated door, clinging to its bars, as birds cling to the bars of their cage, watching hour after hour in hopes of seeing the face of a passing visitor or officer; or they sit on the bed, crying, refusing to sleep or eat.

What they did was to found the Boston Children's Aid Society, with this object:

The chief object of this Society shall be to improve the condition of exposed children, to visit prisons, to provide instruction for young prisoners, and to take such measures as may promote their welfare.

In addition to visiting and teaching the children in jail, leaving them "books to read; slates, pencils and paper; and lessons to learn," they opened in 1864 a Home for boys at Pine Farm, West Newton. We learn from the *First Annual Report* that the Association was later incorporated, to enable it to have *"legal guardianship* of the children *so as to bind them out,* or put them in permanent homes."[14] The Farm was viewed as an experiment by its promoters and "if it proves successful, such homes can be multiplied, until not a child's life is thrown away by the neglect of those who should be guardians of it."

Within two years after Pine Farm was opened, seventy-eight boys had been received, of whom all but thirty had been discharged, fourteen of them to permanent places in the country. Twenty of those still at the Farm were under the legal guardianship of the Association up to the age of seventeen or twenty-one years.[15]

---

[14]Boston Children's Aid Society, *First Annual Report,* Boston, 1865, pp. 5-6.
[15]*Second Annual Report,* June 1866, pp. 3-4.

We soon found that we could accomplish nothing that would be of practical value unless we could retain the boys under our Home influence for months, instead of weeks, as we at first imagined. Boys enter our Home who, from the neglect of parents or the want of them, from early association with vice and crime in the streets of Boston, from the utter absence of anything like love, wear a hard, suspicious and often sullen appearance; but under the kind and gentle, yet firm treatment of those that feel for them, they become gentle and trustful, and all the higher and before-hidden qualities of the nature develop. As soon, then, as in our judgment it is safe, the boys are placed in a permanent home in the country, if possible, or returned to their parents in case we are not allowed to have the disposal of them. Our work does not cease with this: we keep up a correspondence with the boys who leave us to go to distant homes, or if in the city, they are constantly visited and watched over. Your Committee would here say that the thanks of the Society are due to those ladies connected with us, who have been so assiduous in watching over and caring for the graduates of our Home.

Let it be our aim, then, to see to it that our work is *well* done, and that every boy that leaves our asylum is, so far as we can effect it, permanently saved to society.

Such an expression of purpose so early in the work of this Society has a refreshing suggestion of the importance of getting at the needs of each boy individually. It is further interesting to note two points mentioned in this *Second Annual Report.*

First, work with the parents: "Through what we do for the *children* we reach the *parents,* and influence them to think more of what is best for their children." This has a distinctly 1930 sound, as something quite akin in purpose with our efforts toward "parental education," instead of hastily assuming that the only way to save a child of unsatisfactory parents is to take him wholly away from them.

Second, the City Chaplain, Mr. Rufus R. Cook, "Uncle Cook," who was also a paid agent of the Society was

present at all sessions of the Police Court, and constantly on the watch for any cases that should come under our cognizance. His system of taking boys on probation (note the date, 1866) by consent of the Court, instead of, as formerly, having them sent to jail to await trial, has worked most admirably. During the past year Mr. Cook has received at the Police Court 88 boys on probation for six weeks each; of these only four had to be returned to the Court as delinquents, and sent to the school ship at Westboro. At the Superior Court he has received 35 boys, on probation for six months each, all for the crime of larceny; of these only three were surrendered to the Court. These probation boys are obliged to report to him, in person, every week at his house, or at the Court, and so he is enabled to keep an eye on them. It proves a constant check upon them, and their evident desire, in many cases, to improve is very gratifying.[16]

Beginnings among State Officials of Awareness of Need for Juvenile Probation

It is interesting to note the following official words of approval of Mr. Cook's work:[17]

It would perhaps be well if the State consistently provide for every minor, a defender, to whom it should be as much a matter of duty and of pride to acquit the accused, as it is of the State's attorney to convict him.

If this cannot be, then encouragement should be given for some one to undertake, in every court, and before every magistrate to whom young offenders may be brought, the beneficent office which Mr. Cook so beautifully fills in the Police Court of Boston. He watches for the little ones as they are brought in by the officers; and whenever it seems advisable, he interposes the shield of mercy between the sword of justice and its victim. He becomes bondsman for the offender, and takes him tenderly in charge, until some fitting place is found for him. Out of nearly four hundred children whom he has so bailed, eighty percent are now doing well.

The Association felt at this time that something should be done for homeless and friendless girls, believing, in the words of Mr.

---

[16] Boston Children's Aid Society, *Second Annual Report*, June, 1866, pp. 7-8.
[17] *Report of Massachusetts State Board of Charities*, 1868, p. lxviii.

Cook, that "if you save one girl from a life of sin and shame, you save ten boys."[18] A Home at Newton Center was accordingly opened in 1866,[19] but in 1873 the enterprise was abandoned, not because there was no need for it, but because girls whom the directors would accept did not come in sufficient numbers to justify the work, nor under conditions which they deemed essential to its success.

The Boarding-Out Idea Is Planted in the Fertile Soil of The Boston Children's Aid Society

Of the work for boys, this *Third Report* states:[20]

We continue to think (in contrast with the custom of the Rauhe Haus at Hamburg and at the home at Mettrai, both of which kept boys during their whole boyhood) that so secluded a life is not best during the whole of boyhood, though we keep our boys longer than was our first intention. Some of them are so young, from eight to ten years old, that it is very hard to find good places for them, especially this year when the cost of living is so high. They come from the worst homes, are just beginning thieving or vagrant habits, and are generally given by bad parents to our charge till they are seventeen or eighteen years old. *These little boys are our perplexity.* They have improved very much, and are very interesting and dear to us. No one can think that we ought to refuse to take them till they are hardened by two or three years of wrongdoing, when the same years passed with us may bring them well prepared to an age when they can be placed in families. The difficulty of finding places for such little boys, in cases where they are not given up for adoption, is felt quite as much in other temporary homes, or institutions as in our own. *We wish the Society would authorize us to try the plan of paying moderate board*[21] *to families in which we can trust them,* and thus enable us to benefit a larger number.

[18]Boston Children's Aid Society, *Second Annual Report,* p. 10.
[19]*Third Annual Report,* p. 9.   [20]*Third Annual Report,* 1867, p. 4.
[21]We have already noted that this idea of paying board for children above infants in age was also broached in 1866 by the Massachusetts State Board of Charities. It would be interesting to know whether the idea was first broached by the private society or by the State Board.

In getting places for our boys we propose, as far as possible, to put several in one neighborhood, because we can more easily watch over them and learn the characters of the families in which they are placed. We have planted one colony of eleven boys at Wellfleet, on Cape Cod, who have with one exception done excellently well. We began with sending two boys there in our first year, and the people have sent again and again for more of "our boys." We have frequent intercourse, Mr. Cook keeping up his fatherly relation to them, and their bright happy letters show their contentment. We are especially indebted to the Rev. Mr. Morrison and to Mrs. Morrison for their thoughtful interest in choosing good places, and for their great kindness to our boys, befriending them in sickness and in health.

Here again, this Boston Society shows keen interest in three practical steps essential to the welfare of dependent children in foster family homes, namely, (1) the difficulty of getting good free homes for boys not yet old enough to pay their own way;[22] (2) the need for wise and sympathetic choice of individual foster homes; and (3) the necessity for frequent, intelligent and sympathetic supervision. In this connection, it comments also on the special difficulty of getting good homes for difficult boys:[23]

There are many families where a good boy will have a good home, but a bad or trying boy will meet with little mercy, and this is rather the character of New England homes. There is needed to tame them (the difficult boys) a special devotion, patience, and sympathy, which are not universal or even common traits.

This preparatory service it felt Pine Farm was able to give the boys.

In the *Ninth Annual Report,* we meet a refreshing frankness. "We are as successful as we have any right to expect to be. Of our 214 boys a few have turned out very badly, and some of them are at this time in penal institutions."[24] Also we find a growing understanding of the needs of individual boys. "We do need exceed-

---
[22] We have noted this difficulty as recognized in England in the time of James I. See Chapter II.
[23] *Third Annual Report,* p. 6. Order of sentences changed.
[24] *Ninth Annual Report,* p. 3.

ingly a Home for boys who leave us to work in the city, and require to be shielded against the evil that waits for them. All boys cannot and will not be tillers of the ground. Providence in our day will have great cities, and unless we would be found fighting against God we must care for the boys where many of them will be found as 'all the rivers run to the sea'."[25] Mr. Cook cites the cases of five boys who had been placed in the country and who found their way to the city again. Two of them were earning only three dollars a week, not enough to pay for board and lodging. What was to be done with them next? "Have we reached the limits of obligation, or can something further be done?"[26]

In the minutes of the Society for August, 1873, is a paragraph that suggests more difficulties in finding satisfactory homes for placed-out boys, than the printed annual reports show. The suggestion was made by the superintendent of the Home that it would be well to have some printed instructions to be "given to the persons who receive the boys in their employ, as in some instances the only object of the employer seems to have been to get as much work as possible out of the boys and to give as little as possible in return."

The Need for Personal Supervision of Boys in Foster Homes

With respect to the problem of placing out boys, the *Fourteenth Annual Report*, 1879, has this to say:[27]

> Some correspondence is kept with them afterwards. The families are chosen with care and the results are satisfactory. A wish has, however, been expressed, that there should be some one whose charge it should be to keep the run of them for a long time after they have left us, and to encourage their self-respect when they have become their own masters.

In other words, the Society was finding that whatever Uncle Cook was able to do through correspondence, in any intervals of time

---

[25]*Ibid.*, p. 4.   [26]*Ibid.*, p. 7.   [27]*Fourteenth Annual Report*, p. 4.

THE AID OF SCIENCE

left from his exacting tasks as jail chaplain and probation officer for boys in town, was inadequate. Plainly a traveling visitor, such as the State Board of Charities had provided in 1866, was also needed by their private society. It was not until 1883 that such a visitor began to supervise placed-out boys by personal visitation.

Beginnings of Home Library Department

During all the fifteen years of the Society, however, a visitor from the Society had visited the jail daily, "making the acquaintance of all the boys and girls whose unhappy fate takes them inside its walls. All these she sees and talks with, and learns their history and home and family." Books and other suitable reading matter, were also loaned to the little prisoners, "to their great relief and peace."[28]

Here is the germ of the Department of Home Libraries, a phase of the Society's work which, greatly developed, persists to this day. It will be described later.

Children with Differing Needs Recognized

In 1884, in spite of Uncle Cook's illness,

the Home has continued full. Boys are sent to us by the truant officers of the city and by many persons and institutions who have become acquainted with our work. This shows that the Society has proved its usefulness to the community and leads the managers to think that *its sphere of work may be extended* either by duplicating the establishment in some other neighborhood of the city, or *by aiding destitute children* in ways somewhat different from those to which the Society has heretofore confined its labors, but yet within the spirit of its act of incorporation. Up to the present time the work of the Society has been strictly reformative; it has taken into its Home at West Newton only boys who have begun to be bad, who needed moral as well as material assistance. It has kept them at Pine Farm until they had improved so that they

---
[28] *Fifteenth Annual Report*, p. 8.

might safely be placed in families of honest people and grow up in their ways. The managers are considering the advisability of extending their labors to children who are destitute but not bad, for whom homes in the country can be provided but who do not need to be reformed before going to them. They are also seeking to employ a man with the proper qualifications to become an outdoor worker, as it were, among the poor children of Boston, in ways not immediately connected with the Home at West Newton.[29]

This innovation proved to be a vastly important step in the work of the Association.

In the same report of 1884, mention is made of another innovation. Following the experiment with a home for girls in Newton Center, a legacy of five thousand dollars had come to the Society from Miss M. Louisa Shaw, the income of which was to be applied to the uses of a girls' home. This income had been spent under a special committee of the managers of the Society in providing boarding homes for girls not over twelve years of age.[30]

The Society pays their board, about two or three dollars per week for each girl, and sometimes clothes them besides. No girl who is subject for any other charitable institution is taken by the Society. Some of these girls soon become industrious and are now self-supporting and have saved some money, others have given trouble and have been surrendered by the people with whom they have been placed, *one of them has been put in five different places*. . . . Up to the present time ten have come under charge of the Committee, over all of whom (except one who was taken home by her mother without our consent) the Committee still keeps a personal supervision, greater or less, according to the exigencies of the case, by visiting them in their homes, seeing that they are properly cared for and by corresponding with them.

In the next report it is stated that the visitor who had been to see the placed-out boys "has added to her duties that of seeking out boarding places for those who need homes, who are poor but not bad boys."[31]

[29] *Twentieth Annual Report*, p. 6.
[30] *Twentieth Annual Report*, p. 7. Order of sentences changed.
[31] *Twenty-first Annual Report*, p. 4.

Charles W. Birtwell Comes as an "Outdoor Worker" to The Boston Children's Aid Society

From what has already been presented in this chapter, the reader will surely have sensed the quality of the varied pioneering efforts in behalf of the dependent children of Boston, and Massachusetts generally, from 1863 to 1886, both in the work of the State Board of Charities and of the early directors and workers in the Boston Children's Aid Society. Familiarity with these activities has its own value to the American student of child welfare work.

Perhaps it has also been made clear that the situation in Boston, and in Massachusetts as a whole, was ripe for a decided step ahead in philosophy and method. This step ahead was to be taken under the leadership of Charles W. Birtwell. The *Annual Report* refers to his coming in these words:[32]

The plan of having an outdoor worker has been fully developed in the engagement of Mr. C. W. Birtwell. This is a new departure of the Society's work; but it has already shown remarkable results, and will largely increase our work. Mr. Birtwell, in various ways, becomes acquainted with families in the poor and degraded parts of the city, *studies the character of the children, and the best way to help them— whether in their own homes, or by entire removal from their surroundings.* Among the children Mr. Birtwell is trying to help are the juvenile offenders who are put on probation by the court. These children are sent back to the same evil influences that led them into the wrong for which they were arrested, without any provision for their subsequent oversight. In this work among the children's homes, Mr. Birtwell makes use of the existing agencies for the industrial, mental and moral benefit of these children. He places them in industrial schools, evening schools, sewing classes, etc., which otherwise owing to the ignorance and neglect of their parents, would not be used. In addition to his own work among the poor and morally exposed children, he brings to them volunteer visitors, each visitor becoming the especial friend and moral guardian of some particular child or children. He is also establishing juve-

---
[32] *Twenty-second Annual Report,* 1885-1886, pp. 8-11.

nile libraries among these children. Even in the worst localities of the city, children can be found who will act as librarians. On the walls of their homes will hang neat bookcases, containing a dozen or fifteen books and also copies of the best juvenile papers and magazines. Under Mr. Birtwell's supervision, these little librarians will circulate the books and papers among the children of the neighborhood, and when one set has been the rounds of its youthful readers, it is to be changed for a set from another locality. . . .

Our most pressing need now is better facilities for placing in the country the Pine Farm boys, and city children who need to be temporarily removed from their homes.

At present we are restricted to acquaintances made by Miss Washburn in her country visits, and to direct correspondence with farms who may answer advertisements. Miss Washburn's visits are limited; and, while possible homes exist in every township in New England, *there is great chance in their selection, and correspondence is not the same as personal acquaintance with those who are to form a boy's character at the most impressionable time of his life.* . . .

In the permanent engagement of Mr. Birtwell and Miss Washburn, the Society has committed itself to new work that will largely increase its expenses; but they believe that the good accomplished will be fully in proportion to the money spent, and they hope that their friends and the public will give them such support as to enable them to carry out all that they have undertaken.

It is worth special note that, just at this time, when the directors found themselves in the midst of perplexities over the loss of the trusted Uncle Cook, and also of a superintendent who had served for seventeen years at Pine Farm, while at the same time greater need for service to children was daily opening before them, they stress more than anything else the problem of the twofold process of selecting children who are to be helped and of selecting people who can best help them. In short, there is an intimation, after twenty-two years of service, that their greatest job ahead is not merely to apply in a quantitative manner a method, or process, of child care that was already finished and perfect, but rather to discover a process or processes that would be adaptable to a variety of needs.

Mr. Birtwell as a Member of His Board Saw Him

What kind of a man was this Mr. Birtwell who came to the Society in 1886 with the title of Outdoor Man or General Agent? The best answer is contained in a letter sent to the present writer by an intimate associate of Mr. Birtwell in 1921:

> I will try to throw what light I can on Mr. Birtwell's character and habits of thought. I had been a director of the Boston Society for two years before he came to it in 1886, and during his early years with us, before his marriage, he came often to our house, perhaps two or three evenings a week, to pour out his trouble, not that I was any use as an adviser, but as a sympathetic consoler and friend.
> He came of sturdy Methodist stock, his father and uncles were with people who refused to pay tithes for conscience sake, and for greater freedom left England and settled in Lowell. From what he has told me it was a thinking as well as a virtuous atmosphere, and he and his sisters were brilliant scholars. From the time Mr. Birtwell entered high school at twelve his resolve was firm to go into something that should help his fellowmen: he thought of medicine, but was later attracted by social work. He used to speak especially of his studies in college under Professor Palmer and Professor Francis G. Peabody. He tutored to earn his way through college, besides working hard over his studies, broke down, and had to graduate three years later than the class he entered with; he was always at high tension.
> He had a singularly alert mind, novelty made a strong appeal to him, and once a thing was well started he lost interest in it, and began on another; he was a born experimenter and in so far he shared the scientific temper. I should do him an injustice however to imply that he did not keep up the good things that he started, for he did, even while he was taking a warmer interest in some new scheme for ourselves or some neighboring state.
> It has always been our avowed policy, not only Mr. Birtwell's but the directors' handed down from older to newer, to undertake a piece of

work as a needed demonstration and as soon as it was adopted by public agencies to drop it and go on to another. For instance, our Training Farms for boys were given up when the State made provision for the *younger* delinquents at the Berlin School, and the City reformed its truant and other juvenile institutions; our probation work when the Juvenile Court was established; and the placing of "easy" children now that so many other societies will take them, leaving "problem" placing to us, etc., etc. This policy has kept our faces forward and our minds open, and Mr. Birtwell threw himself into it and developed it with great ardor.

Other contributing causes were a fine group of directors who came soon after he did; Miss Annette P. Rogers, Mr. R. M. Staigg, Mr. Robert Treat Paine who had long been a director, and others, who knew social work both from study and practice, and gave him cordial backing and counsel though he was the acknowledged leader. Also he had a *healthy opposition* in his Board and outside. He was not a pioneer in Boston, other agencies had been running longer and looked on him with critical eyes, distrusting his innovations and offended by his criticism. Within his Board too there was a fairly large minority of thinking and reasonable people who kept before him and his admirers the defects in his work.

To sum up—he had a fine mind, and it was entirely bent on his work, no outside distractions, no rest or recreation tempted him from it, and he was always reaching out for new and better methods. He had a clear vision of the worth of an idea, which though sometimes annoyingly concealed by details, came out finely in the end. His surroundings, both as to criticism and judicious encouragement were favorable. Boston being a small and intimate place, all discerning eyes were on this new phenomenon whose vigor and enthusiasm threatened to take them by storm.

Such is the impression of Mr. Birtwell after an acquaintance of thirty-five years, by one of his Directors who was also herself a volunteer social worker.

Turning once more to the contemporary record, the *Annual Report,* we find that the number of boys under care by the Asso-

THE AID OF SCIENCE

ciation, besides those visited in Boston by Mr. Birtwell, had increased from 86 to 116; that "all that he [Mr. Birtwell] does can never be recorded. His energy is endless, and his earnestness a lesson to all."[33]

We learn also that Miss Washburn was continuing to visit placed-out boys, but that "some boys are ungovernable wherever they are placed. They are moved from one home to another until they prove themselves unfit to remain a member of a private family. They are then returned to Pine Farm, but here their influence is bad on the younger boys. The question arises, what is to be done with them?"

We learn also that as a partial, temporary answer, they had been sending more and more younger boys to a farmer in Foxborough until there were sixteen there. The Society paid the board of these children in this home, of which the report says:[34]

> In fact, they [the farmer and his wife] occupy the position of good father and mother to the boys, and fulfill the conditions of family life, in which we believe our work can best be carried on.

How the Work of the Society Looked to Mr. Birtwell

Gradually the office has become a kind of bureau of information in matters relating to needy children. The reference of cases to other societies, especially to the various schools and Homes for destitute and orphan children, has required no little time and thought. The pains taken have been abundantly repaid in seeing cases for which nothing, or the wrong thing, was likely to be done, taken in hand by the very societies that were best equipped to afford the needed relief. It has always been borne in mind that the sundering of family ties—the separation of a child from a father or mother, or the scattering of brothers and sisters—is a serious matter, requiring for its justification grave reasons and evident advantages. Wherever feasible, instead of sending children to "Homes," steps have been taken to place them in families,

[33]*Twenty-third Annual Report*, 1887, p. 5.
[34]*Twenty-third Annual Report*, 1887, p. 7.

chiefly in the country, where the price of board is less, and the life more free from temptation, than in the city. Almost invariably the unfortunate father or mother, and often relatives outside of the immediate family, when informed of a suitable boarding place at a low charge for board, have gladly made every effort to provide for the children in this natural, self-respecting way. When the meager earnings of the natural guardian have proved inadequate, they have sometimes been supplemented by help from charitable individuals, and in one instance from a Church society. Seven boys, also, have been boarded in country homes by means of a few donations, one an annual subscription, for this especial purpose. In three of these cases, part of the cost has been borne by widowed or deserted mothers. Four of the boys have already ceased to be an expense; one was transferred to a "free place" after boarding ten weeks at a total expenditure of $20 for board and $4.25 for clothing; another was similarly transferred at a little less than eight weeks, after an expense of $15.75 for board and $11.30 for clothing; the third, after boarding five weeks at a total cost of $10.00, remained with the family free of charge; and in the fourth case the same result was brought about at the end of two weeks, after an outlay of $4.00. None of the four, however, was under ten years of age. In addition to these, three boys and one girl have been sent directly to free places, and are doing well.

Efforts in this direction have been mentioned in the last three annual reports of the Directors as a prospective line of development of the work of the Society. Not only will money be needed, however, but also assistance in the office, if it is to receive more than present incidental attention. The work ought surely to be done by someone. Again and again children in the direst need—failing to be admitted to any of the charitable Homes, because the latter were crowded, or the children disqualified by their age, religion or nativity—have been forced to remain under conditions of destitution, neglect, and moral exposure; or have been obliged to go to City or State institutions, where hundreds of unfortunate children are gathered together; simply because there has been no one to pay, either wholly or in part, a moderate price for their board in a country home until they should become self-supporting.

The preventive work touches, indeed overlaps, the reformative. The majority of children just referred to, and of the boys who have been

THE AID OF SCIENCE

sent to country homes, came to notice as applicants for admission to Pine or Rock Lawn Farm (the Foxborough farmer home before mentioned) and although not yet wayward, bade fair to be in the near future, unless placed under better conditions. *Moreover, just what cases are best met by one, just what by another, of the three methods of aiding the children—by personal work among them in their own homes, by placing them in families in the country, or by giving them special reformatory training in such Homes as Pine and Rock Lawn Farms—can hardly be known, or the adoption of the best plan in each case insured, until all three methods are adequately and simultaneously tested by one society, or if by more than one, by societies most intimately associated.*

The field of work, mentioned a year ago, among the children who are put on probation by the courts, remains unoccupied. Children are brought into court, placed upon probation, and sent back to the same bad influences that led to their arrest; and at present no efforts are made to help them stem the tide of evil influences that threaten their ruin.

Our graduates, who as a rule return to the city from their places in the country, at the expiration of the time for which they were surrendered to the society, need increasing attention. Although nothing should be done to lessen their self-reliance, yet our friendly relations with them may well be continued, that we may follow up the earlier effort, and know, as definitely as may be, the final results.[35]

Mr. Birtwell's Ripened Philosophy of Child Care

In the next report, after reciting experiences of the year along the different lines above mentioned, Mr. Birtwell boiled down into one sentence *the process* which the Society has since that time followed with rare faithfulness of purpose—*the child welfare process* toward which all the steps we have hitherto described as being taken in England and America were consciously or unconsciously tending. Here it is in Mr. Birtwell's words:[36]

The aim will be in each instance to suit action to the real need— heeding the teachings of experience, still to study the conditions with

[35] *Twenty-third Annual Report*, 1887, pp. 11-13.
[36] *Twenty-fourth Annual Report*, 1888, p. 16.

a freedom from assumptions, and a directness and freshness of view, as complete as though the case in hand stood absolutely alone.

There you have it in a nutshell. First of all, Mr. Birtwell put the question: "What does the child really need?" No question can ever henceforth precede this one for any live child welfare agency or institution.

At this point the reader should remember that in addition to the work for dependent children already described in this chapter, the Charity Organization Society movement, with its new emphasis upon "case work," had been introduced into the United States in Buffalo, New York, in 1877, and had been started in Boston in 1879. The case work ideal was in the air in Boston in 1886. To voice this ideal so that it must be heard by workers for dependent children, was the peculiar achievement of Mr. Birtwell.

In the *Report* of 1890, this courageous statement occurs at the very beginning:[37]

> The simple and yet broad basis for the work of this Society—a readiness to investigate and advise and, if necessary, help in the case of any needy child—may now be avowed more openly and fearlessly than heretofore. During the past five years the Society has been moving steadily toward this position. With this breadth of purpose the constant aim is to combine naturalness of method. We do not say we will do one thing and not another, but we stand ready to learn the need and, whatever it may be, to try either to see that others supply it or to supply it ourselves. It does not follow that every needy child will come to us, but that such a child may; so that while other agencies continue to perform their chosen tasks, and meet as far as they may the wants of specific classes of children, no case need miss the assistance that might be given, because unable to find its way to the appropriate source of help, nor need any that should be aided fall unrelieved into the gaps that exist between the various agencies. We may now venture to say aloud to the community that any needy child may find in or through the Children's Aid Society whatever kind or measure of relief or protection the community

[37] *Twenty-sixth Annual Report*, 1890, p. 5.

is ready to offer. From thirty to fifty new cases, involving the interests of half as many more children, are now reported to us every month.

How the Philosophy Begins to Diversify Work

A circular of inquiry, intended to aid in finding family homes for children of varying needs, suggests the wide variety of such needs which was revealed by the process of really seeking the individual requirements of every child. Such family care was undertaken in addition to all the other activities of the Association. This is the inquiry, as prepared for circulation among interested persons:[38]

The Boston Children's Aid Society wishes to find good homes in the city, suburbs or country, where poor children who are homeless, destitute, or exposed, may enjoy a happy and wholesome family life, instead of being subject to the exposure of the streets, or the crowded, artificial life of institutions. Kind care, good example, moral training, real friends, everything in fact that a welcome in a good home implies— this is what we wish to secure for our boys and girls. We urge you to consider whether your own doors may not be thrown open to rescue, relieve, and protect some unfortunate child, and whether you can tell us of other families with whom these children may perhaps find a welcome. We ask you to help us to find homes of the following kinds:

1. Homes in which children of any age may be adopted.
2. Free homes, that is, homes in which for either a short time or any term of years, without charge, children may receive board and clothing and attend school.
3. Homes for older boys and girls, where they can make themselves useful in return for board, clothes and schooling, or, if sufficiently useful, receive wages.
4. Homes in which a mother, bringing a young child with her, may serve as housekeeper or domestic.
5. Homes in which children of any age may be boarded at a moderate price.

[38]*Twenty-seventh Annual Report*, 1891, p. 13.

6. Emergency homes of two kinds:
    (a) Homes to which a child may be sent on short notice, and cared for without charge, or at a moderate price, for a day or two, or a week, or longer, as may be agreed beforehand, until permanent provision can be made for it—the child being sent clean and in good condition.
    (b) Homes to which, in exceptional cases, with or without charge, a child may be sent without notice, to be made clean, put in good condition, and gently initiated into those decencies of life that, through no fault of its own, it may never have known.

Investigation of Prospective Foster Homes

Of his *method of investigating families willing to take children* on some of the conditions named above, Mr. Birtwell says:[39]

The following system of investigation has gradually been developed, and has been a chief factor in the success of the work.

We learn of families willing to receive a boy or girl—to be adopted, or boarded or given a home free of charge in return for a certain usefulness—either by direct application to us, or through those with whom we have placed children, or through fellow-townsmen or neighbors of the applicants known to us and interested in the work, or through our assistants as they visit children already placed.

By interviews at the office, by correspondence with the applicants and their references, and by visits to the family, we learn the more patent facts, and whatever else we can about the applicants and the home they offer a child. Our inquiries are guided by a detailed and comprehensive list or system of questions: as to the age, sex, occupation, physical condition, church membership and attendance, character, disposition, habits of each member of the family; the character, and degree of association with the family, of any employees; the size of the house, the amount of land and how it is used, the live stock, any special industries —that we may know the material condition of the family, the work needing to be done, etc.; the distance to church and schools, the number

---

[39] *Twenty-seventh Annual Report*, 1891, pp. 10-13.

THE AID OF SCIENCE

of weeks per year the latter are in session; previous experience in the care and training of children; the motive in taking a child; the kind of a child wanted; the terms—as to adoption, rate of board, attendance at school, work required; reading and companions; whether the child would room and sleep alone, and, if not, with whom; whether the child would eat with the family, attend social gatherings with the family, and in every way be treated as a member of the family.

From these inquiries we obtain certain necessary information. But it is idle to think that one can pass judgment upon an application from a mere interview; that would be to decide about a family simply from the appearance of one or two members of it. It is also futile to think that one can surely get an inner view of a family by a visit; if there is a "skeleton in the closet," it will be concealed at such a time. It is clearly unsafe, too, to rely upon what one may learn from references; we must not count upon a frank and unbiased opinion from them; and if they are not known to us, surely some one in turn must vouch for them.

Where, then, is safety to be found? We answer, above all in the verdict of those persons known to us by independent evidence to be people of character, intelligence, and standing in the community, who have had constant communication with and opportunities to judge the applicants as fellow-townsmen or neighbors year after year. From the list of agents of the Society for the Prevention of Cruelty to Children, and of auxiliary visitors of the State Board of Lunacy and Charity, from the Year Books of the various religious bodies, from the gazetteers of the states, giving the names of public officials and leading citizens, from physicians named and vouched for by members of their profession in the city known to us in person, or by reputation, from people of other professions and callings of whom we learn in a similar way, from persons known and vouched for by the directors or officers or friends of the Society, from people with whom children have already been placed to advantage, we are able for each application to make up a list of several people from whom we may seek information and opinion concerning a family, with the assurance that the information will be trustworthy, and the opinion valuable.

Thus, in each case, we discover sources of information that are independent of the references given by the applicants. The fact that we write to these people without the knowledge of the applicants, and with a pledge that answers will be confidential, gives a strong assurance of frank and truthful replies. What we really do is to summon a family for judgment by a jury of their neighbors, and a jury, too, that although it does not pronounce a verdict under oath, does act with a peculiar freedom from selfish motive of fear or favor to restrain it from an honest, thoughtful, impartial decision. The inquiry made of these people reads as follows: "I am considering the question of placing a child with Mr. and Mrs. A——, and am anxious to know whether a child would have with them a thoroughly happy home, kind care and moral training. To decide this important question *I need to know the rugged truth* in regard to their home and surroundings. Will you kindly assist me in my inquiry? Your response will be held strictly confidential."

The information and opinions gathered in these various ways and from these various sources are recorded upon cards designed for the purpose. When the inquiry has proceeded far enough, the home that has asked for one of our children is passed upon, and approved or disapproved. If disapproved, a letter is sent, as follows: "I have considered your application, and find that I ought not to send any child to you." In special instances the letter is softened to read thus: "I have considered your application, and find that I shall be unable to send any child to you. I regret the necessity of this decision." The card referred to is so arranged that if the application is approved, and a child is placed in the home, any further information that comes to us in the course of our relations with the family, any changes that may take place in the home, and the entire story of the child's life there, can be recorded as time passes.

Of course many things have to be taken into account in fitting the children to the families; and it is absolutely necessary that we keep in close touch with the families in order to carry out the purposes of thorough-going supervision. No wisdom, however, in fitting children to places, and no subsequent supervision, can make up for the evils of a slipshod method of inquiry or a lack of real investigation, and careful selection of families at the start. On the other hand the preliminary investigation and the unflinching rejection of all unsuitable or doubtful applications, must be followed by wisdom in matching the children and

THE AID OF SCIENCE

the families, and by that constant supervision, which good families welcome, and which with such families easily becomes a genuine coöperation between them and us to secure the highest good of the children for whom they and we are together responsible.

The Use and Development of Assets in the Child's Own Family

As a summary of his principles—especially as to the relation of children to their own homes—Mr. Birtwell has these things to say:[40]

The true test of work like ours is the ability to lay hold of principles of action which tend not only to reform and educate individuals but also, in the end, to reduce the whole number of unprotected children, and no method ought to satisfy us which does not aim at accomplishing this.

These children cannot be divorced from the natural relations of family life without loss, any more than can those born under more favorable conditions, and therefore we must humbly set ourselves to learn the ways in which family ties may be strengthened and parental responsibilities maintained, while working, at the same time for the reformation of the child.

This method involves more thought and time than any other, but is in itself worth more. It means that before we can decide on the best thing to be done, we must have personal relations, with both child and guardian, and know the whole story of its life and surroundings.

As to acceptance, placement in foster homes, and subsequent supervision, the following passage in the *Report* for 1891-1893 gives a good idea:[41]

These children are sent directly to families, usually in the country, as a rule but one child, except in the case of brothers and sisters, being placed in each family, where they receive the same care and training as sons and daughters of the house. It is evident that this cannot be safely done unless each family has been thoroughly investigated and tested,

---
[40]*Twenty-eighth* and *Twenty-ninth Annual Reports*, 1893, p. 10.
[41]*Ibid.*, p. 13.

and on this previous investigation, together with judicious fitting of children to places, and careful supervision, the success of our system depends.

With regard to the investigation of foster homes, we have already seen the care with which the Association proceeded:[42]

The second element of success, judicious fitting of children to places, may be experimental at first, and sometimes several changes are made before the right place is found for a child. While too much changing should be avoided as tending to destroy the feeling of a permanent family life which we wish to foster in our children, experience often shows that a child who has been a failure in one place may become a success in another.

Our third requisite, supervision, is carried on by correspondence and visiting, and a written history is kept of each child. A visitor accompanies each child when placed, and soon makes a second visit; after this the amount of visiting varies with the child and family. When a child is *well placed* and visited by *respectable parents* less supervision is needed; with troublesome or uneasy children a great deal; but there must *always be enough to establish and maintain the friendly relationship of visitor and child,* that our boys and girls may feel they are not forgotten or uncared for, but have a real friend to turn to for counsel and sympathy. In visiting, both family and child are seen; the latter alone for a part of each visit. The school is generally visited and the teacher consulted as to the child's behavior and progress. Other points to be covered in visiting are whether the child eats at table with the family and has the same food, its clothing, sleeping arrangements, cleanliness, neatness, amount of schooling, church attendance, reading, companions, amusements, punishments, training in house or farm work, its adaptability to the family, its happiness, special failings or habits, and progress in study, work and character.

Responsibility of the Children's Aid Society for Preventive and Constructive Community Programs

That Mr. Birtwell was also thinking of the community and

---
[42]*Op. cit.,* pp. 14-15.

of prevention as well as of the individual child in trouble, this statement is proof:[43]

What is the province of a Children's Aid Society? What may properly be its purpose, its programme, its hope? Is the work it does, or may do, of vital concern, not only to the few but to all? In fine, how lightly or how seriously shall we regard that work, some edge of which this Society has already touched, the heart of which it seeks to penetrate?

Life ought to be worth living to all. How it may become so is the social problem. The first adequate inquiry into the life of the people in a great city, that of Mr. Charles Booth, in London, shows that in that metropolis thirty in every hundred of the population are poor or criminal. So, too, in our American cities, ugly facts stare us in the face, and every thoughtful person is asking how folly, injustice, indecency, misery may be done away with, and the modes of individual and social life become in every way admirable.

Now, the child problem is an integral part of this whole vital and urgent social question. How are the melancholy ranks of the pauper, the criminal, the vicious, recruited? Is it not from "the vagabondage of childhood," from the moral exposure of innocent children and susceptible youth, and from "the dwarfing of childhood by physical and spiritual night?" *The province of a Children's Aid Society, therefore, is to assist the community to see how far the percentage of poor and criminal may be beaten down,* on the one hand by specific work for children and youth, and on the other by such reorganization of the life of the community as may remove the very causes of their degradation. Who shall say how far the number of the wretched might be reduced if, first, every friendless and exposed child should be given such protection and opportunity as an informed and determined community has the power to afford; and if, secondly, the causes that lie back of juvenile exposure should be sought out, and their due recognition secured in education, in industry, in the home, in the Church, in our courts of justice, in state and municipal government, in public opinion—in a word, in all the fundamental institutions of society?

It is by work for individual children that this Society is seeking to carry out the first part of the programme outlined; and it is in such work that we are gaining the information necessary for the second part of the programme.

[43] *Annual Report,* 1890-1891, pp. 7-8.

Dynamic Philosophy as an Iconoclast

At this point it is appropriate to inquire what effect all these elastic efforts to suit the action to the need of the individual child had upon some of the previous activities of the Society. For example, when children were placed directly in family homes "to be made clean" and "without notice," what was the final effect upon the number of boys sent to the Society's Homes at Pine Farm, the Foxborough Home and to Weston? The fact is that these emergency homes of special caliber to deal with children, where they were "to be made clean" and "gently initiated into (those) decencies of life," finally closed all the Homes with a capital H, that the Boston Children's Aid Society had maintained for over thirty years. These Homes, especially the original one—Pine Farm at West Newton—were cherished institutions. It must have caused somebody a heartache to see them go.

Whoever takes as a guide for his action an honest answer to the question: "What does the child need?" may find himself face to face with the necessity of giving up some of his long cherished opinions and institutions. The question for all of us to ask ourselves is: "Have we the courage to follow wherever the answer leads?" It takes courage to believe that we can really find truth in the statement, "A little child shall lead them." It takes courage to ask with all honesty and sincerity, "What does the child need?" There are undreamed of possibilities of danger to some of our dearly loved beliefs if we honestly try "to suit the action to the real need of the individual child." Have we the courage to try?

In 1896 Mr. Birtwell again states his aim:[44]

> Throughout the work of the Society the aim is simply to be human—to understand others as we would be understood—and to get hold at the really right end. One cannot name the misfortune, abuse, fear, hope, sorrow, sin, that is not familiar here. But we are sustained by a cheerful and stubborn confidence in human nature, and by the conviction that in preventive work amongst the young we must win if at all.

[44] *Thirty-second Annual Report*, 1896, p. 34.

THE AID OF SCIENCE

Again the dynamic character of supervision is emphasized. Nothing could indicate more clearly than these passages, the careful and intensive method of work pursued by the Society, and its sense of responsibility for wider generalizations from particular cases.

Placing out is gaining in other cities and states, etc., and

> with the trend toward the newer system a special responsibility for efficient work rests upon those who illustrate it, lest through laxity of method the new should finally prove to be no advance upon the old.[45]

Early in the year the committee entered upon a systematic plan of hearing and taking notes of the details of every case. These notes were kept for six months and classified into groups, so that at the end of that time they could be reviewed. In this way we feel that we have gained a better knowledge of the work and a clear understanding of the reasons for decisions in the various cases.[46]

Through the maze of details in our work run certain broad purposes. These last few years have been years of fulfillment in large ways. Though the individual case is and must be the basis of all we do, results transcending the individual case are the sure fruit of thorough and unfettered treatment of each case as it arises. Public opinion, legislative enactment, the method and growth of charity, after all, do take account of experience gained.[47]

In 1905, we are told that the number of placing-out agents was now seven and that they had the care in homes of 283 children at the beginning of the year, and of 326 at the close, an average of from 40 to nearly 47 children per visitor.[48]

Scattered as they are in New England homes, the wonder is that seven agents can be always ready for the new and urgent cases as they arise, and at the same time able to keep in such close personal touch with the children already placed; the people with whom they live and the communities of which they are a part. It would be impossible without careful organization and distribution of responsibility, a high

---

[45] *Annual Report*, 1900-1901, p. 15.
[46] *Annual Report*, 1903, p. 22.
[47] *Annual Report*, 1900-1901, p. 10.
[48] *Annual Report*, 1905, p. 13.

standard in the selection of agents, and great devotion on the part of the agents. In this department, also, though again the decisions rest with the executive, the fortnightly meetings of the committee with the agents and with the general secretary are a vital feature of administration.[49]

In October, 1911, Mr. Charles W. Birtwell closed twenty-six years of service as General Secretary, and in the report for that year, after summarizing for the period the changes in background of the work of the Society, he says:[50]

The possibilities of a more definite, united appeal by our child-helping agencies to the community to do the things that need to be done to prevent this needless suffering and misery, these needless moral and physical tragedies of childhood and youth, should be thought through to concreteness, and persistently set forth. *A high capacity for united expression and action can only be acquired by practice* [italics by the present writer]. The utilization of the united wisdom and strength of our child-helping agencies is an important and inviting task.

With all this progress, evil, exposure and suffering continue. Children of tender years bear infirmities due to no fault of their own, and are degraded through preventable misfortune and remediable social conditions.

As for the Children's Aid Society, has the past been anything but a *clearing of the ground for the real action?* Its leverage in 1885 was represented by an invested fund one-fifth and an income and expenditure one-tenth as large as now. The aids to inquiry and action have correspondingly multiplied. The opportunity would appear to be at hand, right here among these many children and youth and their families, for experiments and studies that shall prove of the highest value and influence for the prevention of the evils from which children now suffer.

As we here take leave of Mr. Birtwell, we pause yet a moment for a word from him spoken to the writer in the spring of 1928, as Mr. Birtwell looked back over the forty-two years since he came to the Boston Children's Aid Society as "an outdoor worker":

I told my fellow-workers, "Don't say to me that anything can't be

[49]*Ibid.*, p. 13.   [50]Page 16.

done. You find out first what a child needs and we will decide afterwards whether or not it can be done."

That was the good seed that Mr. Birtwell kept casting into fertile soil for twenty-five years: First find out what a child really needs, then face the task of devising ways and means to meet those needs in each individual case.

As the writer has pondered the meaning of this seed-sowing by Mr. Birtwell, these words of the Prophet of Nazareth as to the way a better social order was to come in this world, have come over and over to his mind:

And he said, So is the kingdom of God, as if a man should cast seed into the ground; and should sleep, and rise night and day, and the seed should spring and grow up, he knoweth not how.[51]

We need not interpret this old parable to mean that the speaker belittled the importance of cultivating the soil into which the seed has been cast. That interpretation would be contrary to the meaning of the teaching as a whole. The evident purpose was to emphasize the great fact that, both in the biological world and in the world of human effort, once good seed has actually been cast into good ground, there will be growth, even though the sower and others should forget it—even though they "should sleep and rise night and day."

In what has already been said, and in what follows, there is no intention of setting Mr. Birtwell and the Boston Children's Aid Society upon a pedestal to be worshipped as perfect. Nothing could be further from the truth or could do dependent children more harm. Neither Mr. Birtwell nor his successors have always succeeded in "suiting the action to the real need" of every dependent child in their care. But a man had "cast seed into the ground" and it grew, *and will grow* even though he who sowed the seed and those who followed him should sometimes fail to cultivate it—"should sleep, and rise night and day."

---

[51] Mark 4: 26-27.

The later history of the Boston Children's Aid Society under three successors to Mr. Birtwell, all of whom have honestly tried to cultivate the seed he planted, can be read in the annual reports of the Society, which are worth the earnest student's attention. A quotation from one of these reports—that of 1912—may be found in our last chapter.

Furthermore, in 1929, out of the previous ten years of joint experience of the Boston Children's Aid Society, the Judge Baker Foundation, and other coöperating agencies of New England, came a masterful summary of the best that has yet been learned as to the actual processes of foster home care of destitute, neglected and delinquent children.[52]

In 1930, forty-two years after Mr. Birtwell said that the aim should be "to suit the action to the real need," the Society still finds this ideal process large enough to include help for children in their own homes, in boarding and free foster homes, and occasionally in "some specialized institution." Just what is the need, and just what variation or combination of home and institutional care can best meet the need? During all these years the problem is ever new in each case, and will forever continue to be new.

What Does the Story Thus Far Mean?

Coming back now, as we conclude this chapter, to the professional significance of Mr. Birtwell's principle of suiting the action to the real need of the individual child, these considerations should be emphasized and reëmphasized:

Eventually any agency or institution seeking money and public opinion in support of its efforts to care for dependent, neglected or delinquent children, must also face the same issue. Outdoor relief, almshouse, indenture, orphan asylum, transportation of children in great companies to western villages and farms, one-by-one placement of all children in free family homes as an all-inclusive process

---

[52] Healy, Bronner, Baylor and Murphy, *Reconstructing Behavior in Youth*, New York and London, 1929.

—each at some period has been seen by one and another champion as *the way* to care for all dependent children. Not one of these champions of a panacea has ever consciously and persistently tested out the efficiency of his own service to every child accepted for care in the light of the question, "Son, daughter, what is it that you really need?" However tardy the supporting public may seem to be, it will sooner or later require all agencies and institutions to ask this question.

So far as progress had been made before Mr. Birtwell's time, the needs of children had already been seen and felt by thousands of individuals who had tried to help them. The greatest mistake hitherto made was not in the failure to see some of the needs of children,—the need for bread, bed, and clothes, for example—but the mistake of thinking that there was *just one best way* of meeting all these needs. Some of the pioneers forgot that no two children are exactly alike—even in their needs for bread—and almost all forgot, and still forget, that it is written, "Man shall not live by bread alone." What religion and theology have told us of the further needs of children to whom bread alone has been given, we have often failed to understand; but we are slowly learning to understand it as it is being restated for us in terms of the new psychology of the emotions and of behavior. Dr. Herman Adler, of the Juvenile Psychopathic Institute of Chicago, puts in a single phrase all that was involved in Mr. Birtwell's demand that we find out what every child needs before we try to help him. Dr. Adler says that to answer the question fully as to what a child needs, we must understand "a total personality in a total situation." A total personality in a total situation! Not only must we understand the bodily needs, the emotional needs, the intellectual needs of each child, but we must know also to what extent the satisfaction of these needs is inextricably enmeshed in associations with his own past experiences, with his father, his mother, his brother, his sister, his friend, his locality. We must understand what we actually do to the child when we more or less arbitrarily and by force separate him physically from what we call inadequate, depraved, immoral, vicious parents and surroundings, and place him in what we fondly think is an ideal institution or a good foster family home. Are we sure that for this particular child at this particular time we have really understood what he needs and how, actually, to help him? Have we really understood a total personality in a total situation? If we have not, then we have not in reality used the process described for us by Mr. Birtwell in 1888, when he said to his fellow workers, "The aim will be in each instance to suit the action to the real need, heeding the teachings of experience, still to study the conditions with a freedom from assumptions, and a directness and freshness of view, as complete as though the case in hand stood absolutely alone." In the light of this statement of process, where is the basis for the claims and counter-claims of one method over another as *the only way* to care for every dependent and neglected child? Humility, rather than boasting, becomes all of us in our claims for the merits of our own favorite but partial processes of caring for dependent, neglected, delinquent and specially handicapped children. With what outraged feelings have hundreds of us moaned out our complaint about the boys and girls whom we have rescued from poor and wicked homes, kept for years in our lovely institutions, or in good foster homes, and who, on the day that they were no longer under our legal control, have gone—where do you think? Right back into those very same poor and wicked homes from which we rescued them! What ingratitude! "Man shall not live by bread alone." "It is necessary for us to understand a total personality in a total situation." "The aim will be in each instance to suit the action to the real need."

We have not space, and it is not necessary, to follow in full detail the development of all the subordinate processes of the one great process upon which Mr. Birtwell and the Boston Children's Aid Society had entered. Let any institution or agency once accept this one basic process as the controlling method of all its work, and that institution or agency will go forward. It would be wrong to give the impression that Mr. Birtwell and the Boston Children's Aid Society were the only ones making progress. As we have already said, it would be a mistake for anybody to think that in this Boston Society henceforth no mistakes were made. What is true, however, is that Mr. Birtwell and the Boston Children's Aid Society gained such a clear vision of the process many others were more or less consciously groping for, and became so articulate in describing this process, that they helped enormously to create an attitude of mind, a conception—in short, an all-inclusive basic approach to the process of caring for dependent and neglected children, which all the world must eventually accept and use if we would not publicly acknowledge our inefficiency.

In this process is room for all that has been discovered since it was first described, and for all that will ever be discovered by any branch of science about the nature of children and of any individual child. The discoveries and contributions of medicine, psychology, psychiatry, pedagogy, sociology, social case work, all find a place for all the service they can render in the one process of "suiting the action to the real need" in the case of every child.

CHAPTER VIII

SURVIVALS OF OUTWORN ATTITUDES, AND METHODS IN PRESENT-DAY INSTITUTIONS AND AGENCIES

It would be easy and comforting to think that dependent children no longer suffer from neglect, or ignorance, or inadequate facilities for care, in any community in any state. We like to believe that once somebody, somewhere, has pronounced a formula and has set up in some one agency or institution a fairly adequate program for putting that formula into effect, presto, all the children of every agency and institution everywhere straightway get the benefit of such a program. Alas! agencies and institutions for the care of dependent children do not change so quickly as that. Some persons in charge do not even know there has been a change anywhere. Others know, but think the old ways better. Still others know, but lack the staff and facilities to enter fully upon the better way. Happily there is a better attitude of mind which is typical of many. The superintendant of an agency which places children in free foster families said recently: "What I need is to have some one come in and tell me how I can start *from where I now am* and go as rapidly as possible in the direction I ought to go."

We shall have occasion, in the last chapter, to trace some encouraging evidences of such a desire to give better care to children, and some new efforts toward that end. This will be a pleasant task and will help us to turn our eyes resolutely towards the sunlight of the coming day. In this chapter, however, we must delay long enough to face some discouraging recent experiences of dependent children, away from their own homes and under the care of institutions and agencies in widely distributed states. In some cases—even among the most recent—where unsatisfactory situations are cited, progressive changes have got under way since the data were collected. Even so, and if it could be said with truth that all of the unsatisfactory attitudes and methods had ended prior to January 1, 1930, it might still be helpful for us to realize how recently, and in what a variety of ways, dependent children have been misunderstood and inadequately cared for in many of our states. That such things as are to be described have taken place anywhere in the United States, in the twentieth century, is sufficient reason for everybody who knows about them to inquire in all humility and reverence: Is it I that have in any way betrayed one of these dependent children?

Illustrations Qualitative, Not Quantitative

It should be noted that the illustrations cited are merely descriptive, except in the case of almshouse care. The statements made have no statistical or quantitative value. There is no intention to indict all the child welfare agencies and institutions of the country. The intention, rather, is constructive—to suggest that there is still a great deal to be done, and to stimulate the reader to an honest and persistent inquiry as to the actual situation in his own community—possibly in some institution or agency with which he or some member of his family is very deeply interested as a citizen, as a contributor, or perhaps even as a staff member or director. We shall cite experiences of some dependent and neglected children in fifteen different states. The states are distributed in all the great geographical sections of the country, but where the sources of information are unpublished, and confidential reports by private agencies or individuals, the designation of the localities will be made in general terms, that is: North Atlantic States, Middle Western States, and so forth. It is reasonable to suppose, in view of the wide distribution of these cases, that there is no state in which instances similar to those presented cannot be found. In so far as such cases exist in the states for which we have examples and in other states, the challenge is this: *The processes of care of dependent children by many institutions and foster home agencies are as yet imperfect.*

Survivals of Almshouse Care

In the first place, then, what are the recent facts regarding almshouse care of all dependent children? Almshouse care for children under sixteen years of age was not a thing of the past in 1923. The United States census reported that 4,715 children were admitted during 1922.[1]

We have also the report of a detailed study made in 1923 of the children in the almshouses of twenty-eight counties of Pennsylvania. These counties had approximately 44 percent of the total population of the state. In these twenty-eight counties on the date of visits:[2]

Altogether there were found eighty children residing in the county almshouses investigated, sixty-four of these were two years of age and over. Fifty-nine of these children had been in these institutions considerably longer than two months, the legal maximum allowed by the State law; forty-four of them had been there for more than a year. . . . Only in six county houses of the twenty-eight counties investigated were there no children kept in these institutions, either at the time of the visit or during the last year.

The United States census report above quoted gives, for the year 1922, a total of 541 children under 16 years of age in all the almshouses of the state of Pennsylvania.

Why Children Were in Almshouses in Pennsylvania in 1923

Some of the reasons given in Pennsylvania for keeping children in almshouses may suggest the pertinence of a study of almshouse care of children in other states:[3]

---

[1] United States census report, 1923, *Paupers in Almshouses*, Table 70.
[2] Public Charities Association of Pennsylvania, *The Almshouse Child*, p. 6.
[3] *Ibid.*, pp. 6-7.

SURVIVALS OF OUTWORN ATTITUDES

Manifold were the explanations given by the various poor authorities for the keeping of children in county almshouses. Most officials claimed that the children in the almshouses are usually those who are most difficult to place and who for that reason must be kept in county institutions. One poorhouse steward, in a home where a large number of children were found, admitted, however, that he felt it was difficult to get proper private homes for the children because the directors of the poor limited the amount of payment for the boarding of these children. This was further borne out by the fact that of the counties assigning difficulty of finding homes as a reason for their maintaining children in almshouses for long periods of time, the overwhelming majority provided no payment for the boarding of such children in private families. In three counties the officials declared that the children are kept there only temporarily. In three other county homes the children were obviously idiotic and not placeable. Three additional county boards could assign no particular reason except, perhaps, general inertia, for the presence of their almshouse wards; while the poor officials in three more counties stated that the applications for the admission of their children to the proper institutions have been made for some time, but that they were not admitted as yet. One county home expected to have the children removed soon, while in another instance, the children were in the almshouse at the special request of the superintendent, who was taking personal care of them. In one or two counties it was charged that frequently the poor authorities would keep a child in the almshouse for sixty days, discharge it and then readmit it as new, in order to avoid the legal restriction of sixty days.

Description of Children in a Pennsylvania Almshouse in 1921

Early in 1921 a trained worker visited a county almshouse in Pennsylvania. Her description of the care given children in a Home on the grounds of the almshouse is enough to suggest some of the evils from which dependent children still suffer, who are cared for under almshouse associations and with almshouse standards. The Almshouse and the Home were under the control of the county commissioners:[4]

[4] From a confidential report to a social agency in an eastern state.

The Almshouse was clean but bare. There were no children in the Almshouse itself, but one-half block away, on the Almshouse grounds, is the Home. It had a matron and a cook (colored) for a staff. The house is an old affair, in bad repair and very dirty and disorderly. The kitchen was described as a "hole." There were 17 children in the house at the time—boys and girls—the oldest less than 14 years, 5 under 4 years, the youngest 19 months, several 20 months. The cook said they got regularly two quarts of milk for the whole crowd. Boys and girls use the same toilets and bath rooms. No individual wash cloths, single beds, but much overcrowding. The roof leaked—the place needed condemnation. Three bedrooms—two for boys, one for girls—adjoining rooms. Closet in girls' room opened in boys' room. The place seemed the last spot for children. No books, no toys, etc., etc.

It would be an instructive inquiry for the readers of this book to find out just what are the laws of their several states respecting children in almshouses, how far they are observed, and what the reasons may be for ignoring or breaking these laws. Such inquiries might lead to improvement in the care of at least a few dependent children. Many noble men and women during the past decades of our history have been inspired by similar inquiries to long lives of chivalrous service for children who had no other help.

Reaction of a Young Social Worker When She Saw a Child in an Almshouse

For example, here is the reaction of a young social worker who in 1929 was asked to find a foster home for a child who had been born in an almshouse, her mother being of low mentality and her father an orderly in the institution:[5]

We realize full well that Mildred should never have stayed in the almshouse two years. . . . It should have been impossible for her to be conceived there. . . . When one sees her, and sees the hang-overs of two years at the County Home in her actions and development, one is tempted to cry out to all who will hear, "Did you know they kept babies

---
[5] From a confidential report to the writer by a worker in an eastern state.

at the County Home till they were two, with no chance to play normally or get the right food and training, shut up all day with a bunch of old women of all sorts, in a room reeking with disinfectant and having old stories of any sort mouthed over instead of the songs and stories your babies heard?"

No, even though it be 1930, the almshouse as a home for dependent children is not yet a thing of the past. In many states, for children under two years, it is even sanctioned by law. It might be a good exercise in descriptive imagination for every reader to try to realize as vividly as possible how large a crowd the 4,715 children in almshouses of the United States in 1922 would make. For example, most readers are familiar with school houses for 200, 500, or 1,000 children each. Almost five 1,000-pupil schools would be filled by these almshouse children, almost ten 500-pupil schools, and almost twenty-four 200-pupil schools.

SURVIVALS OF THE USE OF INDENTURE

Concerning indenture in Pennsylvania in 1927, this official statement is recent and suggestive to all those institutions and agencies still using the rigid indenture contract:[6]

There is perhaps no issue in child welfare that has caused as much discussion and difference of opinion as the question of indenture. This was emphasized last spring when the indenture laws were repealed.

It was on May 11th that an Act was passed to the effect "That all Acts and parts of Acts, general, local and special, which provide for the indenture or binding out of minors, are hereby repealed."

The great objection to this practice of indenturing was the implication that the child must pay, as he gets older, for the care he has received during his younger and more helpless years. To insist that any child shall remain in a family or an institution only because he is an economic asset there is surely not just. All children should have the best of care and education as their natural and unquestioned right. There

---

[6] From October, 1927, bulletin, *Hello Central,* Commonwealth of Pennsylvania Department of Public Welfare, Bureau of Children, Harrisburg, Pa.

should be no thought of their paying for this by "working it out" later on. This binding out of children was, without a doubt, quite intolerable.

Outside of this, the rigidity of the measure disqualifies it, as a means of child placing. Such a wholesale, routine method cannot begin to meet the standards of the present day program. All children are different and their needs and circumstances are different. How can one unchanging, rigid arrangement suit all their varying situations?

As a matter of fact one of the most difficult matters to decide when placing a child in a family is the question of how long he shall remain. It depends on so many points of adjustment and acceptance by the child and by the family in working out a happy relationship. This cannot be measured by any hard and fast rule of thumb.

There is another important need not provided for in this method of placing children: The supervision of the child is not emphasized. The standards of today recognize this vital need, and other kinds of arrangements for securing homes have already superseded the indenturing of children.

Method of Study of Children Indentured in Wisconsin

Of indenture in Wisconsin, we have more detailed, but not quite so recent, evidence.

Out of 827 children indentured for the first time by the Wisconsin State Public School during the four year period 1913-1917, a large group of 529 had not been legally adopted in 1923. In that year, 452 of the 529 children in this class were studied by agents of the United States Children's Bureau, under the direction of Miss Emma O. Lundberg.[7] The records of the State School relating to these children were consulted to find data about their original homes, their parents and relatives, also to get the names and addresses of all the homes in which they had been indentured. A study was also made of the records of their supervision by the State School agents of whom, at the time of the study, there were only two charged with the task of looking after five hundred

---

[7]See United States Children's Bureau, *Pub. 150, Children Indentured by the Wisconsin State Public School*, pp. 1-8.

children in all parts of the state. The indenture homes were then visited; the homes of children's parents were also visited if they could be located; relatives were seen wherever possible; county officials, courts that committed the children, social agencies, and others were interviewed in order to get the story of the family both before and after the child was sent to the State School. Of the 452 children studied, 224 were still wards of the state and could therefore be seen. Of the 228 who had been released from jurisdiction of the State School because they had become eighteen years of age, or had been transferred to other institutions, or had been returned to the legal custody of their parents, 80 were interviewed in person.

The indenture contract in use was as follows:[8]

Appendix C.—INDENTURE CONTRACT USED IN 1923

This agreement, by and between the State Board of Control of Wisconsin, by the authority of an act entitled, "An act to establish a State public school for dependent and neglected children," approved April 9, 1885, and acts amendatory thereof, party of the first part, and.... ......of the town of .... county of .... State of Wisconsin, postoffice address .... party of the second part:

Witnesseth, that the said board, in consideration of the agreement herein made by said second party, hereby places ...., one of the wards of this board, in the family of said second party to remain until the .... day of ...., 19.., when said child will be 18 years of age, reserving the right to cancel this contract and require the child to be returned to this school whenever, in the opinion of said board, the conditions of this agreement are not faithfully executed or when otherwise the interest of said child requires it.

That said second party reserves the right to cancel this agreement at any time by returning the child to this school free of cost to the State. Otherwise said agreement to remain in full force.

That said second party hereby receives said child and agrees to keep said child as a member of his family until the said .... day of ....,

[8]United States Children's Bureau, *Pub. 150*, pp. 129-30.

19.., maintaining, educating, and treating .... properly and kindly as a member of his family. That he will provide the child with suitable and sufficient clothing and suitable food and other necessaries in health and sickness; that he will assume the responsibility for the payment of all necessary medical and surgical service required and for expense of burial in case of death. That he will have .... taught the occupation of .... and the branches usually taught in the common schools, causing ...... to attend the public schools where ...... resides at least ...... months in each year, until 16 years of age. That at the expiration of the indenture period he will furnish said child with two new suits of good clothes, and will pay said board or the superintendent of said State school, for the benefit of said child, the sum of $50 or pro rata of that amount for the time .... remains in his family after h.... tenth birthday, if not for the full term of ...... indenture.

That in case this contract shall be canceled, as provided by law, the said second party agrees to return said child to this school at his own expense, when requested by the agent or superintendent of this institution.

That whenever requested by said agent or superintendent the said second party agrees to report to him in writing such facts in regard to said child as he shall request, and that he will furnish said child with materials and opportunity to correspond with said superintendent or agent.

Child must not be removed from place where indentured without the consent of the superintendent.

In witness whereof, the said State Board of Wisconsin, by the superintendent or agent of this institution, and said second party set their names and seals this .... day of ...., A. D. 19...

.... (L. S.)
(Superintendent or agent of the State
public school.)

Indenture as a Stimulus to Overworking the Dependent Child

Under the present system most of the homes secured are on farms because the families there are in constant need of the kind of help that can be given by a boy or girl. The child is expected to earn his maintenance, in part at least, and it is for the service thus rendered that the family pays $50 to the State School in his behalf, when he reaches the age limit, or a portion of this amount if he is released previously. The book of the indenture contract contains the following schedule of pro rata amounts to be paid if the contract is cancelled before the child is 18 years of age:

Age	Amount	Age	Amount
11	$6.25	15	$31.25
12	12.50	16	37.50
13	18.75	17	43.75
14	25.00	18	50.00

The State retains this money until the child is 21 years of age.

In a word, the great state of Wisconsin, from 1885 to 1923, through the process of indenture of dependent children by its State Public School, had expected these children to pay their own way in foster family homes from infancy up to ten years of age. After ten years, they were expected not only to pay their own way but to begin to accumulate a wage surplus of $6.25 a year. Could any plan be devised more likely to appeal to selfishness and greed, and to the tendency to overwork young children, than such a carefully calculated year-by-year insistent suggestion to the family that they were expected by the indenture contract to get out of the child not only all he costs in food, clothing, shelter, medical care, schooling, etc., but a surplus of at least $6.25 a year for each child over ten years of age?

Experiences of Children Indentured in Wisconsin, 1913-1917

And what did the study of the children's actual experiences show? Only a few out of many instances can here be given:

This study has brought out many instances of placement without regard to the histories of children.[9]

Three cases of goiter encountered by one agent (Children's Bureau) had had no medical diagnosis or treatment, either by the State School before placement or by the foster parents. One boy's goiter was so large

[9]United States Children's Bureau, *Pub. 150*, p. 41.

that it was difficult for him to turn his neck. It sometimes hurt him when he worked.[10]

In one home the foster parents were surprised when the father came for his son, whose custody had been restored to him. The foster parents reported that they had been informed by the State School that the parents were dead. Sometimes the State School agents themselves possessed no knowledge of the children, but in several instances knowledge of an unfavorable nature was withheld from the foster parents.[11]

Although in some cases complete separation of indentured children from their own parents was necessary for their protection, the School did not recognize the fact that physical separation does not necessarily mean an emotional separation. It was the general policy of the School not to permit contact or correspondence of indentured children with their own parents. However, 70 out of 123 children went back to their parents and relatives after the period of indenture was over.[12]

Many children visited by the bureau's agents asked about their parents or other relatives. If they did not remember their own homes they were continually wondering about them and wishing to see anyone related to them. When they were old enough at the time of commitment to remember their homes, they worried about the brothers and sisters whom they had not seen since they left the State School to go to indenture homes.[13]

It was the practice of the School not only to separate children while indentured from their parents, but also in most cases children of the same family from each other. There were 113 families represented in the children studied from which two or more children were indentured. Eighty-six of these groups of brothers and sisters were separated from each other during the period covered by the study. . . . Not only were the children placed in different homes, but in the majority of cases they were placed in widely separated counties.[14]

In all, the Children's Bureau agents visited 540 indenture homes:[15]

[10] *Ibid.*, p. 42.   [11] *Ibid.*, p. 43.
[12] United States Children's Bureau, *Pub. 150*, p. 49.   [13] *Ibid.*, p. 49.
[14] *Ibid.*, Condensed from pp. 50-51.   [15] *Ibid.*, Condensed from p. 55.

SURVIVALS OF OUTWORN ATTITUDES

After careful checking of the reports it appears to be a conservative estimate that the conditions in almost half the 540 indenture homes for which there was an apparently adequate basis of information were detrimental to the children placed in them. The figures are as follows:

Character of homes	Number	Per cent
Total homes classified	540	100
High grade	42	8
Satisfactory	236	44
Detrimental	262	48

As many of the children had been indentured in more than one home, the statement is made:[16]

Of the 377 children concerning whose indenture homes there was definite information, only about one-third had had indenture histories that were apparently satisfactory.

Some of the most commonly recorded detrimental conditions affecting 262 different children, were the following:[17]

	Number of children
Deprived of schooling	53
Deprived of schooling, cruelty, too much work	5
Deprived of schooling, too much work	27
Too much work	17
Home morals bad	13
Mistreatment or cruelty	10
Foster parents incompetent	9
Foster parents disliked child (friction or lack of sympathy)	19
Neglect	7
Bad influence in home	9
Bad environment	9
Total	178
42 other miscellaneous combinations of detrimental factors	84
Total	262

[16] United States Children's Bureau, *Pub. 150*, p. 56.
[17] *Ibid.*, Condensed from pp. 56-57.

Not only were children placed once in such (detrimental) homes but they were sometimes removed from one detrimental home only to be placed in another in which conditions appeared no better.

Questions Raised by Such a Recent System of Indenture

If these parents and relatives were fit to associate with these young men and women after indenture, the question is at once raised: Why then an indenture separation at all? If the parents and relatives were unfit to associate with their children when the children were indentured, the questions then are: Were they fit after the children came back from indenture? If so, how did they become fit? If not fit, either before or after indenture of the children, could they have been helped if the emotional tie which brought their children back to them after enforced physical separation had been used as an asset for help to both, instead of being ignored or thwarted? Surely this picture of the care of dependent and neglected children of a great and prosperous American state well along in the first quarter of the twentieth century may well stimulate the citizens not only of that state, but also of all our other states, to ask themselves with persistent earnestness this question: How can we so improve our processes of care for dependent and neglected children that in very truth we may achieve an understanding and sympathetic treatment of every child as "a total personality in a total situation"? We can be satisfied with nothing less than this. Every public and private agency and institution for the care of children—every child welfare worker and board member—every citizen and parent, must eventually abide the application of this test.

SURVIVALS OF OUTWORN ATTITUDES

Some Recent Glimpses into Institutions Other than Almshouses

Institution Number 1

Of children in one of the County Children's Homes of Ohio in 1914, only sixteen years ago, this is the picture:[18]

The children, 44 in number, were in the Children's Home on the Infirmary grounds, the Superintendent in charge of both institutions. The reports indicate "a building in very bad condition, dingy walls with the plastering knocked off in many places, having a so-called playroom without furniture, pictures or toys, except two long benches and a coal stove." The one school room, equally cheerless, was in the same building. All attended this school and the younger children sat all day with only four five-minute recitations to break the monotony. Several of the children were found sitting in school without soles on their shoes and several little toes were peeping through when the inspector called, although it was on a February morning.

Upon retiring at night, the girls had to go upstairs by an outside stairway, which was often covered with ice and snow.

The report continues, "The children do not receive adequate attention owing to a lack of help. It is customary to have two cows driven to the home morning and night, and the milking is done by two girls (the young governesses) during which time the children are neglected as to supervision. . . . There are no records apart from those kept for the infirmary inmates. There is no indication in the record book as to what has become of all the children. However it was possible to locate the placement of a number of these children by going over a lot of indentures. . . . Children are indentured to remain with the family until 18 or 21 years of age and to receive not less than four months school in some instances, while in others it is six. There is nothing to show that any of the children placed out from this institution have been visited."

[18]Esther McClain, *Child Placing in Ohio,* Columbus, Ohio, 1928, p. 33. Quoted from a report of the Ohio Department of Public Welfare, pp. 25-26.

Institution Number 2

Of children in another institution in the North Central group of states, we catch these glimpses in 1925:[19]

The children in the Home eat their meals in silence except as they may ask for something. None of the matrons sit at the tables with them. They eat rapidly and there is no attempt to make meal time anything more than a mere feeding time. On the day we were in the dining room large children were eating hominy with a spoon. Forks had not even been put on the tables. There were no napkins. . . .

The runabout children were having their naps on the bare floor of their play room. This room has one window and the door into the hall was closed. The children had not been undressed but were sleeping in the clothing they had worn all afternoon.

The medical records show that some of these runabouts are rachitic and need special care and treatment, yet the entire group were sleeping on a hard, dusty floor. The fact that small squares of cloth had been placed under their heads is in no wise an excuse for such a plan.

Every child should have an individual towel, comb and tooth-brush and these articles should be kept so that they do not touch. On the day of our visit the towels were hung so close together that the children might just as well have been using a roller towel; the tooth-brushes of the boys were crowded together into one glass jar; and common combs were being used. The manner in which the toilet articles were kept was an indication of a total lack of appreciation of the risks of infection and contagion which are ever present in an institution. The health of the children is constantly menaced by such gross carelessness, particularly as there are cases of impetigo and trachoma under treatment at present.

Institution Number 3

Of dependent little children in a school for delinquent girls in a South Atlantic state, we have this report in 1925:[20]

There are even among these children some little folks who are committed for the crime of their parents, really in themselves only dependents, and yet there is no way to protect them from girls of their own ages who have had the most degrading sex experiences.

[19] From a survey by the Child Welfare League of America.
[20] From a survey in 1924-1925 by the Child Welfare League of America.

SURVIVALS OF OUTWORN ATTITUDES

Institution Number 4

A city institution observed within the last decade in the East South Central area:[21]

A crowded thorofare; an old-fashioned brick dwelling set close to the street and shut in by encroaching business. Barred windows, tiny hands clutching the bars, against which are pressed listless white faces. When it was suggested that it would be better for the children if the extremely valuable city property were sold and the Home moved out into a district which would permit the children to be out of doors, the reply was:

"Those children you see clinging to the bars of the windows bring in thousands of dollars a year to us. Why should we move to a place where no one would see them?"

A glistening white cross over the door. Underneath are those exquisite words of the Master—"Suffer little children to come unto Me." Twenty to thirty white-faced, shaven-headed children, four to six years of age, are standing two by two, tiny hands clasped behind them. No smiles of anticipation, no whispering, no shuffling of restless feet, absolute silence reigns. At the signal from the attendant this tiny "army" begins to sing "Onward Christian Soldiers" and marches down a corridor to a sunless room. Here, after the Blessing, it sits down to its noonday meal of a heap of cold mashed potato, a huge soggy biscuit and a tin cup of skimmed milk, the daily contribution of a charitably inclined milk dealer.

A young board member was aghast to observe that, in preparation for the noonday meal, the faces and hands of these twenty to thirty "Christian soldiers" were being washed with one face cloth and with the same basin of water. What made the situation even more alarming, was the fact that to some degree, each child had the "cold" which, at the time, was prevalent in the "Home." This matter was called to the attention of the board which refused to believe that there could have been any breach of the rules. However, the young board member was insistent and an investigation was made. At the next board meeting the following report was made:

[21] From a private report to the writer.

"Mrs. Young Board Member was, in this instance, correct in her observation. It was deeply regretted. However, the board may rest assured that it will not happen again. In the future, the rule will be adhered to, namely, that the water (no mention of the face cloth) must be changed after every seventh child."

In introducing a health program into the Home, the matron, who claimed to be a practical nurse, was intolerant of any suggestions as to diet and health supervision, as worked out with a pediatrician and the Public Health Nursing Association. The need was repeatedly brought before the board. Finally, the following compromise was made: "The board upholds the position taken by the matron and will not permit the coöperation and supervision of a trained nurse, but sees no objection to a public health nurse's coming in daily if necessary."

Institution Number 5

In 1928 this statement was made as to supervision of the children who had been placed out by an institution in a New England state:[22]

According to records at the Orphanage, forty-six of the fifty-two placed-out children had never been visited since they were placed. Four had been visited once, one twice. There was also one where it seems that there was a pretty close contact with the foster parents, although it is not clear what the nature of these contacts was.

Institution Number 6

In one of our oldest institutions in a South Atlantic state, in 1925 the children were in uniform. Also, after giving details as to a considerable number of inmates present and past who were blood relatives of one another, this statement is given:[23]

The facts brought out by the studies of these families must make it clear that accepting children in an institution and removing them from their parents' home does not solve a family's problem. The number of

[22] From a survey by the Child Welfare League of America.
[23] *Ibid.*

SURVIVALS OF OUTWORN ATTITUDES

these children who are related to one another and the number whose aunts, uncles, mothers or fathers or some member of the family were previously wards of the Children's Institution indicate the ease with which dependency is fostered and transmitted from one generation to the next. The object of modern social service is to cure dependency, not to continue it, and with this in mind it must be evident that it is vitally necessary to recognize the need for social service in these families before and after the acceptance of the children for care.

A "WHITE LIST" OF INSTITUTIONS FOR CHILDREN IN PENNSYLVANIA

It is hoped that the reader will use his constructive imagination as he follows the data given in the accompanying White List, relative to facilities and methods in use in the 240 institutions for children in Pennsylvania in 1926. It is to be hoped also that no reader will fail to read between the lines and to catch the significance of the coöperative and educational methods for better care that are being used in Pennsylvania under the leadership of the State Bureau of Children:[24]

THE MEASURING ROD

Those who were present at the 1924 Institute at Thorn Hill will remember how readily the various points in the minimum standards for institutions were adopted by the group of institution workers present.

Although some of the persons interested in the different children's homes have written asking us for their rating as measured by this "rod," we believe that all would be interested in seeing how Pennsylvania's institutions measure up as a whole. The 240 children's homes were tabulated in 1925 according to these minimum standards and a few of the results are shown here. There have been changes, no doubt, since this original tabulation was made, perhaps yours are among these.

Mary S. Labaree,
Director,
Bureau of Children.

[24] From February, 1926, bulletin, *Hello Central,* Bureau of Children, Department of Public Welfare, Commonwealth of Pennsylvania, Harrisburg.

SANITATION

Cleanliness is the foundation of health.
Individual combs were found in .... 141 of the 240 Homes
Tooth brushes in .... 156 of the 240 Homes
Adequate bathing facilities in .... 147 of the 240 Homes
Standard frequency of use in .... 146 of the 240 Homes
Adequate toilet facilities in .... 173 of the 240 Homes
Hot water provided in wash rooms in .... 186 of the 240 Homes

HEALTH

What do you know about your children's health?
A complete physical examination on admission
    was the rule in .... 51 of the 240 Homes
Regular health supervision in .... 76 of the 240 Homes
Isolation until examined by the doctor in ...... 52 of the 240 Homes
Medical and physical records found in .... 55 of the 240 Homes

DIET

Undernourishment is linked up with many kinds of failure.
Adequate milk supply was provided in .... 104 of the 240 Homes
Fruit, fresh or cooked, served daily in .... 144 of the 240 Homes
Fresh vegetables daily in .... 135 of the 240 Homes

EDUCATION

The child should be given as much education as he can absorb. The educational opportunities afforded the children varied to such an extent that the figures scarcely showed the true situation. In some of the institutions not only were the children given the usual grade and high school courses, but were assisted in completing college and trade courses, while in other homes we found the children being taken from their classes at certain times in order to perform duties in the various industries of the institution.

SURVIVALS OF OUTWORN ATTITUDES

RECREATION

To the child, play is life.

The minimum standard provision for outdoor
recreation was found in .... 140 of the 240 Homes

The minimum standard provision for indoor
recreation was found in .... 172 of the 240 Homes

Books were provided in .... 137 of the 240 Homes

STATE LAWS AND STANDARDS

The law in Pennsylvania forbids the use of common towels, of common drinking cups, and of butter substitutes in charitable institutions. It is interesting to note, therefore, that

Individual towels were provided by .... 149 of the 240 Homes

Drinking fountains or individual cups were
provided by .... 74 of the 240 Homes

Real butter was provided by .... 162 of the 240 Homes

SOCIAL SERVICE AND RECORD KEEPING

It is true that the institution caring for a child who would be better provided for elsewhere, is not rendering a real service to the child, yet there are many homes accepting children without making any effort to determine whether the statements made by the applicant are true. In this study 86 institutions were found to investigate through a coöperating society, 78 institutions made their own investigations more or less carefully. The remaining 76 accepted the child on the say-so of the applicant with practically no investigation of the situation.

Individual records of the important facts relating to the child were kept in 92 of the 240 Homes.

Glimpses of Recent Community and State Standards

In addition to the foregoing glimpses of children in individual institutions, some more general statements may well be given involving, sometimes several, and sometimes all, the institutions for dependent children and the foster home care agencies of a given town, city, county or state. Some of these statements include not only data pertaining to the care of children within the institutions, but also describe with special emphasis intake and after care methods, as well as the relations of children to their own homes, parents, and other relatives.

Community Number 1

The institutions of a certain city of a million people in the Pacific area, as described in 1925, clearly show the need for an application of the Birtwell question "What does the child really need?"[25]

In general it may be said that the children's institutions studied, with some notable exceptions, have admirable plants and equipment. In many instances they are quite new and generally well planned for the purpose. The exceptions we have dealt with frankly in the individual reports.

But while the plants and equipment were adequate and satisfactory, there was great variation in the medical service provided. Private physicians and other medical agencies contribute much good service to individual agencies, but there is on the whole a planlessness for complete medical care which is noted in many of the individual reports.

The criticism made regarding medical service applies even more definitely to social service. This service as it is related to the various children's institutions is almost uniformly inadequate. Children are received by many agencies who do not fit into the plan of the agency receiving them or who are simply received on request from parents without any consideration as to whether they should be cared for by anyone outside of their own homes or immediate family circle.

The care of dependent children in this city is in large measure in institutions, either being committed by court and paid for at regular county and state rates or accepted from parents or guardians, either free or at substantial or nominal boarding rates and supported or supplemented from private benevolence. In addition boarding homes licensed by the Health Department are also used.

The population of institutions under such circumstances easily becomes a conglomerate of early and even serious delinquents, and back-

[25] From a survey by the Child Welfare League of America.

SURVIVALS OF OUTWORN ATTITUDES

ward or defective children mixed in with bright, normal, capable children whom either death of the essential home-maker or some other misfortune has deprived of his chance for home life. The management may seek to guard itself against such a mixture by visits from members of admissions committees or by offhand decisions of superintendents, but the results are well known to lead in the same direction.

To guard against this each institution caring for children *should have social service at the front door, by means of which its intake is carefully studied* [italics by the present writer]. By its means many adjustments are made which make it unnecessary to receive the child at all. In other instances care of the child becomes a very temporary arrangement because plans are set on foot for an early adjustment which would not happen otherwise.

Community Number 2

Of institutions and other agencies for children in a city of about 400,000 people, in a state of the West North Central area, it was said in 1924:[26]

In all of the case work agencies we studied, we found need for better intake investigation; it is at this point in an organization that its policies are in great measure put into effect, and on the adequacy of these investigations will depend most of the future effectiveness of the work done; . . . similarly we find a general absence of planning for cases. At no point in the contact with clients is it common for agencies to sum up the whole situation.

Community Number 3

Of work for dependent children in a prosperous county of more than 50,000 people, in another state of the East North Central area, in 1928, we are told that:[27]

In contrast with several other counties of equal size in this state, very few children have been committed to the State School for Dependent and Neglected Children. The community has not foisted upon the state

[26] From a survey by the Child Welfare League of America. [27] *Ibid.*

the burden of providing for its dependent children, with the usual accompaniment of permanent removal of children from the custody of relatives and the easy breaking up of families when temporary care would have sufficed. . . .

While the child dependency problem does not appear to be as extensive as it is in many similar communities, there has been practically no activity for children on a case-work basis. . . . Institutional care has been relied upon as practically the only method of care of dependent children removed from their own homes. A beginning has been made in providing boarding home care, but this activity must be developed by a worker experienced in the technical aspects of home-finding and supervision.

Community Number 4

Of the methods of dealing with children born out of wedlock, these reports were given in 1926, of a city of nearly 150,000 people in a West South Central state:[28]

Of the nineteen mothers for whom date of their applications and date of acceptance are both reported, thirteen were allowed to give up their babies practically instantaneously, i. e., in less than twenty-four hours. In two instances, the babies were taken the next day. The largest interval that intervened between the Bureau's first contact with the problem and its acceptance of a child was ten days. When it is remembered that many of these mothers and fathers live outside of the city and that consultation with all the people concerned would frequently mean trips of considerable distance, it is obvious that with the high speed in action indicated above, thorough knowledge of all the aspects of each case problem is utterly impossible.

The ages of these babies who were all born out of wedlock are thus summarized:

Fourteen of the twenty babies accepted by the Bureau were only a week or less than a week old, eleven of these babies having been taken from their mothers within a day after birth. Three of them were two weeks or under and only three were older than two weeks.

[28] From a survey by the Child Welfare League of America.

On none of the twenty cases was the case study rated complete. In six cases, a partial study had been made. In the other fourteen, no study was made beyond the statement of the situation given by the person referring the case—information so meagre that it can be contained in one paragraph of about a dozen lines. In some cases, the Bureau's worker had not seen the mother of the child, accepting her information second-hand. Of the thirteen cases referred from January to June, 1925, in only six were informants other than the mother interviewed and in three of these cases the informants were relatives who just happened to be visiting the mother at the hospital at the time the worker called. Of the seven cases referred after December 1925, informants other than the mother of the child were seen in only three. When mothers or other informants were seen, however, the interview resulted usually only in a bare outline of the mother's history with little or no detail concerning her family by which heredity might be judged. Little insight was shown into the emotional problems of the mother or into her ability to resume life without too much suffering. In only two cases was any effort made to establish paternity. This not only leaves the paternal heredity of the child shrouded in doubt but it *leaves untried the metal of the men themselves, their willingness to share the cost of maternity, care and support of the baby, and the salutary opportunity of facing with the girl the practical consequences of their acts* [italics by the present writer].

State Number 1

In Chapter VI, above, the story of the Illinois Children's Home and Aid Society has been told. As the chapter closed some questions were asked about the wisdom of a well-nigh exclusive reliance for care of dependent children upon the two forms, namely, institutional and free foster family homes. It is therefore especially pertinent to introduce here a brief statement of the situation in Illinois when, only ten years ago, the too easy acceptance of children for permanent placement in free foster family homes still prevailed.

Anyone who was familiar with the standards of work of the

Illinois Society prior to 1912, and especially anyone who can at all visualize the work done before Dr. Hart's time, has a background against which he may perceive the full importance of such a statement of contemporary aims and methods as we have quoted from Mr. Reynolds.[29] On the face of it, one might think that a progressive State Children's Home Society, such as this of Illinois, had already approached a standard of care of dependent children that would guarantee to each child full and adequate understanding and treatment as an individual. Yet such is far from the actual state of the case. Mr. Reynolds himself has had the courage to challenge the quality of his own work. He recognized the truth that so many workers with children do not yet dare to face— namely, that we must study our failures as well as herald to the world the story of our successes, if we would be as sure as possible of adequate service to every dependent child. Mr. Reynolds, therefore, in 1921, asked Mr. C. C. Carstens, Director of the Child Welfare League of America, to make a study of the intake of his Society from three chosen Illinois counties, to determine primarily whether or not he had still been taking for permanent placement in free foster homes children who could have been suitably cared for by a surviving parent or relatives, and therefore should not have been separated from them.

The result of this study is startlingly significant, not only to the Illinois Society, but to all societies which are accepting children for permanent separation from any surviving relatives by the process of placement in free foster homes.

There are 102 counties in Illinois, in each of which, under the juvenile court law, the county judge (in Cook County a special juvenile court judge) has the power, after due legal process of notification of parents and guardians, to commit children permanently to an authorized society like the Illinois Children's Home and Aid Society. Efforts had been made by the writer and Mr. Reynolds, previous to this study by Mr. Carstens, to get the com-

[29] See p. 157.

SURVIVALS OF OUTWORN ATTITUDES

mitment papers issued by these various county courts to be legally valid; also to see that the social histories of the children thus committed should contain such social data as seemed, on the face of the record, clearly to justify the acceptance of the children for permanent care. The investigation conducted by Mr. Carstens was intended to show, therefore, as much as possible of the actual personal and family situations, in cases which the county courts or other local officials, such as County Boards of Supervisors, had supposedly investigated and officially decided that the children should receive permanent care away from their own relatives and localities. One hundred and fifty children in all were chosen to be studied—fifty children from each of three widely separated counties. These children were selected by taking the names, in regular order, of children brought to the attention of the Society by the local authorities from July 1, 1921, backward through the previous months and years. In one county this included the intake of children back to 1917, and in the other two counties, back to 1912. The social investigation of the family situations of these 150 children, as of the time they were brought to the attention of the Illinois Society, showed:

County unit number 1 (children from two counties).—The fifty children involved, thirty-two of whom the Society had accepted, were from twenty-five families. In twelve families, involving twenty-five children, family resources adequate either to care for the children entirely or in part were found to have been available at the time the decisions as to the disposition of the children were made. The Society had accepted sixteen of these children for permanent care, although eleven of them were from families who could have cared for them with some assistance and five others were from families who could have cared for them without assistance. Entire lack of investigation, or incompetent investigation, looms up as the most prominent defect. In a word, in only eighteen out of the fifty cases did the opinion of the local court and other officials, that the children be taken for permanent care in foster homes, seem to the surveyor to have been justified by the social and personal facts in the case, and only nine of these cases were based on adequate information.

Furthermore, among the families involved, there were thirty-four other children under juvenile court age, ten of whom needed care but were ignored in the court and other decisions rendered in the cases of the fifty children directly concerned.

In this county there had not been, until very near the time of the study by Mr. Carstens, a local worker qualified to make an adequate social investigation, or to give careful probationary supervision in homes of neglect, delinquency or destitution. Boarding homes were then unknown in this county. The Society had, therefore, been faced by three alternatives: first, to take no children at all, and thus leave many urgent cases to local neglect; second, to equip themselves to make their own complete social investigations in all the counties not locally equipped with capable case workers; or third, take the children who on the face of the record and on superficial investigation seemed to need their care. The last alternative was the one chosen.

County unit number 2 (children from two counties).—These fifty children were from twenty-one families. Defects in the Society's procedure were of the following nature:

1. Failure to place proper responsibility on parents and relatives, either by making them responsible for the child's entire care, under court probation or supervision, or by collecting financial support from relatives for the care of the child outside its own home. This defect involved thirty-two children.

2. Failure to consider the whole family situation, evidenced by assuming the care of some children and leaving others in the same families uncared for. At least eight children were so neglected.

3. Other defects were: failure to follow up the families involved; lack of institutional care for, or discipline of, adults; lack of diagnostic study of at least one child of doubtful mentality given for adoption.

In these counties, as in County Unit Number 1, there were, during the ten years or so covered by the investigation, no adequate local facilities for social investigation or probation. The criticism by the investigator is, that lack of these facilities was accepted as inevitable and that the Society merely tried more or less blindly to serve the children they were asked to take. Whatever service was given should have been accompanied by vigorous effort to educate these counties to the possibility of preserving, through case work service, the integrity of many families that for lack of such service were disrupted.

County Unit Number 3.—The summary of action taken in the cases of the fifty children of this county involving nineteen families was: unsuitable twenty-four, suitable twenty-six.

Taken as a whole these studies indicate the important truth that, in spite of the advance made by Mr. Reynolds, the influence of the Society in the less developed counties of the state in 1921 was still toward a too easy excuse of parents and relatives from their responsibility to care for their own children, toward an easy final separation of children from relatives by placing them in permanent free homes, and toward a toleration of easy-going local inadequacy of social ideals and methods in care of dependent and neglected children. Of the fifty children involved in this third county unit, sixteen had at some time been inmates of the county almshouse, or farm, as it is locally called.

State Number 2

In a state of a million people in the Mountain area, the situation in 1924 is summed up as follows:[30]

The present opportunities for the care of children not eligible for adoption is extremely limited in every locality studied. Widowed mothers are working out of their homes everywhere for want of sufficient money for food and shelter.

[30] From a survey by the Child Welfare League of America.

The provision during the illness of parents, for the temporary care of children, looking toward the re-establishment of the home is available in only a few instances. In one county only has there been any recognizable service and that not satisfactory to the social workers. No state can feel that it is giving its children a square deal until there is service available for all its dependent children.

State Number 3

In another state of over three million people in the Pacific area, a state-wide agency for the placement of children in foster homes was acting in 1925 upon inadequate information, thus described:[31]

It would appear that the proportion of non-acceptance of children to acceptance equals only about one-eighth. This would mean that the Society separated eight times as many children from their natural families as it enabled to stay with them. . . . "From the records the case work on application to place children appears to be largely limited to an interview with the parent in the office, resulting in the filling out of an application blank usually by the supervisor of placing. In certain cases a legal surrender is signed on the day when the application is filled out. No application is to be acted upon without a visit to the home by the field worker but these 'visits' usually result in a recapitulation of the history already given in the office. Again, judging from the records, nothing approaching a real case study is made." . . . Because of inadequate investigation the Society has incomplete and sometimes erroneous knowledge of the real situation and has developed no other practical help for these needy families except *the drastic action of permanent surrender of their own children which violates one of the deepest human instincts* [italics by the present writer].

State Number 4

In a state of three million people, in the South Atlantic area, a state-wide agency for procuring foster homes for children used methods, in 1923, of dealing with children of unmarried parents, which are thus described:[32]

---

[31] *Ibid.*   [32] From a survey by the Child Welfare League of America.

The records of the Society will run about as follows: Conference with mother or mother's representative. Application of the Wasserman reaction. Decision to take the child. In one case the Society accepted a child with a positive reaction of the Wasserman test. We find no records of any attempt to interest the fathers, no records of attempts to help the mothers to keep the child, or any efforts to place financial responsibility on the fathers. The evidence goes to show that the Society has made it easy for the young unmarried parents to cover up their wrongdoing and to shift their responsibilities to other shoulders.

It is a rather striking discovery that among these 50 cases there is only one in which an illegitimate child is not received by the Society. And in that particular case the Society had decided to accept the baby and then the mother stated that she had found a relative who was willing to take it.

In the same state, out of another group of 28 children of unmarried parents:

The records of the Society indicated that in only one instance was the father of an illegitimate child interviewed and in only one-half of the cases were the unmarried mothers interviewed.

And of 108 children placed out in foster homes by this Society, the survey reports comment:[33]

Among all the histories of these 108 different children, as far as the record goes, there is only one lone child who appears to have had the intimate and continued personal interest of a member of the staff. One cannot read these histories without getting the impression that these children have not been regarded as impressionable, eager, affectionate human beings whose loyalty is worth cultivating, but rather as the outcast products of society to be disposed of as soon as possible. It is rarely that one sees a friendly letter to a child or from a child—there are probably not a dozen in all these case folders.

Another right of the child—the right to have the care and protection of its kinfolk—has been almost totally disregarded. This is evident not only from the ease and speed with which children are separated from

[33]From a survey by the Child Welfare League of America.

their parents and natural guardians, but also in the regulations under which the Society places children. It is not the separation of brothers and sisters that comes in for criticism; it is the fact that they are so often not allowed to know or hear anything about each other or their parents. This is a condition which the public has already sensed. There is grave doubt whether children with living parents should be put out for permanent placement and a rule of silence imposed.

State Number 5

In another state of over one million of people, in the West North Central area, some of the methods of a state-wide foster home care agency were the basis in 1924 of these statements:

From the figures it is clear that not even one visit was made to each (every?) child in 1924 for whom the Society is responsible....

The Superintendent estimates that 70% of the field workers' time goes into raising money, which leaves something less than eight days per month for work with children.

As these workers had not only to raise money but to find foster homes, receive children, and supervise those who were placed out, the report concludes:[34]

The task is physically impossible. In 1924 the Society [with six workers] was responsible for 443 children placed in 91 different counties. An active worker in good health can supervise about 65 children if they are not scattered over too great an area and if she does not have to collect money, find homes and investigate new cases. To expect elderly men with [no?] training to do this while loaded with all these other duties is to insure the neglect of the children.

ILLUSTRATIONS OF RECENT PROCEDURE IN ADOPTIONS

Even in Massachusetts, the state in which Mr. Birtwell pioneered for "action suited to the real need," the state more praised than any other in the whole forty-eight for its more nearly adequate care

[34]*Ibid.*

of dependent and neglected children, a judge, in 1927, could still make a mistake like this:[35]

> At the age of three years, Edward's large blue eyes were wistful with longing for a mother. Deserted by two mothers, toted from house to house by a drunken man called father, cold, ragged, dirty, unwanted and unloved, Edward was rescued by the S. P. C. C. and committed by the court to the State Department of Public Welfare.
>
> Edward's own mother deserted when he was three weeks old. The police found her. The court put her on probation to care for her baby. She gave him away in adoption.
>
> Edward's adoptive mother played with him for eight months. Then she disappeared. His adoptive father was an illiterate, simple-minded wood-chopper who spent his wages for drink. He never had any money to buy Edward shoes or to pay his board. He said he had adopted the child to keep his flighty wife at home.
>
> The judge who signed the adoption papers had accepted the statement of the lawyer that the adoptive parents were a very reliable couple. The lawyer did not know them. They had lived in his town only a few weeks. They had paid him to get the adoption. It was not his duty to go out of his office to seek information detrimental to his clients. A chief of police in a neighboring town knew that the adoptive father had a long court record for drunkenness. A State detective knew that the adoptive mother had a Superior Court record for forging and uttering, and breaking and entering, and larceny. A social agency knew that the adoptive mother was promiscuously immoral before marriage and unfaithful after marriage. The police knew that this couple's married life had been punctured with numerous separations following stormy scenes. But there was no one to tell the judge these facts. Nobody appeared in court in Edward's behalf.

The foregoing story of unfit adoption is not an isolated case. Ample evidence of that is given in a recent study[36] of adoptions

---

[35]Massachusetts Society for the Prevention of Cruelty to Children, *Annual Report,* 1927, p. 40.

[36]Ida R. Parker, *Fit and Proper,* Church Home Society, 41 Mt. Vernon Street, Boston, 1927, pp. 30-36.

in Massachusetts, especially in the chapter entitled "Means Employed in Placing Children." As to one of these methods, namely advertising in newspapers, we may quote from a study of adoptions in New York made in 1922 by the State Charities Aid Association. This New York study summed up its findings in conclusions which were said by the writers of the above 1927 Massachusetts study to be as applicable in Massachusetts as in New York:

Adoptions in New York in 1922

1. It is clear that large numbers of unmarried mothers are surrendering their babies to strangers about whose morals, personality, financial standing and standards of living they know nothing.

2. Married couples are surrendering legitimate children without adequate reason in the same haphazard method.

3. Children of unknown history and family traits, and who are possibly feeble-minded, psychopathic or tainted with inherited disease, are being foisted upon ignorant but in many cases well meaning foster parents.

4. Indiscriminate giving away of children not only works great hardship upon individual children and individual foster parents, but also, has the effect of discrediting conscientious and intelligent home-finding done by competent child-placing agencies.[37]

It is evident that so far as legal adoption occurs in cases like these, a socially-minded judge with a social case-worker at hand to secure the facts before signing a decree for adoption, could be an invaluable influence in the direction of better processes of care for these dependent children.

Fit and Proper Homes for Adopted Children in Massachusetts in 1927

The following statement is evidence that the judge could not have acted intelligently, because often he could not have had

[37] Parker, *op. cit.*, p. 34.

SURVIVALS OF OUTWORN ATTITUDES

adequate information, in a great number of cases in Massachusetts where adoptions were secured without the assistance or knowledge of any social agencies.[38]

Decrees affecting 365 minors—approximately two-thirds of the children (544) comprising Group II (those adopted without assistance of any social agency) were signed on the day filed. 140 of these children were legitimate; 224 illegitimate.

Some of the adoptive parents were people of sound character and intelligence who recognized the seriousness of voluntarily through legal process becoming the parents of a child of other blood. They faced squarely the responsibility and risk involved as well as the possibility of disappointment, but were willing to assume all obligations for the sake of the happiness which they and the child might give each other. Others apparently did not reckon the cost of upbringing in terms of effort, patience, money or sacrifice and soon tired of the undertaking. Still others were totally unfit because of ignorance, lack of understanding of their duties, insufficient income, mental defect or instability, or vicious habits to be entrusted with a child's life. There were sixteen families with which high-grade social agencies had refused to place a child for adoption, each of which obtained one in some other way.[39]

One of the recommendations of this study is:

That every adoption petition filed should be investigated by a person competent to make the inquiry for the purpose of supplying the court with the social facts which bear upon the situation. . . .

The 952 cases which form the basis of Parts I and II taken together show that legal adoption is a complicated child-welfare problem of such importance that it "cannot be entrusted altogether to good will or to intuitive impulse or even to unaided common sense." The facts show that adoption may bring tragedy or great happiness to child and to adoptive family. Properly safeguarded, adoption may be a social asset as well as a social expedient. How much longer must helpless children of Massachusetts wait for their state to extend that measure of protection against unsuitable adoption which they sorely need?

[38]*Ibid.*   [39]Parker, *op. cit.,* p. 60.

Adoptions in Pennsylvania in 1925

A similar study[40] was made in Pennsylvania in 1925 for the State Department of Welfare. In this study it was found that, in addition to the usual method of adoption by court decree, of which there were, during 1922-1923, 1,160 in the thirteen counties studied, twenty-seven cases of adoption by deed had been recorded in these same counties. Of this form of adoption the writer says:

> A deed of adoption is a legal instrument by which the natural parent transfers all his rights to his child to the adopting parent who is given complete responsibility and control of it. It is similar to a deed of property, and is acknowledged before a Notary Public. This document is filed at the office of the Recorder of Deeds where it is copied into the deed books with records of mortgages, etc. A person may thus deed away his child with as little ceremony as he disposes of a bit of real estate. . . .[41]

Out of 1160 adoptions through courts, 380, or almost 33%, were granted the same day as the petition was presented; an additional 391 (another 33%) were granted within less than a week; that is, in at least two-thirds of the cases the time between the date of petition and date of decree was so short as to preclude any adequate investigation of the fitness of the adoption home.[42]

[40] Clara Josephine McDonnell, manuscript, *Adoption Practice in Allegheny and Twelve Other Counties of Pennsylvania*, Carnegie Institute of Technology, Pittsburgh.

[41] *Op. cit.*, p. 10.

[42] *Op. cit.*, p. 22. The student who would like to compare experiences of immigrant children in Canada with the glimpses we have thus far given of foster family home care of children in the United States is referred especially to three publications: (*a*) *Canada's Child Immigrants*, published by the Social Service Council of Canada, Ottawa, 1925; (*b*) Publication No. 15, "Juvenile Immigration Report No. 2," published in 1925 by the Canadian Council of Child Welfare; (*c*) Publication No. 39, *Several Years After*. In these publications the reader will find data regarding dependent children in Canada to compare with the data collected in 1866-1867 in Massachusetts by the first visiting agent of the State Board of Charities, and with data already presented in this chapter relating to children indentured previous to 1923 from the Wisconsin State Public School.

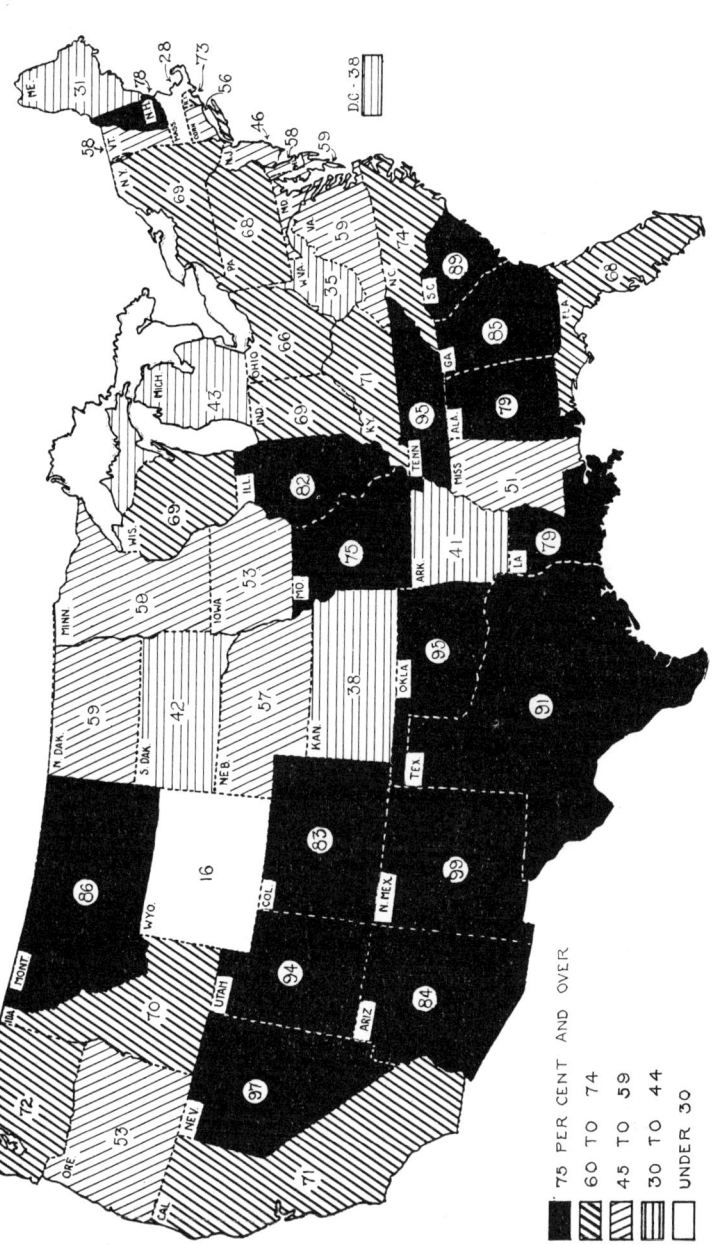

CHART I

PERCENTAGES WHICH DEPENDENT CHILDREN IN INSTITUTIONS CONSTITUTE OF ALL DEPENDENT CHILDREN CARED FOR OUTSIDE THEIR OWN HOMES. FEBRUARY 1, 1923

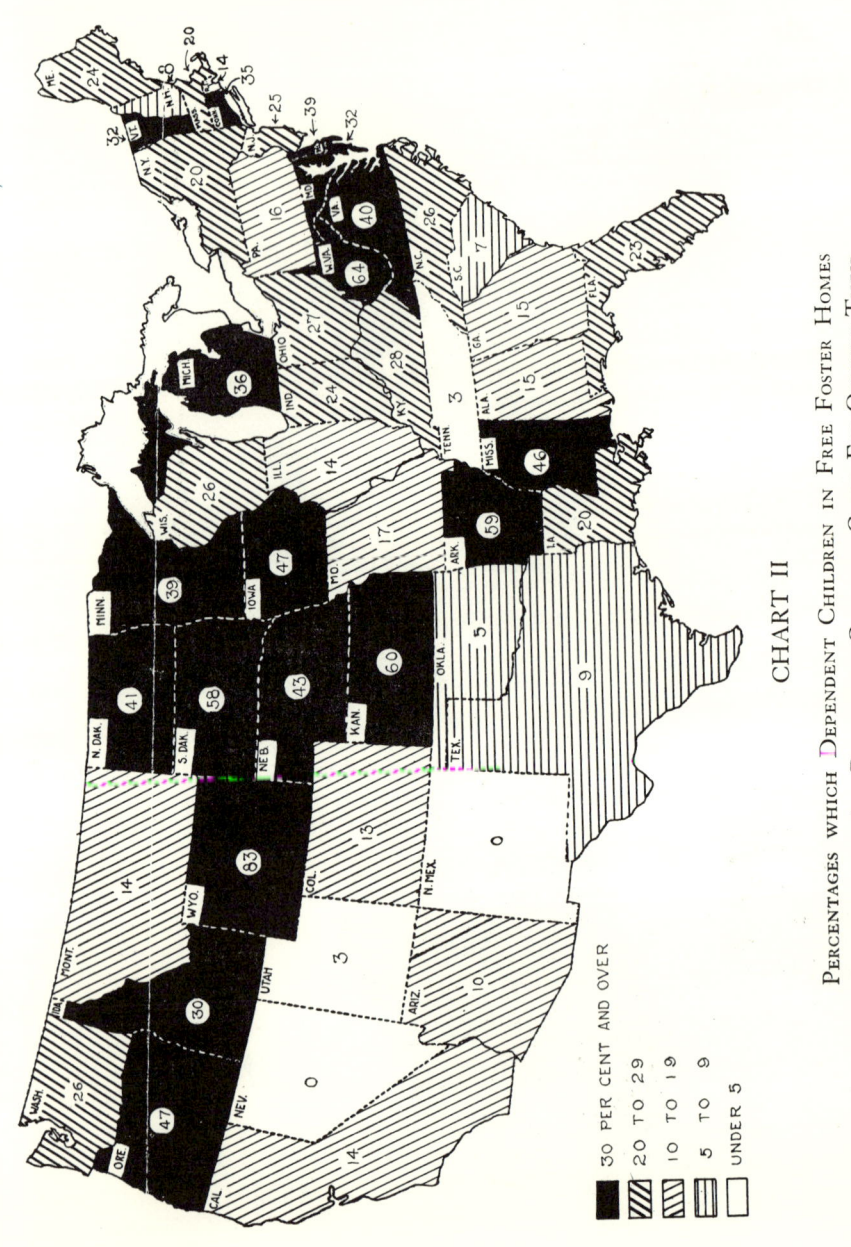

CHART II

PERCENTAGES WHICH DEPENDENT CHILDREN IN FREE FOSTER HOMES CONSTITUTE OF ALL DEPENDENT CHILDREN CARED FOR OUTSIDE THEIR

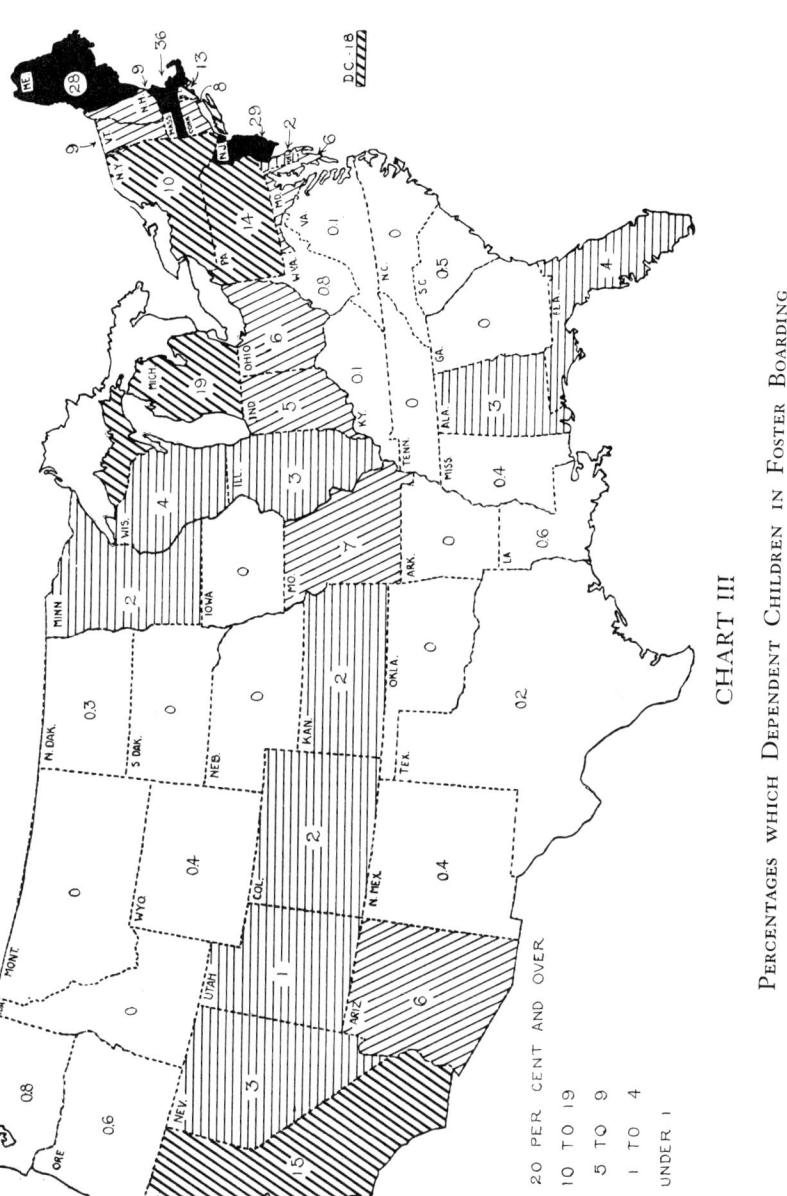

CHART III

PERCENTAGES WHICH DEPENDENT CHILDREN IN FOSTER BOARDING HOMES CONSTITUTE OF ALL DEPENDENT CHILDREN CARED FOR OUTSIDE THEIR OWN HOMES, FEBRUARY 1, 1923

SURVIVALS OF OUTWORN ATTITUDES 237

Charts of the Census Figures of 1923

The only attempt that has ever been made to show in figures for every state how many dependent and neglected children, away from home on a fixed day, were in institutions, how many were in free foster family homes, and how many were at board in foster family homes, was made for February 1, 1923.[43] The percentages of these figures for each state are shown on these charts so as to make an appeal to the eye. The queries are almost automatic in the mind of the observer: Why is the distribution thus in my state? What does this distribution mean to the dependent and neglected children of my state? What have I to do about it?

In bringing our illustrations to an end, it is hoped that the descriptive facts given will be challenging to the reader. They will have served their purpose to the degree that those who read are moved to ask: Are these things true in my state and community? They will serve the lives of children still better if readers begin to make first-hand inquiries,[44] in detail, into the processes of care in actual use by the nearest and most accessible institution, placing agency, almshouse, overseer and superintendent of the poor, city and state department of welfare, foundling asylum, maternity home, juvenile and adoption courts and any others.

Put Yourself in the Child's Place

After all, the final test of all our work for dependent children is its effect upon the children themselves. The illustrations and autobiographies with which this chapter closes may help the reader to look out on life through the dependent child's eyes.

---

[43]United States Census report, 1923, *Children under Institutional Care*, Table 2, pp. 18-19.

[44]For census data relative to any institution for dependent children or any child placing agency in which the reader may be interested, consult the census volume, *Children under Institutional Care*, 1923. For data on institutions, see Table 22, pp. 50-139; on child placing agencies, Table 26, pp. 170-187.

The following description of the process of sending a boy out from a County Home at a recent date in Ohio is fact, not fiction:[45]

"Come on, boys. Some folks here want to see you all in the parlor." This was the announcement that sent some twenty curious boys scurrying from their institution playroom to the front of the "House of Seven Gables" to be looked over individually by a man and his wife who had just driven up to the Children's Home to get a boy. The Superintendent had never seen these people before, but the man introduced himself as "Dr. ——" and that was enough.

"Here, no, look up, and don't hang your head, Sam, just when the Doctor might pick you out and take you home to be his boy." "Jim, your hands and face show the usual 'lick and promise.' How do you think you'll ever get a home looking like that? Pretty good looking boys, Doc, eh? John, there, leads the boys in school work and can beat them every time, even if he isn't their match on the playground. Bill, here, is a good worker but a bit sassy at times. They are all good boys, Doc, and just take your pick."

The boys shifted about, shrugged their shoulders, and some looked anxious and hopeful, others sullen and uncomfortable, especially those who had been out and had returned.

The "Doctor" and his wife could not agree. He intimated his preference for Bill, a strapping boy who looked good natured. His wife spoke up for John. They finally agreed on Bill, however, and stated they would like to get started home. Billy's face at first glowed with triumph over being first choice, but his steps and attitude when he was hurried into the "Doctor's" gig a half hour later indicated that some serious thoughts and questionings were beginning to work within. Then, too, he hadn't lived at the institution eight of his ten years without feeling that he was leaving his world for parts quite unknown. A child's fears half felt, inarticulate, had he tried to express them; an institution's system of child placing; a child turned over body and soul to the understanding or misunderstanding, the unselfishness or selfishness, the kindness or cruelty, of total strangers.

[45] Esther McClain, *Child Placing in Ohio*, Columbus, 1928, pp. 13-14.

SURVIVALS OF OUTWORN ATTITUDES

A Girl's Autobiography[46]

I was nine years old when I came under the guardianship of the Children's Agency. I am now fifteen. I have been in quite a few homes. I have had my good days and my bad days, my happy days and my sad days as everybody has. But no matter. What I am going to write about, is the difference between an orphan home and a private home. I have been in both and so I am going to give my views as I see them.

When I was eleven years old I entered an orphan asylum. I shall not state the name of it, but suffice to say that it is considered one of the best in the city. I was in there six weeks but the memory of those six weeks will always remain in my mind very vividly. If I were married and had any children I would never put them in an orphan home. So you see I am not overfond of one. I had my happiness as others probably did but the happiness in an orphan home is not to be compared with the happiness one has in a private home.

First I shall talk about the pleasure side of the orphan home. Every year the XYZ club would give a picnic. As it came during the six weeks I was there I went, and incidentally, had a nice time. We went to the Theatre once while I was there. I went to the Municipal Opera also. Every other Friday night we would dress in masquerade and have a jolly old time. We always held these parties in the gym.

The younger children had to go to bed at seven o'clock while we older children could remain up till nine o'clock. We used to sit on the front lawn. The lady who had charge of us would tell us stories which sometimes took three or four nights to finish.

In the back yard were seesaws, slides and rings on which we spent much time. Every other Sunday was visiting day. These days our parents could visit us and bring us anything they wished in the line of candy, fruit, etc. They had to give these to the matron who locked them up in a closet. Then after every meal time she would give us a portion until it was all gone. She would serve us while we were at table. I do not think this was right as there were some children who didn't have any folks to bring them anything.

---

[46] The Executive of this Agency in a large city in a North Central state gave this autobiography for publication.

Now, for the other side. We never could leave the grounds. We had to sit behind high iron fences and there gaze longingly out at the people walking or riding by. (I like to do that from a private home but not from an orphan home.) Many were the times I longed to be able to do the same thing.

Now to go on with the work. Every morning each child had to do some kind of work before going to school. Then about every month or so we would do another kind of job. The job I did most while I was there was washing dishes. There were practically a hundred people in the place. There were three children to help do the dishes. I always wiped the dishes and whenever I picked a dish up to wipe it, it almost sickened me. The back of the plates were never touched, consequently they were very greasy. We had to do this before going to school at dinner time so you see we had to hustle to get through.

When I look back upon it now the children there remind me of a bunch of cattle. They were shown how to do a thing and they did it. There was no display of affection. There was no explaining the why and wherefore of doing this or that. There were no talks exchanged of the incidents and happenings of the day. Many were the times that the children ran away. So you see they did not like it either.

We were underfed, also. When I entered the home I weighed seventy-one pounds; when I left, sixty pounds. I lost eleven pounds in six weeks. I could not keep anything valuable there as it was stolen. There is no other word for it. I had both a silver and gold eversharp. They were taken out of my locker. We did not have locks. If you had any games the children took them out and played with them whenever they wished. While I was in the home the thing I felt the worst was the lack of affection. I felt so lonely and forlorn.

After I left there I came under the guardianship of the Children's Agency again. After being in several homes I came to the home where I am now at. The lady in this home is the sweetest lady I have ever known. She is past middle age and is an invalid. She is also very small. Such suffering as has been hers! She cannot walk. Still she sees the bright side of life. I know when she passes from this earth she will surely be rewarded for the sweet patience and the wonderful courage which has been hers while here. She has a big understanding of the people in this world and their weakness. The memory of this dear little lady will always be a beautiful one in my memory.

In being in different private homes I have gained a knowledge of human characters such as I never would have had, had I been raised in my own home. On the other hand it has been hard to adjust myself to so many places. But as it has been impossible for me to have been raised in my own home, I prefer a private home.

"The Kids with Fathers and Mothers Have the Edge on Us"

A sixteen-year-old problem girl whom an organization was asked to remove from a "free" home said to the worker[47] in an outburst of resentment:

I guess no one would be what you call normal, if they'd lived as I have. My parents parted when I was a baby. First one relative took me, then another. My mother's people criticized my father and my father's relatives had no good to say about my mother. After I'd been shifted all around both families I went to the orphanage. Then I was put out in a home. Mrs. Alvord pretended I was to be one of the family, but my new "mother" met me with an apron in her hand and left no doubts in my mind as to what my relation was to be to the rest of the family. They took me to save a maid's wages, and then scolded because I couldn't do all the work. It was so lonesome sitting alone in that kitchen I just couldn't eat. They had a lovely house, but I couldn't make friends with the furniture, and I wouldn't bring my high school friends there to see that I was only a servant. Mrs. Holmes was so busy doing church work that lots of times she forgot to order food for me to eat when they all went to the church suppers. . . . Well, I got tired of it all, and I was sassy. When I knew they were going to be out late, I'd go out too, and stay late. Mrs. Alvord only came to visit me when she was invited to dinner, and of course I had too much sense to try to tell her my side. She just didn't want to hear it. So now I'm a bad girl. Nobody can do anything with me. But if you are going to put me in a home where I'm to be the servant, I'll be glad to go if I get wages. Then I'll save until I

[47] A social worker connected with an institution in 1928.

have enough to go back to school. Only it's not fair to expect me to make good at school and on a job, and get nothing for my work. I've been in thirteen homes that I can remember, and believe me, the kids with fathers and mothers have the edge on us!

Chapter IX

TRENDS IN ENGLAND SINCE 1834

There were no very distinctive differences in the practice of dealing with the dependent child in the United States from the system we inherited from England, until the peculiarly American developments associated with the names of Charles Loring Brace and Martin Van Buren Van Arsdale, previously discussed in Chapter VI. The influence of English social procedure up to that time and to some degree since, however, justifies at this point a brief review of developments in Great Britain. In the United States the importance of almshouse care was emphasized by the Yates Report of 1824, and most of the substitutes for care in the mixed almshouse, both in England and the United States, have grown up since that report was current. How, therefore, do these substitutes, as developed in England, compare with those of the United States? Of the situation in England in 1834, ten years after the Yates Report, we read:[1]

The Almshouse in England in 1834

In 1834, when the Poor Law Commissioners began the execution of their great task of reform, they seem to have found, in the existing four thousand parish work houses or poor houses, something like forty or fifty thousand children in residence, in numbers varying from a dozen or two in the majority of small parishes, up to several hundreds in such larger institutions as that of Liverpool and those of St. Martins-in-the-Fields and other considerable parishes in the metropolitan area. Such descriptions of the provision made for the children as appear in the re-

[1] Webb, Sidney and Beatrice, *English Local Government—English Poor Law History*, Part II, "The Last Hundred Years," 2 Vols., Longmans, Green & Co., 1929. p. 256.

ports of the Assistant Commissioner in 1833 reveal[2] not only a shocking neglect of proper nurture, but also an almost total lack of education. In the majority of parish poor houses there was no effective separation of the children from the adult inmates, and no teacher of any sort; in many the children of all ages and of either sex were nominally in charge of an aged pauper man or woman, very often feeble-minded and occasionally an actual lunatic.

From this description we can see that two urgent things to get under way were segregation of the children from adults, and efforts to educate them. The first attempts were in respect to segregation, but we are told that

for many years there was apparently improvement, if at all, only in classification, order or discipline, even for the larger workhouses, where there were scores, and in a few cases hundreds of children, trained leaders were, at that date, not to be had.[3]

The Workhouse School

In spite of these difficulties some of the larger parishes and, later, groups of parishes called "unions," established schools on the workhouse grounds that were called workhouse schools. These schools, it should be noted, did not remove the children from the workhouse atmosphere, and from a certain amount of contact with adult paupers. We are told[4] that

during nearly the whole of the second half of the century the conflict of opinion for and against the workhouse school, as the most appropriate provision for pauper children, was maintained among the Assistant Commissioners and Inspectors, and the few Guardians and outsiders who interested themselves in the subject.

It was not until 1911 that Poor Law Commissioners were peremptorily told by Act of Parliament to take all children over three

---

[2] Cf. description in Royal Commission Report for 1832, quoted in Chapter IV.
[3] *Ibid.*, p. 257.   [4] *Ibid.*, p. 265.

years of age out of the mixed almshouses.[5] Meanwhile, prior to 1834, private enterprise and a desire for financial gain had pointed out a way to something better in both residence and schooling for the dependent children. These undertakings, called Farm Schools, were later adopted as models by joint action of some of the most enterprising smaller unions, and by some of the larger unions acting individually. Of the origin of these Farm Schools, we read:

The Farm School and District School

For the convenience of parishes having no "Infant Establishments" of their own, there had grown up various commodious establishments in which enterprising contractors relieved parishes of the care and trouble of maintaining the child paupers in return for a payment of a few shillings per head per week.

And again:[6]

These Farm Schools, in which the stimulus of profit-making was at the period far from being objected to, seemed at least superior to the workhouse schools in that they were, at any rate, separate institutions for children.

While in some of these Farm Schools high rates of sickness and mortality prevailed, in one, administered by Aubin in Norwood, the sanitary conditions and schooling became so good that in 1837 it was definitely recommended by the national Poor Law Commissioner as a model. Influenced by this recommendation, Parliament, in 1844, gave power to Guardians of different unions to cooperate in founding and maintaining residential schools for their children. These were called district schools, and were in reality what in the United States have been called orphan asylums. Altogether, about a dozen such district schools were established, only three of them by rural unions.[7]

[5] *Ibid.*, p. 259. [6] *Ibid.*, p. 260.
[7] *Ibid.*, pp. 264-65.

Meanwhile, in the larger parishes and in the unions of the principal cities . . . where each Board of Guardians found on its hands as many as one to five hundred children of school age, it became increasingly frequent to establish for them, as Birmingham, St. James's, Westminster, and a few other parishes had done before 1834, an administratively and sometimes geographically distinct residential school; and in this way to secure for the children of each particular Poor Law area that complete separation from the General Mixed Workhouse for which the Poor Law Board was persistently pressing. Notwithstanding the serious capital cost of these separate Poor Law Schools, there were gradually established, in the course of the second half of the nineteenth century, about sixty such institutions—some three dozen of them being the more expensive "Cottage Homes" type—accommodating in the aggregate some 12,000 children, leaving in more than five-sixths of the unions the children still in the General Mixed Workhouse.

Scattered Homes

In addition to, and in contrast with, these institutions for dependent children in "Cottage Homes," frequently referred to in English reports as "Grouped Cottages," or "Grouped Cottage Homes," there are, since 1893, what are called "Scattered Homes." This plan of care was originated by the Board of Guardians of the Sheffield Union. Of these Scattered Homes it is said:[8]

There were in 1896 nine homes (two with fifteen beds, one with sixteen beds, three with seventeen beds, two with twenty-one beds, and one with twenty-eight beds). The home with twenty-eight beds is for boys alone, and in the others the children are mixed. Seven homes are assigned to Protestant children and two to Roman Catholics. The homes are ordinary dwelling houses rented by the Guardians, but indistinguishable from other dwellings of respectable artisans. They are scattered about in different healthy suburbs of Sheffield. . . . Each house is presided over by a foster mother who washes, irons, cooks, cleans, and mends for the children, with the help of the elder children, and a char-

---

[8] *Ibid.*, pp. 288-89, quoted from *Report* of Departmental Committee, p. 123, and *Second Annual Report* of the Homes.

woman one day per week. The cooking is done with ordinary utensils, and by an ordinary fire, and its preparation affords the children some knowledge of cooking, as well as instruction in methods of economy, cleanliness and domestic management. The same may be said with regard to house-cleaning and the mending and washing of clothes. In the day rooms are pigeon holes or lockers for the children's possessions and playthings, and in the bedrooms there is a box for each child containing its clothes. Every effort is made to cultivate the children's individuality and the personal attention given to them renders it possible for their natural characteristics to be studied and guided aright.

As a supplement to the experience which each separate group of children could get within their cottage home, each cottage was selected for its nearness to a "board school" which was public, and which the children of school age attended. The Sheffield Guardians said their plan could not succeed without access to a public elementary school:[9]

It is our rule not to send over thirty children to one school. This number is comparatively lost in the large number of other children; owing to the two sexes and different standards, there are rarely over two of our children in any one class.[10]

So far as permitted by the residents of each community in which a scattered home was located, the dependent children could also enjoy the religious, recreational, and other social facilities each neighborhood afforded. Two other unions followed the Sheffield plan in 1897.[11]

In the course of the next decade a number of other unions, in rural as well as urban areas, adopted the same expedient for some, at any rate, of the children for whom the Guardians felt themselves responsible. The Sheffield idea increasingly commended itself, in fact, to the more enlightened of the local administrators.

It should be noted in passing that, although supervised from the

---

[9]*Ibid.*, p. 288. [10]*Loc. cit.*
[11]Webb, Sidney and Beatrice, *op. cit.*, p. 289.

central office of each union, the success or failure of each of these scattered homes depends, in the nature of the case, primarily upon the housemother.

Certified Homes and Schools[12]

In addition to the care of children in the public institutions already described, namely, workhouse schools, separate schools, and district schools—whether of the congregate or "grouped cottage" type or the "scattered homes" type—all of which are administered directly by the Poor Law Guardians of the unions—large numbers of dependent children have been paid for at public expense in private institutions and agencies called "Certified Homes." In 1915 there were 291 of these and in 1920, 266. These figures include a large variety of establishments ranging from small training homes for perhaps twenty or thirty children to large institutions housing several hundred. Many of these Certified Homes are for children with special handicaps—the blind, deaf, crippled, feebleminded, etc. Some of them are of a particular religious faith so that dependent children can be sent to institutions of the faith of their parents.

Training Ships also are certified to receive dependent children from the unions.

Boarding-Out

There has been also a development in England of foster family home care, but with emphasis solely upon boarding-out. Free foster home care of young children, except for adoption of infants, is practically negligible in England. Although the practice is known to have been followed in occasional instances ever since 1597-1598, it "received no notice in the 1834 Report [of the Royal Commission]," and

neither the Commissioners (established 1834) nor, for its first twenty

[12]*Ibid.*, pp. 267-71.

years, the Poor Law Board (which succeeded the Commissioners as the national agency for supervision in 1848), gave any approval or sanction to placing out orphans in the homes of foster parents.

Not until the sixth decade of the century, when the general interest in public education had greatly increased, does the question of boarding out the orphan children seem to have been expressly raised in England and Wales.

However it was found in 1869 that twenty-one different unions had made a beginning on their own initiative and already had 347 children boarded out. Accordingly an inspector was sent to Scotland, where the system was general and, following his "somewhat grudging and qualified admission of its success,"[13] the Poor Law Board, in 1869, decided that it "In view of the Scottish experience, would no longer, where Boards of Guardians pressed for it actually discourage a trial of the system."[14] In 1870, a general order was issued allowing boarding-out, not only within the union area, but beyond it.[15] After 1889 boarding-out may be said to have been permanently adopted as part of the English Poor Law system.[16]

All this agitation for boarding out, as also for scattered homes and grouped cottages, was stimulated during the last three or more decades of the nineteenth century, not only by a growing recognition of the pauperizing and debasing influence of the mixed almshouse upon dependent children, but also by a violent reaction against the institutionalizing evils of the large congregate, separate and district schools which some unions had established.[17] These schools, the largest of which housed from one thousand to two thousand children, were condemned as "Barrack Schools."

Persistence of Workhouse Care of Infants

In England, as in the United States, there has been a persistence of the method of caring for infants and children under three in the general mixed workhouse.

[13]*Ibid.*, p. 272.   [14]*Ibid.*, p. 273.   [15]*Ibid.*, p. 274.
[16]*Ibid.*, p. 275.   [17]*Ibid.*, p. 283-86, and references there given.

The members of the Royal Commission had been shocked in 1906-08 at the condition in which they found the nurseries in the Workhouses where the Boards of Guardians were attempting to rear the four or five thousand infants under three years of age, who had either accompanied their parents into the institution, or had been brought as orphans or foundlings. . . .[18]

Whilst the persistent efforts of the Inspectors (and especially the scrutiny of the women Assistant Inspectors), which were resumed after the Armistice, have, we believe, resulted in a continuous and almost universal improvement in the conditions of the Workhouse nurseries, we cannot learn of any successful attempts, apart from those made in Nottingham, Birmingham, and a very few other unions, to remove the children under three years of age—even if without mothers—from the General Mixed Workhouse. There are now, 1928, still some 3870 children under three, not being sick, in the Workhouse Nurseries.[19]

Indenture

Ever since the time of Elizabeth, and even during this last hundred years, the final way out into the community for those dependent children who did not return to their own parents, has been by some form of apprenticeship or indenture. Before the beginning of child labor legislation[20] these unlucky parish apprentices were often sent off in wagonloads to the mills, mines and factories, where they were without any inspector and doomed to unlimited hours of toil, until in the humanity of the year 1802, an Act was passed restricting their hours of work to twelve.

As child labor legislation has improved, and especially since the development of the various substitutes for the mixed almshouse, which have herein been mentioned, these and many other abuses of apprenticeship have been discontinued. The usual age of apprenticeship of children by Poor Law Guardians has now become sixteen. Especially since 1911, the unions have been urged by the national authority

---

[18] *Ibid.*, pp. 753-54.   [19] *Ibid.*, p. 755.
[20] Robinson, M. F., *The Poor Law Enigma*, London, 1911, p. 86.

that endeavors should be made to start them not in "blind alley" occupations, such as that of errand boy, but in skilled employments; and that training for domestic service should be provided for the girls.[21]

Ins and Outs

On the intake side, the problem of infectious disease has been found a serious one in the various institutions and agencies of the English Poor Law Unions, because of the great number of children who have always come in and gone out with their parents who were in temporary financial distress. These children are called in England by the vividly descriptive name of "Ins and Outs."[22]

Children of this class give great trouble to the Guardians everywhere. They are sometimes discharged and readmitted several times in the year; they often bring back disease, dirt, and bad habits, and though permanently belonging to the pauper class, are unable to receive regular instruction and discipline in either the District or Separate School.

For these "Ins and Outs," as well as for a quarantine period for children who come for a longer stay, some three dozen of the larger unions have established an "Intermediate School"; other unions [23] have to use the workhouse itself for this probation or quarantine purpose.

Allocation of Children under Public Care in 1923

In 1923 the children, *not including the sick and specially handicapped in body or mind,* who were cared for in institutions and family homes at the expense of the various unions of England and Wales were as follows:[24]

---

[21]Webb, Sidney and Beatrice, *op. cit.,* p. 731.

[22]*Ibid.,* p. 278. Quoted from *Report* of Departmental Committee on Metropolitan Poor Law Schools, 1896, p. 8.   [23]*Ibid.,* p. 280.

[24]Persons in Receipt of Poor Relief (England and Wales) 1923, *Report of Ministry of Health,* 1923, pp. 22, and 25.

Separate Schools:
  Grouped Cottage Homes   6,559
  Other schools including (one) Training Ship   5,757
  Grouped Cottage Homes other than Schools   4,540
  Scattered Homes   9,184
Other Homes
  Large   5,784
  Small—accommodating 15 or less   335
  Training Ship and other training and industrial homes   7,500
  Children boarded out within the union   8,405
  Children boarded out beyond the union   1,715

  Total   49,779

Institutions under Private Auspices

In addition to the children cared for directly by the public in their various institutions and boarding homes; and in addition to other children sent at public expense to certified institutions under private management, there are in England, as in the United States, a multiplicity of private institutions and agencies that care for children by direct arrangement with parents, parent, or guardian. There were some such institutions even before the days of Queen Elizabeth, and as in the United States, the sufferings of destitute children in the community at large and, since the founding of the mixed almshouse, the woes of children therein, have stimulated humane persons, especially during the nineteenth century, to found other private institutions.

Barnardo Homes

The famous Barnardo Homes, started in 1866-1867, are good examples of this type. They were begun for reasons similar to those which moved Charles Loring Brace in New York City, and were carried on in much the same spirit. Up to 1918 these Homes reported 26,281 who had been sent overseas as emigrants.[25] On the same date they reported 7,131 children in their institutions in England and 3,421 boarded out.

THE FOUNDLING HOSPITAL

The Foundling Hospital of Bloomsbury, London, founded in 1746 by Thomas Coram, who had spent most of his life in America, is another example. Upon his return to England, it was the sight of new-born infants lying in the streets exposed and starving that moved him to found the Hospital, which task took him seventeen years. A basket was hung outside the door into which a mother could deposit her baby after dark, ring the bell and depart. Although moved in 1926 to a new site, the following account of a personal visit by an American student to the Hospital on its original site in 1921, may here be quoted:[26]

The Foundling Hospital is one of the famous "sights" of London, and hundreds of visitors come on Sundays to hear its famous organ, which Handel used to play, to see the Hogarths and Raphael cartoons, and to gaze at the little foundlings in their quaint uniform. But besides being a "place of interest," the Foundling Hospital is also the home of some four hundred boys and girls between the ages of five and fifteen, who have been separated from their unmarried mothers at infancy, have been boarded out in country homes during their babyhood and then at the age of five are brought to the institution for the ten long years of their childhood, and it is from this point of view, as a home for children, that we must consider it. Built in the first half of the eighteenth century by a certain Thomas Coram, a retired sea-captain, it stands in what were originally the open fields of Bloomsbury.

Though it is now in the very heart of London it has retained spacious grounds with room for lawns and playing fields, but the buildings themselves are still of the old-fashioned congregate type. The boys' and

---

[25] For recent evidence as to the experiences of some of these children in Canada, see references cited on p. 236, Chapter VIII.

[26] From a manuscript in possession of the present writer, written by Miss Margaret Timpson, Bryn Mawr Fellow for Study in England, 1920-1921.

girls' sides are absolutely separate, having even separate dining halls. All the rooms are large, bare, immaculately neat and depressingly dreary and comfortless. The children live by bell and schedule and do everything in large groups. They sleep in long dormitories of thirty or more beds, they eat at long tables, they play in huge halls. They have their own schools on the institution grounds and attend their own chapel in a body. The uniform[27] of the Foundling Hospital is distinctive; in the days of the good Captain Coram dark brown stuff dresses with white kerchiefs, voluminous aprons and stiff upstanding caps may have been the proper dress for little girls, and scarlet vests, brass buttoned jackets and flowing ties the ordinary costume for small boys, but in the twentieth century, not only does the uniform have the usual effect of wiping out the individuality, but it succeeds in making the children look ridiculous (or pathetic, according to one's point of view) and ruthlessly marks them out as belonging to "the Foundling." Following the traditional policy, the girls are at fifteen placed out as domestic servants. Their mistresses send an annual report as to their characters to the home, and on a certain day in each year these reports are read out and those fortunate ones who have achieved "good characters" are allowed to return for a day's holiday at the institution. As from the Poor Law schools, many of the boys enter the Army or the Navy. A special feature of the after-care is the Benevolent Fund which is devoted to the assistance of the children after they are placed out in the world, and at the age of twenty-one they also receive "rewards" in money if their "characters" have been uniformly good.

Infant Adoption

To complete the list of varieties of care of dependent children away from their own homes, mention must be made of infant adoption. Two private societies have recently been organized for the special purpose of promoting and arranging for the adoption of infants. These are the National Children Adoption Association and the National Adoption Society, both caring almost entirely for illegitimate children. The former was organized during

---

[27] The uniform is still (1930) worn by the children, in the new institution.

the War for the purpose of caring for Belgian babies. It was soon discovered that there was a large and practically untouched need for the same sort of care for British babies, and accordingly the work was rapidly extended.

The other agency for the adoption of infants, the National Adoption Society, was started in Cambridge by private effort before the War. Its original work was very limited in scope, but in 1917 it became registered under the Friendly Societies Act of 1896 and in January 1919 began work with London headquarters and a paid office staff. Thereafter its chief object was to provide homes for children bereaved in the War or those who were "legally fatherless."

Summary

This sketch has made no attempt to discuss the relative merits of public and private care of dependent children in Great Britain. No reference has been made to the broad field of industrial and reformatory schools; to the enforcement of the Children's Act of 1908; to relief in the form of medical treatment; to the feeding of school children; or to the work of care committees.

In summarizing what has been said in both chapters treating of Great Britain, it is reasonably clear that an adequate statement of the sequence of facts would show these trends:

(1) A converging of factors in England before 1601 led inevitably toward a recognition in legal form,[28] of the obligation to support the destitute poor, including children, out of taxes.

(2) In the slow working out of this principle, the local overseers of the poor and justices of the peace who were charged with the collection and expenditure of taxes for the care of dependent children, developed four main methods: apprenticeship; the mixed workhouse; outdoor relief for the child with his parents; and later, various certified institutions and agencies, supported and controlled in the main by private persons, but subject to public

[28] See 43 Eliz. Cap. 2.

inspection and entitled to public assistance when acting as agents of the public.

(3) The dominant idea of the public authorities for at least two hundred years after 1601 was to get as much as possible of the public expense of maintenance out of the work of the children themselves. This idea led to an excessive use of apprenticeship of individual children at first, and later, after the introduction of the factory system in the latter half of the eighteenth century, to the wholesale apprenticeship of groups of children from workhouses to manufacturers.

(4) The pauperizing condition of masses of children in mixed almshouses increased with the growth of factory legislation for the protection of children in industry, and with the legal restrictions that came also to be placed upon unsuitable apprenticeship to individuals. This situation forced the problem of segregation and education of the workhouse children upon public attention.

(5) The ensuing segregation of children in workhouse schools, in huge district schools, and in the separate schools of urban unions, forced attention further upon the problem of life and education for children in huge congregate institutions.

(6) A shifting of emphasis from the dominating idea of a zero or minimum immediate investment in a dependent child to the idea of sufficient investment in his care and education to take him out of the pauper class and to make of him later an efficient worker, resulted in the development of grouped homes, scattered homes, and boarding out.

(7) The development of the idea of an efficient citizen led to specialization of industrial training, especially of the boys, in the big district and separate schools.

(8) Once started, the idea of differentiated treatment and education, for efficiency, has resulted in the use of emigration for selected boys and girls, and in the use of a great variety of certified institutions and agencies for the deaf, blind, feeble-minded, crippled, and mentally defective, dependent children.

(9) The idea of differentiation of children is still, in the main, confined to variations of treatment within the dependent group, and thus tends to limit the child's future career to that of domestic service for girls, and to manual labor—often in the Army or the Navy—for boys.

(10) Because of the magnitude of the problem, and because inadequate income does not permit individualized education and training in many independent working-class homes, all these trends toward a recognition of individuality in dependent children too often stop short of a conscious purpose and procedure to discover and utilize to the utmost the potential capacity of each dependent child as an individual.

(11) In boarding-out, especially "without the union," great use is made of the volunteer and unpaid services of local citizens.

(12) Beginning with individual local freedom of boards of guardians in interpretation and administration of law, there has been a slow development of guidance and integration under national authority which still leaves the union boards of guardians responsible for the expense and details of administration.

Chapter X

TRANSITIONS TOWARD BETTER ATTITUDES AND METHODS

I. Retrospect and Questions

What is the present after all but a growth out of the past?

In the preceding chapters of this book we have traced the slow stages of growth in the methods of care accorded the dependent child. We have glanced at the period when the care of children was determined largely by their status in a manorial community under the feudal system. As this period passed and children whose parents were dead or unable to care for them were shaken loose from local and customary sources of support, it was a step ahead for the waif and stray child to be indentured, or bound out, to some person whose duty it was to give him at least a minimum of food and a roof under which he belonged. Similarly to such waifs and strays the almshouse was an open door to food, clothing and a bed, no matter how poor each might be, and no matter what and how many bedfellows he might have. Accordingly, until well toward the close of the nineteenth century, we have seen in England and in our states generally, dependent and neglected children gathered into the mixed almshouse. In the United States we have seen institutions for children only, usually called orphan asylums, founded by sympathetic, humane, and religious people, to take children out of the mixed almshouse, and to prevent other children from ever going into the almshouse. We have seen children indentured on their way out, after a period of life within almshouses and orphan asylums. We have seen poor law and other public officials, and even poor parents, indenture children direct, that is, without first sending them to almshouse or orphan asylum. We have seen Charles Loring Brace and the New York Children's Aid Society reject almshouses, orphan asylums, and the form of indenture, as methods of care for dependent and neglected children, and attempt to find for hundreds of emigration parties, foster family homes in which the need for a child to work should be softened by a genuine feeling of Christian charity. We have seen Martin Van Buren Van Arsdale found, in Illinois, the first of the more than thirty State Children's Home Societies to place dependent and neglected children, one by one, in free foster family homes where they could stay, as presumably real members of the family, and often by legal adoption, until they should grow up.

For each of these forms of care—almshouse, indenture, orphan asylum, and foster free home—we have found avowed championship, or tacit acceptance, as a well-nigh universal system of care for most dependent and neglected children. We have also seen the gradual emergence, particularly in Massachusetts, of a supplementary, and rival, system of care, called boarding-out in foster family homes.

And finally, in striking contrast with a belief in any one or all of these forms of care as rigid systems for all the children of any state or community, we have heard Charles W. Birtwell of the Boston Children's Aid Society give eloquent expression to a new and inclusive ideal of suiting the action to the real needs of the individual child.

Each one of these stages was a forward step in the process of development; but as we look back now, in the light of this ideal, upon the experiences of dependent and neglected children, we can see, as could not have been seen so clearly at the time, the peculiar weaknesses in each method of care, and the hardships and injustices each system brought to many children. For example, some faint outline of this ideal, seen "as through a glass darkly" in the first half of the nineteenth century, brought to the people of the latter half of the century a growing conviction of the ghastly injustice of the mixed almshouse for any child. In the light of the same ideal we can now see what a Procrustean bed of torture each of the other forms of care—indenture, orphan asylum, foster home care, both free and boarding—may be when it is not suited to the needs of the particular child concerned.

How then, in the light of the past, out of which a better present in the care of dependent and neglected children has grown, can we help a still better future to grow?

Two things, which *some of our leaders have already begun to do,* are still needed practically everywhere in the United States.

First, in each state and community there are needed extension and improvement of our intake processes. Such changes should be designed to show us as clearly as it is humanly possible what kind of care each child, as an individual, and as a member of a particular family group, needs—not only on the day he becomes dependent, but as year by year he himself grows older, and as his relation to his kin may change.

Second, we need to make available in the community not only such a variety of resources for care as will best meet every variety of child need, but also such a balanced and flexible supply of each variety of care as will meet the need of every child as soon as the need is discovered. At present in most communities and states there should be great humility in face of the fact that the best we can do is to make a partial adjustment only. Whether or not this or that kind of care is known to be really needed by child after child after child, the only thing that can in fact be done with him now is to send him here or send him there to such institution or agency as exists.

How have we already begun to do these two things? Not in most localities rapidly. Not in any two localities, perhaps, in exactly the same way. A description of the procedure of some persons, institutions and agencies that have already entered, or are just now entering, upon the new way will be the best answer.

II. Some Evidences of an Attitude of Self-Criticism among Leaders in the Care of Dependent Children

Self-Criticism as a Basis for Better Administrative Standards in The Boston Children's Aid Society

When Charles W. Birtwell left the above Society in 1911, he was succeeded by J. Prentice Murphy. In the *Annual Report* for the next year Mr. Murphy formulated standards of child-placing work for the use of his own staff. While these standards were in some respects colored by the facts of the Massachusetts situation, in the main they are still worth careful study, and are still far from general realization in practice.[1]

Free homes—that is, families taking homeless children, are not easy[2] to find. Public authorities board their wards, and this makes many people inclined to ask for support from other applying agencies. Good boarding homes and good wage homes, however, can be found. Through payments we are able to secure many high-grade people as caretakers who cannot afford otherwise to give their services to this work. About 66% of all the children we receive go into boarding homes.

It is not the practice of the Society to agree to very many adoptions of its children. It cannot guarantee physical and mental soundness for some of them, and for others it is anxious to exercise supervision until majority is reached and in some cases long afterwards. In view of the vast importance of this branch of child-helping, and also in view of some recent tendencies, it is well for us to reaffirm our position.

A society is really doing placing-out work when it places its children for days, weeks, months or years deliberately, and after careful inquiry, in good normal family homes, where the individual, physical, mental, moral, religious, social, and industrial development of each child is a matter for careful and constant supervision and oversight—oversight at once sympathetic and elastic in its understanding.

It is not placing-out work, in the standard meaning of that term, to

---
[1] Children's Aid Society, *Annual Report*, Boston, 1912, pp. 15-16.
[2] This is not true for young children in many other states.

make a small institution of a private family by placing three, four, or more unrelated children under the same roof. It is not placing-out work to place a child in a home free of cost, when its real needs can only be met by an expenditure of money such as the receiving family is unable to make unaided.

It is not placing-out work to coerce a child into an economic state which it hates, as, for example, farm work for a boy with a mechanical bent, or ordinary housework for a girl with tastes for other things.

It is not placing-out work to take a child when it reaches fourteen or fifteen years of age from a boarding home where it has been doing well, and where it has become an integral part of the family, and to place it in a free home for no other reason than to save money for the caring society.

It is not placing-out work to permit the transfer of children from place to place, so that they have no real home life. Families must be selected and used with discrimination.

It is not placing-out work to crowd a visitor with more children than she can know intimately or plan for unhurriedly.

It is not placing-out work to fail to keep in touch with the children in care. Faith here is no substitute for knowledge.

It is not placing-out work to fail to keep in touch with changing conditions in receiving families. They need training and supervision as well as children.

It is not placing-out work to be ignorant of the exact physical and mental condition of each child in care, and to neglect to have such information carefully recorded for frequent use.

It is not placing-out work to fail to see that there are certain disciplinary tasks which are not for family homes to solve. In other words, even the thing we urge and advocate has its limitations.

The Boston Society Begins to Look at Itself in the Mirror of Research

In 1913 Mr. Murphy began a research study of the actual results of the work of the Boston Children's Aid Society, in terms of the lives of the children who were, or who had been, under its care.

Mr. Murphy and Miss Ruth Lawton, research worker, thus describe their purposes at the beginning of their efforts to evaluate the results of the work of their own Society:[3]

> This paper . . . was written partly to present some findings of our study which we have been conducting for the last year and a half, and partly as a protest against the tendency of social agencies to understate the great fallibility of their work. If social work is ever to develop into a profession, searching analysis and criticism of methods and results, no matter what the consequences may be, become prime essentials.
>
> As the study went on, the records of the Society were found inadequate for any trustworthy evaluation of what the Society had accomplished up to that time.
>
> So we decided on three things: (1) a statistical schedule to be used in interpreting records from October 1913, on; (2) the completion of at least a certain number of our history records, so as to build up a certain amount of information adequate for future research work; and (3) the making of an intensive study of the children over twelve years of age in care on October 1, 1913.

In the paper from which the foregoing quotations have been made, the reader will find, even in this Boston Society of which Mr. Birtwell had been the head, further illustrations of the survivals of outworn and inadequate methods which were cited in the preceding chapter. However, our purpose in referring to them here is not to repeat them but to give sharper point to the plea that one of the greatest things that still needs to be done by great numbers of institutions and agencies caring for children, is to begin the same honest and courageous procedure of self-study and criticism that Mr. Murphy began seventeen years ago.

Mr. Birtwell's ideal of suiting the action to the real needs of each child is, in practice, a counsel of perfection. But we shall never even approximate such an ideal until we try, and try hard.

---

[3] "A Study of Results of Child Placing," National Conference of Charities and Corrections, *Report* for 1915, pp. 164-74.

Mr. Birtwell tried hard. Mr. Murphy began to ask, "How far have we succeeded?" And now Mr. A. F. Whitman and his staff are carrying on, reinforced by the insight, in questions of mental hygiene, of Drs. Healy and Bronner of the Judge Baker Foundation. From this combination have come the understanding and sympathetic services to dependent, neglected and delinquent children which are described in the remarkable book, *Reconstructing Behavior in Youth.*

Self-Criticism within a Protestant Religious Denomination

One of the difficulties in the way of making changes in method, or even in reducing the number of children a given institution or agency is to accept, is often a certain loyalty to a given religious denomination. We must keep up the size or scale of a particular institution or agency and in just the way it always has been kept up, lest our sect suffer in prestige. A convincing answer to this argument, both for Protestants and Catholics, is the one below:

A certain institution had been found doing poor work for the children accepted; furthermore it was accepting children from distant states, thereby unnecessarily separating them from their kin. One of the leaders in the church under whose auspices the institution in question was conducted said:[4]

No care for the dependent child is sufficiently good so long as better is available.

In all work for dependent and neglected children the child is, or should be, the end; all else is or should be means only. . . .

Genuine loyalty to a Christian denomination is identical with loyalty to Christ, and whenever a child welfare institution is created or sustained for its own sake or for any denominational glory, it becomes disloyal to Christ. In other words, what is frequently thought of as church loyalty in work with children is frequently nothing more than misdirected sentiment.

[4] Dr. George C. Enders, of the Christian Divinity School, Defiance, Ohio, in a Child Welfare Conference in New York City, April 21-22, 1927. Quoted in *Christianity and Social Adventuring,* New York, 1927, p. 144.

Self-Criticism as Outlined by a Catholic Leader

There is also an encouraging note in the spirit of self-criticism implicit in the words of a great Catholic leader in child welfare work. Dr. John M. Cooper, director of a committee of the National Conference of Catholic Charities on Study of Catholic Child-Caring Homes, included these directions among others which he gave to the members of his survey staff who were to visit nearly a hundred Catholic institutions in all parts of the United States:[5]

We are interested more in "hows" than in "whats.". . .

Find out what by experience has not worked well although it promised well in the beginning and particularly find out why it did not work or would not work well. . . .

On any given good feature get as precise and minute details as possible. . . .

Be insistently and consistently on the lookout for the intangible things such as spirit and attitudes in staff and children, and so forth, and particularly endeavor to find out how such desirable intangible things have come about. . . .

Do not look for evidence to prove theories you already hold, but instead look for what actually works well, get the evidence that it works, and find out why and how. . . .

Wherever possible, get concrete factual evidence, statistical or otherwise, that proves impartially and objectively the success or failure of any particular device, policy, or program. . . .

Perhaps the greatest single thing upon which we need detailed information *is individual treatment as contrasted with mass treatment throughout all phases of the institutional program* [italics by the present writer].

Studies in this spirit may yield their fruit slowly, but a quest of what actually proves good to the child will lead earnest seekers on and on until, throughout the country, all Catholic institutions

[5]*Report of the Fourteenth National Conference of Catholic Charities,* Catholic University of America, Washington, 1928, pp. 240-46.

and agencies will approach nearer and nearer to suiting the action to the real needs of the individual child. All success to Dr. Cooper's quest! May the little child in very truth lead him and all his fellow workers on!

Readiness of a Jewish Leader to Follow Wherever the Welfare of Children Leads

An unusual readiness to follow wherever the welfare of dependent and neglected children may lead, is found in an outstanding man of the Jewish faith who has just passed his eightieth birthday. His words must be quoted from memory, but there is no mistaking their import when one knows the quality of his acts both before and since his public utterance. The speaker in question is Adolph Lewisohn of New York, president of the Hebrew Sheltering Guardian Society, which has a remarkably complete institution on the cottage plan, built about twenty years ago at Pleasantville, New York. The Society has also been developing, especially during the last fifteen years, a Home Bureau for the placement and supervision of Jewish children at board in foster family homes. In an honest attempt to suit the action to the real needs of each child who has been accepted for care away from its own home, the number of children in the institution has decreased and the number of children in foster family homes has increased. With this situation in mind, Mr. Lewisohn recently said, in substance:[6]

We have a cottage institution for dependent children at Pleasantville that cost us a million dollars. But *if it be proved that children can all be better cared for in some other way I am willing to see it scrapped tomorrow for their good.*

A Protestant Denominational Program Based upon Self-Critical Study

Still another encouraging illustration of this new attitude of intelligent and courageous self-criticism is found in the Social

[6] At a Child Welfare Conference called by the Child Welfare Committee of America in New York City, May 15-20, 1925.

Service Commission of the Reformed Church in the United States. From recent reports[7] these facts have been summarized:

The Executive Secretary of the Commission, Rev. James M. Mullan, assisted by H. W. Hopkirk of the Child Welfare League of America, made a detailed study in 1928 of the five institutions for dependent children maintained under the auspices of the denomination. The "Summary of Needs" in the report of this survey is given in full for its valuable suggestions to those persons who in other religious communions are responsible for the welfare of dependent and neglected children in their institutions.

1. A new statement of child welfare policies should be drawn up as a substitute for the limited policies suggested in the charters of the orphans' homes. New policies should reject outworn practices such as the use of surrender or indenture forms, entire reliance upon institutional care and limitation of the work by the use of the term "orphans" or "half orphans." Positively stated, the policies should allow somehow or other for the care of children according to their special needs. Children of all ages, including the feeble-minded, convalescent, crippled and sensory defectives, as well as those who are dependent and neglected, should be considered. This does not mean that the Church should provide care for all kinds of children, but that it should stand ready to see that a child with any special need receives the care which he requires if facilities therefor exist or can be created. This implies a close cooperation with other private institutions and with public institutions for children exhibiting mental, physical and conduct problems. The policies should provide for the use of homes of relatives and foster homes, as well as institutions.

2. Because of the distressing lack of interdenominational planning in the care of children, the Reformed Church should plan to exercise some initiative in stimulating cooperative action on the part of all Protestant communions engaged in this kind of work. This exploration of the possibilities of interdenominational planning should aim at a

---

[7]Preliminary report before a Conference on Child Welfare in New York City, called by the Child Welfare League of America, in June, 1928, and printed report cited below, footnote [8].

minimum of duplication of work for dependent and neglected children and a maximum of specialization wherever special services to children are not yet organized. It should extend to a cooperation of the Protestant Churches in the support of adequate child welfare legislation wherever it is needed.

3. Executives now employed by Reformed Church institutions should secure technical training in social service. If this is not practicable in any case, eventually an executive should be secured who has had training in social service, even if this requires the use of a layman rather than a clergyman for the position.

4. Various improvements in the care given children in Reformed Church institutions should be provided. The improvements needed in some institutions are not needed in others. A separate list of these needs will be submitted by the survey staff to the management of each institution, if requested. These will include subjects such as the following:

Employment of substitute cottage mothers.
Increases in salaries and improvements of working conditions for cottage mothers.
Centralization of sewing and mending.
Regular medical and dental examinations.
Additional medical service for the prevention of disease and correction of defects.
Better equipment and supervision for recreation.
Improvement of diet.
Regular fire drills.
Use of the public schools.

5. Any future developments or replacement of institutional facilities should allow for small cottages. Cottages never should have capacities for more than 20 children. The most desirable, and in the end the most economical, unit is a cottage for 10 or 12 children, with its separate kitchen and dining room. No additional capacity should be provided by any of the existing institutions until there have been case-by-case studies of the children and families now served. These studies, to be effective, must be made by skilled workers who know how to help in the rehabilitation of family homes and who know how to use other social agencies to the greatest advantage.

6. At this time no institutions for children should be built by the Reformed Church. This survey indicates that there has been almost no attempt on the part of existing institutions to use family homes. If in the future foster family homes, homes of relatives, and mothers' allowances are provided by the Church, then these institutions need be used only for those clearly requiring institutional care. By using these different methods, the Reformed Church can provide suitably for at least three times as many children as it now serves.

7. Uniform financial accounting should be developed by all Reformed Church children's institutions. Until this is done, the administration of some of the institutions will be hampered by unbusinesslike and insufficient budgeting.

8. More and better social service should be provided in connection with admissions and discharges to Reformed Church institutions. Above all else, this will require the employment of social workers whose professional training and experience have prepared them for this kind of work. Adequate social service will include efforts at rehabilitation of the families of children while the children are receiving care in institutions or foster homes. Various plans may be followed in the employment of social workers.

(a) Each institution may secure its own case worker.

(b) Two or more institutions may cooperatively employ one case worker. This may be arranged by cooperation of Reformed Church institutions or of institutions within a limited region representing various Protestant Churches.

(c) A bureau operating as a part of the Social Service Commission of the Reformed Church, with headquarters in Philadelphia, could be set up, (1) to provide social service for those children and families for whom the Church, through its institutions, has already accepted responsibilities, and (2) to serve and advise pastors of local churches in helping individuals or families in need of social service. The field staff of this bureau should be professionally qualified to do intensive social case work. In addition to an intimate acquaintance with the various institutions operated by the Reformed Church, each worker should develop a working knowledge of the social service agencies of the territory to which she would be assigned. This would allow a maximum use of the social service resources of each locality in preventing family breakdown and in caring for those who must be separated from their families. This kind of service would avoid removing many children from the states in which they have legal residence and allow the most economical use of Church institutions by referring to them only those for whom suitable plans could not be made locally. In developing an interchange of service with other institutions and agencies in all parts of the country, the Child Welfare League of America can be used to good advantage. (The Child Welfare Division of the American Legion has made extensive use of the local institutions and agencies which are members of the Child Welfare League of America.) Service developed by a social service bureau of the Reformed Church could secure splendid results in getting at cases of distress before they are beyond the point where preventive work may be done.

In organizing such a central service, it should be clearly understood that this would not necessitate any change in present synodical or classical control of the institutions or the surrender of the right of the institutions to decide finally upon all admissions and discharges of children. After investigating applications for admission to these institutions, the staff of the social service bureau should submit only the information secured and only when requested should accompany this information with recommendations for the individuals concerned.

A central social service bureau could provide suitable cooperation with the organizations of the various states which administer mothers' aid and with child placing agencies, family welfare societies, juvenile courts and other organizations.

9. A conference of official representatives of all Reformed Church institutions for children should be held in the near future to consider the findings of this survey.[8]

It should be noted that the foregoing "Summary of Needs" has been given here to describe a desirable attitude toward a problem— to give expression to a statement of *next steps* in a concrete situa-

[8]*Study of the Work for Dependent Children (Orphans' Homes) under the Auspices of the Reformed Church in the United States*, pp. 23-26. Published by the Social Service Commission of the Reformed Church, February, 1929, Philadelphia, Pa.

tion, not to record actual changes for the better care of children in the institutions concerned. These changes will at best come slowly. Whether they come at all will depend upon the degree to which superintendents, staff members, board members and the supporters of individual institutions respond to the same dynamic ideal of suiting the action to the real needs of the individual child which has led to this survey, and to the publication of this "Summary of Needs."

In this connection, we may hope that responsible persons in general will take the attitude toward self-criticism and the need for charting a new course that the following quotation assumes:[9]

> The Cincinnati Orphan Asylum is one of a considerable number of institutions throughout the country that within a ten year period have faced the problems of reorganization due to changing social conditions in their respective communities. Thus the Orphan Asylum is not peculiar in that on the eve of its hundredth birthday it is taking stock of itself and attempting to chart a new course for the future. It is merely doing what most institutions with a hundred years of child care to their credit find necessary, if they are to meet present day needs.

III. Some Evidence of Progressive Transitions within Institutions

Whenever executives and board members of any institution have attained an attitude of genuine self-criticism, they have found increasingly available, during the last twenty years, a wide variety of new philosophies and techniques to help them in making this attitude effective. Among these philosophies should be mentioned that of the new education associated with the name of Dr. John Dewey, whose phrase, "education is not a preparation for life, education is life," has been literally "heard around the world." An earlier and partial expression of the same philosophy—"we must get the whole boy to school"—is that of Colonel Francis W.

---

[9] Child Welfare League, *Report of a Study of the Cincinnati Orphan Asylum*, 1929, pp. 56-57.

Parker, pioneer educator in Quincy, Massachusetts, and Cook County Normal School, Illinois. This educational philosophy is helping to revolutionize not only the experiences of children in the day schools, public and private, but also the lives of dependent boys and girls in institutions.

Likewise in the first White House Conference on Dependent Children, called by Theodore Roosevelt in 1909, there was a pronouncement that even dull ears could hear as to the value of the experiences of family home life to the child: "Except in unusual circumstances the home should not be broken up for reasons of poverty."[10]

The second White House Conference, called in 1919 by the Secretary of Labor at the request of President Wilson, reaffirmed the conclusions of the 1909 Conference[11] and added many other resolutions, including some which emphasized the rights of the child to education, recreation, vocational preparation for life, and physical, moral and religious development. This second conference also urged more adequate support of "Mothers' Assistance" work,[12] and the necessity of using all the new techniques of social case work,[13] and mental hygiene clinics,[14] as well as the scientific study of all the methods in use by child care institutions and agencies, including the results of such methods.

In what follows, describing the progressively transitional efforts of different institutions and agencies to apply new philosophies, and to use new techniques, there is no intention to urge the reader to become a literal imitator of any one. Mistakes have been made,

[10] Proceedings of the Conference on the Care of Dependent Children, 1909, p. 10.
[11] United States Children's Bureau, *Pub. No. 62*.
[12] This work was started in Missouri and Illinois in 1909. For *Extent* and *Fundamental Principles* in 1928, see United States Children's Bureau, *Pub. No. 162*.
[13] Richmond, Mary E., *Social Diagnosis*, 1917, and *What Is Social Case Work?* 1922.
[14] Dr. William Healy started the first Mental Hygiene Clinic for juvenile court children in the Chicago juvenile court in 1909. For clinics now, see *Directory of Psychiatric Clinics for Children in the United States*, Second Edition, Commonwealth Fund, Division of Publications, New York, 1928.

but progress has also been achieved. How in the future to minimize mistakes and to accelerate progress, is among the reader's problems. In particular, he is urged to give critical attention and study to the conditions that are essential if mental hygiene philosophy and mental hygiene clinics are to make their best contributions to the understanding of the behavior of the individual child. Such attention and study are especially necessary on the part of all those who may contemplate the use of existing institutions for children as centers for social case work and mental hygiene clinics.

A brief description of the transitional experiences of eight institutions will now be given.

The New England Home for Little Wanderers

The New England Home for Little Wanderers was incorporated in Boston in 1865. Among the purposes mentioned in its charter were to "take any destitute child without regard to race, color or parentage, feed, clothe and care for its bodily wants and cultivate it in mind and heart." As developed during the rest of the nineteenth century and the first decade of the twentieth century, it became largely an agency for the permanent placement of children in free foster family homes in the New England States. The Home also maintained a small institution for the temporary care of children on the way from their own broken family homes to permanent free foster family homes, and also for the temporary care of children who were taken in while their parents were sick or destitute.

In 1907 a new superintendent came, Rev. Frederic Howard Knight. Within the first five years of his direction of the Home, three thought-provoking things, to which reference has already been made, were happening in the country, namely: first, the White House Conference on the Care of Dependent Children was called by President Roosevelt in 1909; second, Dr. William Healy was beginning his remarkable mental hygiene studies of problem children in connection with the Chicago Juvenile Court, and Dr. Henry H. Goddard of Vineland, New Jersey, was introducing the Binet-Simon system of mental tests in the United States; third, the Widows' Pension or Mothers' Allowance Movement for providing public funds to keep children at home with their own mothers, especially widows, was gathering headway in Missouri, Illinois, and other states.

Dr. Knight caught the new idealism that was in the air and recognized the latent possibilities for bettering both the foster home work of his agency and the temporary institutional care which the Home afforded to dependent children. He saw that for children prior to placement and for many of his children who were already under supervision in foster family homes in all the New England states, he needed competent medical, psychological and psychiatric advice. His plan was to provide all this in his small institution in Boston, which most child-placing agencies operating over a whole state call a Receiving Home. Here children could live for a period varying from a few days to six months in order that he might try to discover what their physical, mental and emotional needs really were.

By 1922, the plan as Dr. Knight himself conceived it was substantially as follows:[15]

1. To receive from all parts of New England for foster home placement children whose homes are disintegrated because of poverty, unemployment, immorality, disease, desertion; children who because of lack of adaptation to their home environment have fallen into delinquency; children of unmarried mothers whom we try to place together where both can be guided.

2. To receive for diagnosis and temporary treatment in the Study Home difficult behavior problems. These come from any part of the country on application of charitable organizations, juvenile probation officers or parents and friends. Some children come from well-to-do families.

[15]Summarized by Dorothy C. Cobb, from *Little Wanderers' Advocate,* Boston, June, 1922, pp. 3-6.

3. To receive for after-care delicate but curable children whom the hospitals are unable to keep for a long period of convalescence after operation. Many of these are infantile paralysis cases.

PROCEDURE IN THE STUDY HOME

First comes the medical examination. During this period which usually lasts about three days the child is kept in temporary isolation. The child is examined, vaccinated, cultures taken and specific tests given.

Second come the school and recreational facilities. In school the "observation teacher by means of specially assigned tasks is able to gauge the ability of the child to do both mental and hand work, and to instruct him in the academic subjects required by the public schools for his grade in order that he may not fall farther behind his class than need be during the period of his stay in the Home. By maintaining a school of our own we avoid the danger of contagion which is so serious a problem to institutions whose children attend public schools."

Each child old enough to assume such responsibility is given some small task which must be performed before he enjoys the playground.

Children are instructed in the fundamental religious and ethical principles that underly all creeds, in the daily chapel service. When possible special arrangements are made to allow them to attend Sunday services of their own denomination.

WORK OF THE DEPARTMENT OF CHILD STUDY

Each child is given a detailed mental examination by the staff psychologist to determine his intellectual rating, adaptability, natural aptitudes and deficiencies. This is supplemented by an examination by the psychiatrist. Most of these examinations are so informal in character that the child does not realize he is being studied.

When the Home feels that they understand the child, which process takes from a week to six months, his case comes up for discussion in the weekly conference of the Behavior Clinic. "At this conference his whole past history is reviewed, reports of all examiners and observers are presented, and then in a round-table discussion the plan for his future is discussed." After this discussion, if the child is fitted for a free home he is placed in one. "Temporary boarding homes are found for children whose parents are unable to care for them on account of sickness or other misfortune, and in such cases parents are asked to cooperate to the extent of their ability in paying for the support of their children." Supervision is maintained until the child has attained legal majority or until legally adopted, or until parents receive him again. The parents are helped in readjusting the child in his own home as long as necessary or as long as parents wish it.

To the reader of the foregoing, its courage and idealism are evident. The intent is plainly to suit the action of the real needs of each child.

The services of the Temporary Home in Boston, with its expert medical, psychological, psychiatric and educational staff, have not been confined to the children for which this agency is permanently responsible; they have been available to others in all parts of New England.

Light on Next Steps from Case Work and Mental Hygiene

And yet, only to the degree that at least the inherent limitations and conditions of success are recognized and provided for, could the Little Wanderers Boston Clinic possibly do for children all that Dr. Knight hoped it might do. These limitations and essential conditions for success were at first seen only in part by Dr. Knight. They have become more clearly recognized as the work has developed. It is important that others elsewhere who undertake to work out something similar to Dr. Knight's project should, from the first, see all that has now been made clear by experiment.

There is a difficulty inherent in any clinical study of the needs of a child on the sole basis of his behavior while he is in the new and strange environment of the Receiving Home or institution. Unless we have also the record of what is called a social investigation made by a competent social case-worker, the child as a "total personality in a total situation" cannot be understood.[16]

When a child is committed to the Industrial School in reality his

---

[16] From a private report on another institution by the Child Welfare League of America.

whole family comes with him. The kind of parents he has, the type of home they maintain, what the weaknesses in the home are, what the parents' attitude to each other is, what place the boy or girl occupied in the family circle and dozens of other closely related facts must be known. Without such family background and without definite information as to a child's school record, his attitude towards school and the various other factors which go to make up his previous environment, it is not possible to make an intelligent plan of institutional treatment for him or to determine what should be done when he is ready to leave. Should the objective be to return him to his own family? If so, what needs to be done to help the family get ready to assume its responsibility for the child at the end of a year and a half or two years? If the family is utterly unfit, how is the child to be safeguarded and protected until it is clear that his training has taught him to be a responsible member of the community? These questions can only be fully answered when the institution has a department whose job it is to seek the answers.

Without a competent case-worker, then, to help get *the whole boy and girl to the clinic,* the best possible medical and mental hygiene clinics have serious limitations. There is equal need for the work of an efficient case-worker when the child leaves the institution, should he go to any other home than his own.

Suppose that a perfect understanding of a child's needs has been reached and he is recommended for a particular type of foster family home or institution, who is to select such a home and institution? These foster homes and institutions cannot be brought to the clinic for evaluation, except through the agency of the case-worker. And yet the child's future welfare depends just as truly upon the correct diagnosis of the persons in the family home or institution to which the child is to go, as upon an understanding of the child's needs. This responsibility is primarily laid upon the social case-worker who visits the family home in person.[17] Without a competent case-worker, the whole child cannot

---

[17] See "Evaluation of Homes for Child Placement," by Charlotte Towle, Supervisor, Home-Finding Department, Children's Aid Society of Pennsylvania in 1927 *Report, National Conference of Social Work,* pp. 429-30. Also reprinted as a *Bulletin* of the National Committee for Mental Hygiene, New York, 1928.

be got to the clinic. Without a competent case-worker, the right foster family home cannot often be selected for the whole child who has been studied and understood in the clinic. Without a competent case-worker, the relations between the child and his foster family home, between the child and his own home and surviving kin, and between the foster home and the own home and kin, frequently go dangerously awry.

We do not cite these limitations and essentials of a successful clinic to imply that Dr. Knight and his successor have ignored them.[18] But, as we have said, they were not so convincingly evident to Dr. Knight at first as they have become later. Any child-caring agency or institution seeking now to follow in the steps of the New England Home for Little Wanderers should, from the beginning, be as sure of the competency of its case-workers as of its doctors, psychologists and psychiatrists.

Self-Study and Transitions in Coit House

Two other illustrations of the establishment of study centers as next steps in care will now be given. Both of these projects are by institutions. The first, by Coit House, Concord, New Hampshire, is hardly out of its first year of development.

Coit House was incorporated in 1874 as the Orphans' Home in Concord. It was founded in 1866 by Rev. Henry A. Coit, rector of St. Paul's School, "whose attention was drawn to the needs of certain children left destitute by the Civil War. With the earnest coöperation of Mrs. Coit its work began, very modestly, in a cottage not far from the school, in the year 1866." Under the act of incorporation, its purposes included "maintaining, educating or otherwise aiding children who have lost one or both parents, or are otherwise destitute." In 1923, the charter name was changed to Coit House.[19]

---

[18]For illustration of the present technique of case work, mental hygiene clinic and home, see "Case Record of Edward," *Little Wanderers' Advocate*, September, 1929, 161 S. Huntington Avenue, Boston, Mass.

[19]*Annual Report*, 1926, Coit House, Concord, N. H., pp. 2-3.

One of the trustees in a letter, February 13, 1928, to Cheney C. Jones of the New England Home for Little Wanderers, Boston, set on foot a movement for enlarging its function, power being given in the words of the charter, "or otherwise aiding destitute children." In the words of the letter: "We want to be a study home, capable of doing a good job in all but the very exceptional cases. We are ashamed to have to send children to you at the Little Wanderers, or to the Judge Baker Foundation, because we are not equipped to diagnose and deal with them properly here. And we believe there is need of a proper diagnostic clinic in New Hampshire."

After study by Mr. Jones, in coöperation with the Child Welfare League of America, these recommendations were made.[20] Note the first, under (a).

1. In view of the present situation in New Hampshire as well as in Coit House itself, we would not recommend that it be developed into a full-fledged diagnostic study home but that the next steps in that direction be taken by providing:

(a) *more adequate social service,* linked up more definitely with the location and life of the institution.

(b) the appointment of a pediatrician, part of whose time could be under the command of the institution in return for a modest salary.

(c) an accessible psychologist should be appointed for part time service.

(d) psychiatric service should be sought from the New England Home for Little Wanderers, if it can be made available there.

(2) that a better record system and better statistics be developed.

Transition from an Institution to a Children's Community Center

Another institution which has already gone a long way on a new stage of its journey of usefulness to dependent and neglected children, is the New Haven Orphan Asylum. This institution,

---

[20] *A Brief Study of the Plans and Work of Coit House,* Concord, N. H., 1928, pp. 7-8.

with its name significantly changed to *The Children's Community Center,* issued its ninety-sixth report in 1928. The Center has a group of small buildings adapted to all the various needs of children whose average stay is less than six months.

The 300 children under care December 31, 1928, were thus distributed:[21]

In institution (Community Center)	103
Adoption homes	6
Free homes	44
Boarding homes	126
Work homes	9
Schools and institutions	12
	300

It should be noted that there is here no rigid allocation of all the children to any one method or system of care. To the real needs of each individual child, so far as sympathetic and intelligent study can find these out, the action can be suited.

The Center serves not only the city of New Haven, but the surrounding towns and counties:[22]

Applications for the care of children in 1928 came from relatives, county organizations and selectmen of towns and a variety of services were rendered. The Children's Community Center is rapidly becoming the private agency to which county child caring problems are referred, and the services which this organization can render are limited only by the funds available.

Results of Self-Criticism in Harrisburg, Pennsylvania

During 1924 the Harrisburg Associated Aid Societies made a population analysis involving 105 children in two private Children's Homes. It was found that 37 could be returned to relatives at once; 5 could be returned to relatives at a future date; 36 could be placed in foster

---
[21] *Annual Report,* 1928, Children's Community Center, New Haven.
[22] *Annual Report,* p. 17.

TRANSITIONS 281

homes; and 6 could be better cared for in other specialized institutions. The remaining 21 were to be provided for in a new institution to be constructed as the result of a merger of the two Homes whose populations were studied. The new building will have accommodations for only 50 children as the population analysis clearly indicated that institutional facilities for 105 were not needed.[23]

Transitions in a North Carolina Institution

From another institution, the Thomasville Baptist Orphanage, Thomasville, North Carolina, comes a message of the beginnings of a more elastic process of dealing with applications for care of dependent children in the institution. The superintendent, M. L. Kesler, in the thirty-eighth annual report, not only tells us something of the new service to children but of how he was led to see that there ought to be a change in his procedure. Mr. Kesler says:[24]

The members of this Board will recall that for several years I have insisted that we should address ourselves to a wider task of child welfare.

For these years I have kept in close touch with child welfare agencies, attended various conferences, visited many other institutions, and have had good opportunity to make close-up observations for myself. In the past much well meaning philanthropy has been turned into blind alleys of failure, or has fallen far short of the success deserved, because of poorly matured methods of doing the work. Orphanage workers have not been entirely exempt from these blunders.

A large percentage of the applications we receive are from children who have strong, capable mothers, but altogether helpless in making a support for their children. As you know, it has become a firm conviction of mine that these children should not be separated from this type of mother, but that she should be aided in rearing them in their own home. You agreed with me, and for more than two years we have been slowly and carefully inaugurating this work. We are now visiting . . .

[23]From a Child Welfare League summary.
[24]*Thirty-eighth Annual Report*, May, 1923, pp. 6-7.

227 children and 49 mothers. You authorized an increase of ten thousand dollars, making fifteen thousand to be spent annually for this cause. I was also authorized to employ a field worker to supervise this work and other needed work in investigating cases. . . . So far the results have been all that we could have hoped. We have been able to adjust a number of urgent applications without putting them on the aided list. This has left a better feeling behind and enabled us to devote the funds we had to the most needy cases.

A few have been taken off the list because of changed conditions in the family for the better.

The work has been well received.

By 1927, Mr. Kesler reports that the number of mothers helped by the institution to keep their children at home was 99, and the children involved 448. He further says: "We have in the past been advising this mother to send her children to the orphanage. This seemed to be the only thing to do. But we have had the growing conviction that this was wrong. This mother should not be relieved of her responsibility, but be helped in bearing it."[25]

Transitions in Rhode Island

The Rhode Island Children's Friend Society affords another illustration of changes in method resulting from the honest effort to suit the action to the real need of the day. The Society looked back in 1928[26] upon an honorable career of ninety-two years, in the early days of which it had been the pioneer worker for better conditions for children. It saw the gradual development of other organizations, and it continued to do well its part in giving good care to the children in the institution which it maintained. There was nothing spectacular in its experiences to lead the trustees to desire a reform program, "but slowly the conviction was being driven home that there was more to be done in taking one's part in a child welfare program in a city or state than the giving of

[25] *Bulletin,* "Mother's Aid," Thomasville Baptist Orphanage, 1927.
[26] *Annual Report,* Rhode Island Children's Friend Society, 1928.

even the best of care to a few children." A study was made of the situation, as a result of which "it was decided unanimously . . . February 2, 1926 . . . to close and sell the institution, and to develop the placing-out method of caring for children on a basis of careful case work in connection with each application."

Medical service was provided; also mental and psychiatric service.

Of the relations between Board members and the trained workers of the staff, we find a statement that is commended to the careful reading of Board members of other agencies and institutions for its suggestions as to the attitude to be taken in deciding upon a division of labor between volunteer Board members and trained staff members.[27]

Seldom, if ever, has there been a finer spirit shown on the part of officers and Board, or greater willingness to leave the details of the case work which they had previously controlled to the staff, while holding themselves in readiness to cooperate, assist and help in every way possible. To their credit let it be recorded that of their own free will the Board voted unanimously to refrain from visiting the children in their foster homes or from seeking to know the family history of the new children as they came into care.

The Staff, on its side, grew to appreciate increasingly the wisdom and sound advice of the various committees of the Board in all matters brought before them, while being constantly aware of the steady support and willingness of the Board to adopt new methods and make changes as the need was clearly shown.

There is no trace here of the stiff employer attitude of members of the Board toward members of their staff which limits the latter to the rôle of mere employees.

The report goes on to state: "One of the first duties was the amending of the charter which authorized the binding out and indenturing of children, a method of care long ago found wanting and abandoned"—a statement too optimistic to be backed up by

[27] *Op. cit.* See Coöperative Undertaking.

facts in some quarters even yet, as the recent experiences of indentured children in Wisconsin and Canada indicate.

The immediate results of this experiment are thus stated:[28]

By engaging trained case-workers and developing foster home care the society has been able to help a greater number of children than in the days of its limited institutional capacity; it has helped solve many perplexing problems in other ways than by separating the child from his parents, and in its Department of Foster Home Care has had the satisfaction of seeing children for whom no other provision than placement was possible, being built up physically, receiving moral and religious training by foster parents of their own faith, attending public schools regularly, entering into all the normal, wholesome activities of good homes in good communities. Not the least enlightening part of an interesting venture has been the spontaneous, entirely unsolicited comments of the older children themselves and their outspoken joy at the greater feeling of ease in their foster homes, with their greater opportunities for individual effort and accomplishment. While they still inquire with affection for those they knew in the Home they nevertheless have a frank satisfaction in their having their own bedroom, for instance, in their share in the foster parents' plans and interests, *in the privilege of entertaining their own parents at an occasional meal or holiday picnic. The parents themselves, without exception, have responded well to the foster home care of their children and have themselves many times received help and inspiration in the acquiring of new friends in the foster parents of their children* [italics by the present writer].

Of the care taken in selecting foster homes from the 581 applied, we are told that there were:

Approved	68
Disapproved	222
Declined	34
Withdrawn	122
Transferred to other societies	42
Pending April 1, 1928	93
Total	581

[28]*Op. cit.*

TRANSITIONS

A South Carolina Institution Gets a Case Worker

An illustration of another "next step" that some individual institution can take is found in the experiences of the Connie Maxwell Orphanage in Greenwood, South Carolina, under the leadership of its superintendent, Dr. A. T. Jamison. The institution is of the cottage type under Baptist auspices and receives children from all parts of the state. Its capacity is inadequate to meet the requests for admission. Accordingly Dr. Jamison in 1925 found a young college woman who was interested in the institution and willing to try to study the needs of individual children for whom admission was asked, and also the plans for those who were leaving the institution. Although not without some preliminary training, this worker felt the need of better preparation. Arrangements were therefore made for a school year of attendance upon social work training courses, combined with supervised case-work experience in child welfare agencies. For the past two and a half years she has been with the Connie Maxwell Orphanage. Dr. Jamison has this to say in regard to the function and training of the case-worker:[29]

For a few years our best managed institutions have shown their appreciation of the importance of studying the intake. Now it seems there is very much more general recognition of the value of such study. We note that many institutions are employing workers for this purpose. It is a good sign. In the good old days when we knew no better, it was a very simple proposition to decide whether children ought to be received into the institution or not. If we had room we would take them, if we did not have room they were refused or postponed. That was as simple as A, B, C. But we have almost unanimously passed that point, and now all want to study the environment of a child, his heredity, his mental ability, his behavior problems, his disposition, and a number of other things. A number of institutions are now employing persons to go to the community from which the child makes application to secure such facts as may be had.

[29] Condensed from "Investigating the Intake," in the monthly *Bulletin*, by Connie Maxwell, Clinton, N. C., April, 1929, pp. 7-8.

While the movement is encouraging . . . there is one feature that causes concern. There could not possibly be a reasonable objection to the visit of an officer to a community to make inquiry as to the status of a child, but there is very grave objection to the tendency to call such investigators by the title of Case-Worker. The title Case-Worker has come into vogue from the social field and stands for something very definite. When a person is called an M.D. we know very well that he has pursued a certain course of study and that he is trained to practice medicine. This should always be so with the case-worker, though some are assuming the title without having done the work that wins the title. Any common sense person may secure a great many interesting facts in making an investigation, just as any average person may give a dose of salts or a headache tablet, but in the one case we certainly could not call him a case-worker, nor could we in the other case call him a doctor. It is pretty well agreed that if a teacher is employed for our school he must be a trained person. If we need the help of a secretary in the office, we prefer one who has had the training that fits him for the job. If we want a trained nurse, we get one who has had a course in a hospital. In neither case do we think that merely a person of good common sense could fill the job in the school room, the job in the office, or the job of taking care of a sick person. And yet strange enough we are taking people who have been trained to teach and giving them the job of investigating cases, and though they have no training in the work of investigation we give them the title of Case-Worker. The training that one receives in a hospital does not fit one to be a case-worker. The training offered in a school of social work does fit one to be a case-worker. Here is the main point of our anxiety—that we are about to cheapen the title of the case-worker. The service demanded of such a person requires highly specialized training. In none [sic] of the schools for social work will a candidate for this office be received unless he can certify that he is a full college graduate. Only such a person is thought to be capable of becoming a candidate for such a delicate and highly specialized form of service. It seems a pity that a number of our institutions are calling certain persons case-workers when they have no right to hold such a title, having never been trained for such service. . . . Probably no argument is called for to support the thesis that such an important form of responsibility should call for special training. . . . It ought to be apparent on first thought . . . that no person who has been trained for one job is therefore competent for another job of different quality. . . .

If any of our brethren in institution work should take time to read this article, we hope they will give consideration to the honesty of bestowing a title upon a worker when such person has never done the study to merit the title. To be sure . . . many a real case-worker has made errors of judgment, but in such an instance we have the satisfaction that we did our best in trusting the case to a person who had been certified to as competent to study it. It is well known that case-workers are expensive people in a financial way. Certainly no criticism should be directed against an institution not in position financially to indulge in the luxury of the real article. Nor should any one offer criticism against an institution too small to justify the employment of such an expensive officer. But we should guard ourselves against the error of bestowing the title Case-Worker on a person who has been trained for another form of service.

Another Institution in South Carolina Gets a Case-Worker and Also Better Medical Service

The Thornwell Orphanage in Clinton, South Carolina, under Presbyterian auspices, also secured for itself a trained case-worker by selecting a young college graduate and arranging for her to attend a training school for social workers for one full academic year. Of her work during the past two years a competent observer says:[30]

There has been a great change in the practice of the institution with reference to admissions and discharges. There has been a substantial amount of family rehabilitation which previously was impossible. In most cases this rehabilitation has avoided the necessity of admitting children to the institution or has speeded up the discharge of children already in residence. In one case the management provided regular aid

[30] H. W. Hopkirk of the Child Welfare League of America, private report, January, 1929.

for a widow so that she might keep her children with her rather than send them to the institution.

Early in 1928 Dr. Lynn [Superintendent], the case-worker and Mr. Hopkirk conferred at Thornwell Orphanage in order to determine ways and means for securing improved [medical] service, including estimates of the cost. A plan was agreed upon and within a few months was placed in operation.

The results were as follows:[31]

In the past there has not been a careful and exhaustive examination of the children on admission or at any time during the year. A "family physician" has been employed at a nominal salary, and he has been called as occasion has arisen. The smallness of the fee has not been the measure of his interest and attention. The work has always been given faithful attention.

But as this was not deemed sufficient, arrangements were made in September with a skilled diagnostician in Greenville, S. C. (forty-three miles from Clinton), to come for a careful examination of all the 320 children then in the orphanage. He brought an assistant from the City Hospital in Greenville. It required nine trips and the doctors worked from four till eight o'clock with an intermission for dinner. The Child Welfare League's medical blanks for making the records (Child's Medical Record Form C-a) were used.

It was found that four children had incipient tuberculosis. It was thought that three of them needed hospital care. Seventy children showed a deficiency in diet which if allowed to continue might lead to pellagra. A number were under weight; a number were found with enlarged tonsils and adenoids. Blood tests and other more detailed examinations were made of such children as seemed in any way suspicious. A few were found who called for a little follow-up work. These latter are being sent by auto to Greenville for laboratory tests and further study. Suggestions as to an improved diet were made and the diet has been improved. A graduate of an agricultural college has been employed for the farm and garden with a view to securing a better vegetable supply from the garden.

[31]Child Welfare League *Bulletin*, December, 1928.

Brewers' yeast has been given to seventy children and cod-liver oil to thirty. One child has been gotten into a tuberculosis hospital. Another has been sent to Florida and will be placed in a camp if he needs it. Steps are being taken to get a third into the hospital.

The children themselves have responded to the program. They have been delighted to report: "I have gained seven pounds," or three, or five. For several years this diagnostician has done considerable free work for the orphanage in his office and because of his great interest will continue to do this, but he has been paid for his services at the institution. In the light of the service rendered and results secured, Dr. L. Ross Lynn, president of the Orphanage, has felt that the compensation was pitifully small. Although it only amounted to about $1.50 per child the cost represents a substantial amount from the point of view of most institution executives. The precedent established by Thornwell Orphanage will help other institutions to understand that painstaking preventive health service is worth paying for.

As to future plans, it is proposed to give greater attention to diet, to have all new children examined in the Greenville office, to have an occasional visit from the doctor to the Orphanage, and to have the whole group gone over once a year.

Transitions in a California Institution

Our illustrations thus far have come from the East and South; now we give one from the far West. In the *Fiftieth Annual Report* of Homewood Terrace in San Francisco, March 23, 1922, is told the story of the evolution of a Congregate Institution into a Group of Homes for Children, each for ten boys and ten girls, on a high, curved, and tree-shaded street. We are told that in 1912, after forty years of experience "in every period of which there is evident an eager desire to do that which, at the time, represented the best thought of the day," the institution needed a new plant. A new superintendent also succeeded a man who had served for twenty-three years. The *Report* describes as follows the attitude of the management toward the problems presented and the lines of effort soon laid down:

This was the period when the problems of education were increasingly engaging the attention of laymen. The schools were being subjected to searching criticisms of results, and from results the investigations went deeper, to curriculum, methods and housing. Such was the impetus which started psychologists at work devising tests to measure the actual achievements of pupils with scientific accuracy instead of leaving us to vague, unreliable information given by the traditional examination and marking system. It was natural that the leaders of an organization like ours, who were devotedly applying themselves to the task of securing for unfortunate children a fair chance in life, should share this thoughtful attention to measurements of achievement in education and to means of raising the standard of achievement. It was thoroughly understood that, at this time of planning for a new home, the whole subject of the institutional care of children should be studied from every viewpoint, for many generations of our wards would thrive or suffer as the decisions were wise or mistaken. So once more, and very deliberately, the whole life scheme of the Institution was re-examined, and every phase, no matter how firmly established by custom or authority, was reconsidered. It is this process, steadily pursued these ten years past, which has resulted in Homewood Terrace as it is today.

Certain very definite lines of effort were laid down. The Institution must provide for these things:

1. A home where regulation shall be so overlaid with love that the harness of discipline will support and guide the tender body of childhood without galling or needless stress.

2. A religious training which shall make religion part of life itself and not a matter of times and places. It must include common worship, ceremonial experience and formal instruction.

3. An elementary education in the public schools.

4. Abundant opportunity for varied hand work, for the double purpose of giving every child the needed skill in home-making exercises and of disclosing every child's special aptitudes.

5. A vocational training following the lines of special aptitudes which have been disclosed, whereto high schools, special schools and home exercises must all contribute.

6. Economic education, including discrimination of materials, knowledge of costs and discretion in expenditure.

7. Adequate physical education, including expert management of diet, medical attention, bodily development and knowledge thereof, and play.

8. Social education, including normal intercourse, the use of leisure, development of social accomplishments and experience both as hosts and as guests.

9. The preservation of family ties so as to prevent residence in the institution from destroying natural feelings of mutual responsibility and willingness to make sacrifices. This particularly in regard to surviving parents.

10. Such relationship to us that former inmates of the Institution shall neither unduly lean on us, nor yet fear to turn to us in case of failure, misfortune or ill health.

In pursuance of these objects, and recognizing that the genuinely effective factor in education is the personality of the teacher, and not the house or equipment, the staff was so reorganized that none but chosen, trained workers were in authoritative control of the children. The staff was differentiated from the help, and every staff member, including the superintendent, assistant superintendent, governess, housekeeper, matron and nurse, was a teacher. The atmosphere at once became more genial, as it must when changed from driving to leadership. From 1873 to 1912, practically every annual report made specific mention of disciplinary problems. Since 1913, this has not been mentioned even once.

Our children live in groups so small that every one will know intimately every other member of the group. Every one in each family must make some contribution for all the rest. The little ones contribute their helplessness, and themselves to be loved and taken care of. The bigger ones give their growing powers and derive a double satisfaction from "doing for" the little ones—the egotistic pleasure of showing abilities which others have not yet developed and the unselfish pleasure of making others happy by personal exertions.

The groups are so constituted that all normal relationships can be normally, unconsciously developed. Not only the relationship of older to younger, of stronger to weaker, of brighter to slower, but also of boy and girl and of "handy man" to "home-maker." The cottage families consist of ten boys and ten girls, each with children from youngest to oldest. And every cottage is headed by a "cottage mother"—a true home-maker, who guides and teaches and loves and works with all her children, so that her children work heartily and lovingly with and for her. There is no "help problem" in our households, for there are abundant hands to carry on all the work, under the wise guidance and direction of the mother.

There is a note of finality in this report that is somewhat disturbing. A reader of the report who has not had an opportunity to visit the institution wonders if the dynamic force hidden in item 9 is allowed to be sufficiently potent to disturb the perfect serenity of the institution life.

IV. Transitions in Foster Family Home Methods and Philosophies

In Ohio

Coming back now from California, we stop in Ohio. Inasmuch as we have previously given at some length evidence of inadequate care of children by some of the County Children's Homes of Ohio previous to 1913, we are glad here to present, also at considerable length, more recent evidence of progress toward the ideal.[32] We include a statement of "Ohio Trends and Goals in Child Care," as seen by the Department of Public Welfare in 1928. There is no claim by Ohio or by the present writer that Mr. Birtwell's ideal has been reached. The evidence is given to suggest to the reader something of the methods by which the child care processes in Ohio are being changed in the direction of the ideal.

STATE ASSUMES CHILD-PLACING AS WELL AS INSPECTIONAL FUNCTIONS IN 1913

With the crying need for the placing of children from the public

[32] *Child Placing in Ohio*, by Esther McClain, Division of Charities, Department of Public Welfare, Columbus, Ohio, 1928, pp. 17-20.

TRANSITIONS

Homes all over the State where children were found, in many instances, to be eking out pitifully narrow, dreary existences, with their young lives spent fruitlessly performing the changeless drudgery of the institutions, the State began to take over certain children for placement. County after county requested this service in the face of its own limitations.

STATE CHILD-PLACING IS COUNTY SERVICE

As fast as the legislature provided funds for field workers the children in a continuous stream were brought in to Columbus for examination, observation and placement in free or boarding homes, after passing through the State Receiving Home. This service by the State had a twofold objective as conceived by the far-seeing, energetic friend of children, Mr. C. V. Williams, who came to Ohio as Director of the Children's Welfare Department when the work was started in 1913.

The objectives were:

1. To give these hundreds of homeless children a chance in real homes.

2. To demonstrate the possibilities in home-finding and child-placement an idea which was then new or had fallen from grace in many communities due to the tragedies to children that had resulted from the kind of placing that had been done.

Both objectives have been fairly well accomplished. The State has assumed the guardianship of 3784 dependent children since that time, all of whom have been placed in family homes, free or boarding. This does not include the 1901 dependent, crippled children who have been received for orthopedic service and after-care which is frequently that of boarding-out in private families during certain stages of convalescence.

As to demonstrating in the State the possibility and value of foster homes, both to the child and to the community, the demonstration has been highly successful, for hundreds and hundreds of children that undoubtedly would have stayed on and on in the institutions, have been happily absorbed in family and community life. The acceptance by counties, of the demonstration has not been as rapid nor as complete as anticipated for there are today, still hundreds of children in the County

Children's Homes of Ohio that should have been placed out long ere this. The need for the turnover of children under care in many institutions is still their greatest problem.

COUNTY CHILDREN'S HOMES AND CHILD WELFARE BOARDS IN 1928

Of the eighty-eight counties in the State, sixty-three have a county organization for the care of dependent children. Fifty-five have an institution known as the "County Children's Home" and three carry the name of "County Children's Home" but operate without an institution, having abandoned their old-time institutions within the past few years (Hancock, Hocking and Lawrence Counties) and use instead a receiving home and foster homes (free and boarding) with a placing agent to engineer the receptions and placements.

Five others, Lake, Brown, Ross, Morgan and Mercer Counties, have County Child Welfare Boards as made legally possible by the law of 1921,[33] providing for the abandonment of children's homes in counties so desiring and setting up a county child welfare board in any county not operating a Children's Home. Of these five counties, two (Brown and Morgan) abandoned their former Children's Homes in 1922 and 1923, respectively, and adopted in their place the Child Welfare Board plan with a placing agent in charge and a number of boarding and free foster homes in which to place the children, using a special boarding-home for receiving purposes. The other three (Lake, Ross and Mercer) had no county system of child-care prior to the creation of the Welfare Boards.

Thus eight of the sixty-three counties that have some form of child-care organization aside from the juvenile court, have a non-institutional plan, each with a social worker or placing agent in charge of the case work and child placing, some operating with, others without, a receiving home but in each case foster home care, free or boarding, is the medium for child-care and adjustment.

CHILD PLACING AGENTS

This subject brings up the question of how far we have kept faith with those early pioneers who emphasized this need in our County Chil-

---

[33] Section 3092 of the General Code of Ohio.

dren's Homes fifty years ago and later secured a permissive law to that effect in 1889. At that time, the possibilities of case work as we now understand it, were not appreciated, so that the term "placing agent," was quite descriptive of the principal duties involved, namely, home finding, placement and supervision of children.

Today with our appreciation of case work principles and the great value of treating the family social problems to the end of preventing the removal of the children whenever possible, the term, placing agent, has a far greater connotation. It carries with it the responsibility of securing and recording all the facts of the case, a full family history, a formation of some plan for the family as a whole, as well as the children individually, and working tirelessly to a goal of self sufficiency for the family, or, if that is impossible, foster home placement and supervision of the children.

Several county placing agents, especially those who have had the advantage of case work training, are actively and conscientiously pursuing these principles in their investigation and treatment of family problems involving child dependency. Of the sixty-three counties having a children's home or a county child welfare board, twenty-two or thirty-five percent of them have the services of a placing agent or agents, some of them over a period of years, although seventeen of the twenty-two have been secured within the past eight years, i. e., since 1920.

The mere fact of the employment of a placing agent or agents has not, of itself, always assured adequacy or efficiency of service, but an appreciation of training and experience in children's work as qualifications for placing agents, is coming more and more to be in the minds of the Board responsible for their appointment. . . .

In recent years the recognition of social case work, child-placing and supervision as an important function of the county, has been infinitely greater than in previous decades. We have not kept faith, however, in the degree that it should have been kept with those early pioneers whose ideals and beliefs in this regard were expressed a half century ago. The process has been almost discouragingly slow. The institutions for years have provided shelter and maintenance and the officials did not see beyond this for it is so much easier to keep children there under their eye than to seek homes. Then, too, the former tragedies of "out of sight, out of mind" made of child-placing itself a hazardous and gloomy picture.

However, since 1913, with state inspection and an annual check-up on the visitation of placed-out children, they are not placed and forgotten as in the early days. A law requiring, as a minimum, annual visitation of placed-out children is rigorously enforced by the State or the license to an agency or institution is withheld. A few agencies are visiting their wards regularly three or four times a year. Several have the six-month limit between visits, and the twenty-five agencies placing children in boarding homes are trying to visit such children monthly.

OHIO TRENDS AND GOALS IN CHILD CARE[34]

The future of the world is limited by ourselves.
Maeterlinck

1. That county child welfare boards be made possible by future legislation, the latter coördinating all the public welfare work within the county, including such activities as public health, care of the aged, care of children, mothers' pensions, court probation service, blind relief, school relief, soldiers' relief, township trustees' relief, etc.

2. That the County Children's Homes become receiving homes for children for short time care, using foster homes, free or boarding, for long time cases.

3. That there be at least one social worker in every county. Social work is a profession that calls for considerable training and preparation. Salaries commensurate with this preparation and service rendered must be paid.

4. That the educational social service training centers make additional efforts to attract more of the right type of students. The demand for trained, efficient workers in the children's field today so far exceeds the supply that it is discouraging to communities and agencies.

5. The trend in child-care work is to make the agency or institution program more flexible by providing the kind of service and care a child needs rather than merely what the organization has to offer. Therefore adequate social service, mothers' aid, funds for boarding out, and the development of boarding homes are among the matters for

---
[34]McClain, *Op. cit.*, p. 87.

TRANSITIONS 297

earnest consideration by agencies and institutions heretofore thinking in terms of giving the child what they had been providing in the past and not considering other plans.

6. Know the child. Individual study of the child, his mental capacity and mental processes, and helping him to build the right habits and attitudes is perhaps the greatest movement in child welfare today. Hence the emphasis on parental education, child study clubs, child guidance clinics and similar movements.

In Illinois

We have already considered the origin and development of the work of the Illinois Children's Home and Aid Society.[35] This Society, it will be recalled, was the pioneer among the thirty or more private Children's Home Societies, each of which operated over a whole state, and followed Mr. Van Arsdale's lead in almost exclusive reliance upon free foster family home care, aided by a small institution for temporary care called a Receiving Home.

We have seen a further development of the Society's methods under Dr. Hart's leadership, when he began an Aid Department in the Society to pay board for some children in foster family homes. This Department had so developed in 1921 that $28,000 were paid for such service. We are recently informed that the Society now carries an average of five hundred children at board in foster family homes, at a cost of $153,000 for board in a year.[36] The distribution of the total number of children under the care of the Illinois Children's Home and Aid Society on May 31, 1929, was as follows:[37]

Children in free family homes	1119
Children in boarding family homes	547
Children in our three institutions	87
Children in other institutions	79
Elsewhere	66

[35] Chapter VI, Part II.
[36] In a letter from the superintendent, C. V. Williams, January 3, 1929.
[37] Given by Roy James Battis, Department of Public Welfare, Springfield, Illinois, in a letter June 20, 1929.

Thus in its efforts to suit the action to the real needs of the individual child, this pioneer free foster home society for a great state is finding its next step to be an increasing differentiation of treatment. Full justice to all dependent children cannot be secured by exclusive reliance upon the free foster family home.

In Michigan

A significant departure has been made in Michigan from the exclusive free foster family home philosophy and procedure of the State Children's Home Societies that follow Martin Van Buren Van Arsdale as their prophet. A brief statement of the present methods and of the reasons for this departure in Michigan is herewith given. By studying the maps following page 236, the reader can see how Michigan in 1923 contrasted with many of these states in the degree to which it had developed boarding foster family care work for dependent children.[38]

In the early days the whole program of work consisted of temporary care of children in a "Receiving Home" and placing out in free foster homes usually for adoption.

The present situation shows nearly a thousand children in care at any one time, practically all in foster homes and by far the greater part in paid boarding homes. This has come about as a gradual transformation caused by definite considerations.

In the first place, we began to discover that infants and young children would thrive better in good family homes than in an institution. Accordingly instead of keeping them all in the Receiving Home we began to place them out in temporary foster homes pending their future disposition—a permanent placement for adoption,

Again, social case-workers were learning that a large percentage of the children who came to our notice did not need to be separated permanently from their own people. Therefore, they should not be placed

---

[38] In a personal letter to writer in 1929, from Albert H. Stoneman, many years superintendent of the Michigan Children's Aid Society; now head of South End House, Boston.

for adoption although they did need foster home care for a time. But suitable foster homes could not often be found excepting on an adoption or permanent basis. To secure proper temporary care for younger children in family homes it was found necessary to pay board. Moreover it was learned that better supervision of the homes was essential to the welfare of the children.

Thirdly, in an agency extending over a whole state and helping children in various sections, it was found desirable to provide care for them in the vicinity of their parents if the children were not to be adopted or taken away permanently. The boarding home system fitted well into this plan because foster families could be selected in different sections of the state. The number in each group of such homes could be adapted to the needs of the district. A local worker could be made responsible for the selection and supervision of these homes as well as the case work with the families of the children. And not only for social reasons but also for saving in transportation was this system advantageous.

Finally, it was found that the per capita cost of child care by the boarding-out plan was lower than by the institutional. It actually costs less to properly select and supervise foster homes than it does to care for children in an institution with proper equipment and personnel.

To sum up, the Michigan Children's Aid Society learned by its own experience that for the sake of the personal health and social development of the children, as well as for reasons of administration and finance, the boarding-out system of child care was justified.

V. Some Illustrations of Free Foster Family Home and Boarding Foster Home Philosophies

As Seen by an Institution

Of the 188 children received into the institution, 115 had brothers or sisters who were also admitted. This is a very important consideration in connection with the types of family homes that may be found for the children who should be cared for out of the institution. Free home placement is rarely available for groups of children. The result of using this method without doing boarding home placement also is likely to be that only those children are placed in family homes who are the only members of their families, or else that children from the same family are placed in different homes, and some members of the group may be kept in the institution. With the use of boarding homes as well as free homes and wage homes, it becomes possible to place in the same home two or more children who should be kept together.[39]

Standards of Boarding Foster Home Care as Adopted by Foster Mothers Themselves

Since our foster mothers have always helped us to find successful foster homes, and as we have always felt that their recommendation meant a great deal, the last Foster Mothers' meeting was turned over to them, and they told us just what they expect of a foster mother and her home. Here are some of the most important points they raised, this is the standard they have set for the new foster mother and her home:

1. You must know that the child will be treated as their own.

All agreed that this was essential. The child should feel at home, and no distinctions should be made.

2. Must encourage them to see their own people, must make their relatives welcome.

Foster mothers told stories of their own experience, they insisted no child will be happy if the foster mother does not help it to accept and love his own people. This is part of the foster mother's service to the child.

3. Must love them, but not so much that they will be unhappy when they go home.

They said part of their job is to prepare the child for the time when it must leave them, and to give it a feeling of security even when that time comes.

4. Be interested in the things the child is interested in.

The foster mother has to be young enough in spirit and patient enough to understand the child's interests and to make it feel that she too is interested.

5. Be successful in raising own children.

[39] *Analysis of Data on Admissions and Population of the Indianapolis Orphans' Home*, p. 6, 1928. This analysis was made by a private survey agency at the request of the managers of the institution.

No mother who has failed or is failing to raise her own children successfully can undertake to raise a foster child.

6. Must be prepared to look after the child's health.

The new foster mother must be aware of the importance of health and of the modern ways of keeping a child healthy.

7. The home must be one where there is plenty of food, plenty of rest, and play.

Children must play, they have to be free to play and no home which does not allow this is a good home. Food is of primary importance, say our foster mothers. Children all need a certain amount of rest, of quiet. A good foster home should provide these.

8. The home should be happy.

Peace, warmth, love—all these are essential for normal happy children. A home where parents are happy with each other, where there is no friction between parents and children will be a good foster home.

9. The whole family must want the child.

Foster mothers say they will not recommend a home where they know that some members of the family will not be interested in the child, or will be opposed to the mother taking the child. This is important—the child must be welcome.[40]

For evidence as to the possible influence of the boarding foster family home upon the child's relations to his own parents and kin, the reader's attention is directed especially to sections 2 and 3 above and to the following two stories:[41]

Bennie

Little Bennie had a very young and devoted mother. She visited him frequently. She always brought him plenty of sweets, which Little Bennie usually ate and promptly got sick over. Then the doting mother would examine him minutely, question him and watch the foster mother to see if she was giving him the proper care. Little Bennie soon

---

[40] *Home Finder* of the Home Bureau of the Hebrew Sheltering Guardian Society, Mary E. Boretz, superintendent, New York City, February, 1928.

[41] Taken from *The Home Finder,* of the Home Bureau of the Hebrew Sheltering Guardian Society, New York City, January, 1928.

found his mother's questionings and excessive attention tiresome. Besides, he found that it was not pleasant to have an upset stomach after eating the sweets mamma brought him, so gradually he refused to eat her offerings and besides was cranky when she visited. The poor mother was heartbroken. But the foster mother, who had not reproved the mother for her interference, now stepped in. She called the mother aside one day when Little Bennie had been particularly peevish and spoke to her.

"You know," she said, "you do not need to worry that I will neglect your child. I promise you that I will give him very good care, for I too love him. But it hurts me that he does not act more friendly toward you. Try to win your child. Next time you visit bring him a bright toy, don't question him, play with him. Let him think of your visits as something to look forward to. Always bring him some little thing that he will like. Soon he will be waiting for you to visit him."

The mother took the advice. It has worked. Now Little Bennie and his mother are both looking forward to each visit, and there is room in their lives for the foster mother too.

"Sharing the Child"

Take the case of little Joe and Mamie. Their father used to come to see them regularly. He was devoted. He brought them gifts and his visits were the biggest thing in his childen's life. Then suddenly he stopped coming. For nearly a year they did not see him. The children did not understand, they were hurt at their father's neglect and spoke of him bitterly to their foster mother. She immediately began to defend the father. She explained to them that they could not judge him as they did not know the facts; that he had always loved them, and she felt sure he would come to them if he could.

Finally a letter came. The father had been ill, he had been in a hospital in a southern city for nearly a year. Now he planned to come back, and hoped he would see his dear children very soon. The foster mother explained to Joe and Mamie that their father had been ill, that he had not worked for a long time, and that he had little money. She told them that when he came to see them they were not to expect gifts. They agreed they would be so happy to see their father, they would need nothing else. When he came, there was a happy reunion. He offered the children a little money. Both put their hands behind their back, and said: "No, papa, we know you have not been working, you keep the money. Auntie gives us the pennies we need for spending money. All we want is you, Daddy." The father who had been so hesitant about approaching his children, who felt he could not go to them empty-handed, was relieved and grateful.

Attitude toward Kinship Ties, 1856, Contrasted with that of 1924-1930 New York Children's Aid Society

We have already devoted considerable space to the objectives and method of the free foster family care of the New York Children's Aid Society. On account of this emphasis, and because of the prominent place the work of this Society has always held in the public consciousness all over the United States, a further statement of present trends in the Society should now be made. We shall close with a story illustrating present attitude and methods in the new Department of Boarding Homes, in contrast with the easy philosophy of separating children from parents which prevailed some years ago, and which was followed in the case of Nancy T—— and her parents, described in Chapter VI.

During the first seventy years of its service to dependent children, the trend of development within the emigration department of the Children's Aid Society had been the slow modification of a fixed and persistent ideal—that of placement in free foster homes for all dependent children as a class. The placement work was accomplished from the first by means of public distribution of large groups of children. In the very nature of the procedure there was possible only the minimum of knowledge of the child as an individual who, on the one hand, was to be placed; and, on the other, of the foster parents who were to receive the child. In the case of these parents, too frequently their need for child labor was frankly accepted along with their assumed willingness to give Christian service to the child. The early successes of the Society, which were many, were due first to the marvellous inherent capacity of children to grow, and to take advantage of opportunity; and, second, to the general decency and sense of fair play to children among foster parents, rather than to any well worked out method in placement, or skill in supervision. However, the method of free home placement by public distribution of children, which has prevailed right up to the year 1929, does violence to the sensibilities of dependent children as individuals, even though it has of late been associated with some previous study of both child and foster parents by the Society's agent and by a local committee of citizens.

Since 1869 the Society has slowly been developing resident workers for supervision of children in foster homes, in partial recognition of the trend toward treatment of dependent children as individuals.

The stream of childhood flowing out from New York City under the auspices of the Children's Aid Society has grown smaller as the city has grown larger, until the annual average of the ten years, 1915-24 was only 239, or practically one-fourth of the annual average (946) for the first ten years, 1865-74. This is evidence of at least an increased difficulty in finding children whose parents, relatives, or custodians are willing to see them permanently placed in family homes scores or hundreds of miles away from New York. In short, the tendency in New York City, toward a recognition of the dependent child as an individual member of some family group—although the group may have been in fact physically broken, has in later years been in itself one factor in changing the size of the stream of child emigrants.

The Kimbark Family

The story of the Kimbark family is given as an illustration of the extent to which the Children's Aid Society is now willing to go in its effort to recognize and build upon the intangible foundations of actual and potential affection among the members of a family group.

In August, 1924, Mr. Kimbark, a man about forty years old, came into the office of the Department of Boarding Homes of the New York Children's Aid Society, and asked that a boarding home be found for his boy Steve, two and one-half years old. His situation as revealed by his own story, supplemented by investigation, was as follows:

Although he and his wife were both Slavs and born in the same Polish city, they did not know each other until they met and married in the United States about 1910. They had three children, all born in the United States and therefore citizens—Nicholas, 12; Anna, 7; and Steve, 2½. Mr. Kimbark was an unskilled worker, but the family had been on the *independent home level* until the birth of Steve. Soon afterward Mrs. Kimbark's mind became seriously affected with a manic-depressive type of disease and she had been taken into a hospital where, two years later, the prognosis for recovery was distinctly unfavorable. It was at this time that Mr. Kimbark asked help in a boarding home for Steve. The family was already scattered. From the time Mrs. Kimbark had been taken ill until he was two years old, Steve had been in an infant asylum. He was then taken into a farm home of a fellow countryman of Mr. Kimbark in New Jersey, where he could not stay longer. Anna was in an orphan asylum. Nicholas and the father had been living with two brothers of Mr. Kimbark, Michael and William, in a two-room apartment on the lower East Side of New York City. No one of the three brothers was a citizen of the United States. Michael was a steady worker in a restaurant and had a wife and children in Poland whom he could not bring here on account of the immigration laws. William was unmarried, and not a steady worker. These three brothers and Nicholas did their own housework. There were no other relatives of either Mr. or Mrs. Kimbark in the United States except a brother of Mrs. Kimbark. He lived near the Kimbarks, but he had a sick wife, was not able to help, and was not on very good terms with Mr. Kimbark who thought his wife's brother had not treated Mrs. Kimbark right.

At the outset, therefore, here was the situation of an unskilled man, not a citizen of the United States, whose prospect of again having the help of his wife was almost hopeless and whose three children were living in three different places, having seen very little of each other for two years—Steve, indeed, was almost a stranger to sister, brother, and father. What was the action that was suited to the real need of Steve? How could the Department of Boarding Homes get such an understanding of a "total personality in a total situation" as to do the right thing, as nearly as possible? Seventy years before, with the awful pressure of numbers of destitute and neglected children in New York, it is easy to see how a separate free foster home in the West for each of the three Kimbark children would have seemed the best possible thing.

In August, 1924, however, there was at least a chance to build up a family solidarity in the Kimbark family. The philosophy of the Department of Boarding Homes of the New York Children's Aid Society is to save both the child and his own home and kinship relations if it can possibly be done. Therefore, Steve was accepted, given the best possible medical attention, and placed at board in a family home, the father to pay what he could afford, the amount being determined by study with him of his family budget. Attention was given also to the health of Nicholas, and arrangements were made for him to take his luncheons at a school near the one he attended which did not serve luncheons.

Mr. Kimbark and Nicholas were invited to spend Christmas Day in the foster home of Steve. The foster father kept himself out of the way as much as he could lest Steve should show more affection for him than for Mr. Kimbark.

Early in 1925 Mr. Kimbark said one day, "I wish I could get my kids all together." Soon afterward the Department found a boarding foster home for Anna near Steve where the two could meet often. Mr. Kimbark and Nicholas could now see both Steve and Anna on one trip from New York City.

In the fall of 1925 a great question came up. The foster parents of Steve were to move to another state and wanted to take Steve with them. The distance from New York was so great that frequent trips to see Steve were impossible. Mr. Kimbark and the Department of Boarding Homes stared into the face of the old, old question—shall we give up Steve to what in all human probability will be a permanently good home for him, but which will also effectually prevent the building up of any real family consciousness in *all three* children and the father?

The father hesitated, and was willing to accept the decision of the Department. The Department thought not only of Steve but of Nicholas and Anna. Especially did they question what ideals of family loyalty, and of obligation of parents to children the separation would develop in these two, Anna and Nicholas, and what influence such ideals might exert upon the homes they might have later on. The decision was finally made to keep on trying to get the children and their father closer together.

A new home had to be found for Anna, on account of the death of the man in her first foster home, so Steve and Anna were placed in another home together. This home had promised sympathetic opportunity for Nicholas and his father to visit, but the foster mother proved herself unable to help the Department in its great central purpose, not only to care well, for Steve and Anna, but to help build up a stronger family feeling with Nicholas and Mr. Kimbark.

Another home was therefore found for Anna and Steve in which Nicholas and the father were welcome. In this home, however, where the children stayed two years, an emotional difficulty developed with Steve. The foster mother grew to love Anna better than she did Steve, and Anna herself, as sisters in other families have been known to do, felt so much responsibility for Steve that she became quite bossy with him, which Steve resented. As Steve felt himself growing insecure he developed obstreperous behavior at home and school, and also curried favor at school by various devices such as taking flowers and little articles from one person and giving them to another as if they were his own gifts. As he had also at intervals been troubled by eczema, stringent advice by the Department's doctor and nurse to the foster mother about his diet had deprived him of some articles of food. He retaliated by prowling around waste baskets at school in which there were stray remnants of the luncheons of other children. Also the foster mother grew unwilling to let the two children visit their father and Nicholas and Uncle Michael (William had disappeared) in their New York City apartment as frequently as the father and the Department wished.

For the next year, therefore, the children were in a home of one of Mr. Kimbark's fellow-countrymen in the Bronx. The father found this home himself and the Department approved, after investigation. There were two children in the family, a boy and a girl who were not far from the ages of Anna and Steve. The home was one of thrift and physical comfort—the house had a yard—the man owned a car—and there was a piano in the house. The woman was a strong personality who, without very much show of affection, tried hard to do right by all four children. The necessity of treating Anna and Steve as nearly alike as possible, and the reasons, were fully talked over with her. Anna also tried hard to be more understanding and less bossy with Steve, so that the tension between them grew less. The question of diet for Steve was studied again by the most competent medical men, and some food restrictions were removed. His behavior also was thoroughly studied by a competent mental hygiene clinic. Although the psychiatrist thought he had missed the security of the foster home that wanted to adopt him, and that a mistake had been made in not letting him go to that home, Steve stopped his food foraging propensities, made his first grade in school, got along better with Anna, grew proud of his big brother Nicholas and very fond of his father. *He came to feel very clearly that he belonged to his own family group.* Still, there was some question as to the advisability of a temporary separation of Anna and Steve, and this has now been done. Steve is in another boarding home which he likes and from which he makes occasional week-end visits to his own home, where Anna now is. He is also having expert tests for foods and other stimuli which tend to bring on asthmatic attacks from which he is not yet free. Both Steve and Anna have made good progress in school. Anna has just been given an I.Q. of 106 in an intelligence test. Nicholas reached the middle of the second year of senior high school in January, 1930. He then felt that he ought to go to work to help out on the family budget. He therefore got a job and attended evening High School until the close of the school year in June. Since then he has worked steadily and pays his father part of his $50 a month wage in a chemical supply house. He also worked for money during the two summer vacations of 1928 and 1929.

Uncle Michael has returned to Poland and as Uncle William has disappeared, Nicholas and his father and Anna are keeping house by themselves. A motherly woman of the same nationality as the Kimbarks, who lives in the same building who also has a girl about Anna's age, keeps a kindly eye upon Anna. Mr. Kimbark is working steadily in a laundry for less than $30 a week but is given a two weeks' vacation. He pays all that he can squeeze out for the board of Steve, which is less than it costs the Department. The mother's prognosis is well-nigh hopeless for recovery, as in addition to her mental disease she now has tuberculosis. Nicholas has been most insistent through the years that he and his father visit the mother; but she never recognizes them or pays any attention to them. Nicholas has never been able to speak to her without tears in his eyes. Anna also has recently been to see her mother, who did not pay her any attention.

In June, 1929, after much saving for new clothes for the children, and after much planning, the father had a group picture taken of himself and the three children to send to his brother Michael in Poland.

And there you are. The family is not yet on a wholly self-supporting basis; Steve is only nine, and many years stretch ahead before he can become self-supporting; Anna is only thirteen and though well grown and skillful with needle and housework, her father is the real housekeeper and the three are not yet equal to the job of keeping a safe home for themselves and Steve as well. Nicholas just about earns his own way. The family group may never have a home where all four can be physically together. Who can tell, even after six years, what the result, in terms of a sense of family affection; of belonging to each other and of sharing in a common family heritage; of character and preparation for playing their full part in homes of their own, these children have acquired? Who can now tell what the struggle of Mr. Kimbark to "keep his kids together" at least in awareness and affection has wrought in the fiber of his own soul?

The story of this family has not been given to prove beyond any peradventure to any doubting Thomas that the boarding foster home process, by which a family like this can be kept in touch with each other, is better than the free foster home process that would have separated these three children permanently from each other and from the father. Readers will disagree on this point and neither can prove his case. The story has been given to show in living human terms the contrast between the philosophy as to the value of natural family ties held by the Society in the Fifties, when it took Nancy T— from between her weeping parents, and the philosophy of the Department of Boarding Homes of the same Society today, when it has worked and spent money for six years, and perhaps will have to work and spend money for six years more, to save whatever assets there may be within the family circle of foreign-born Mr. Kimbark and his three American-born children permanently bereft of a mother's care. The reader must take his choice, but he is urged to give this matter most careful thought and study. Upon the issue hang momentous decisions as to the future of the family as an institution in the United States, and the welfare of untold thousands of individual children in homes that are already beginning to break—that every day in the future will be beginning to break.

Along which road, that of light parental responsibility for children, and the easy severing of kinship ties, or that of heroic loyalty to offspring and the cherishing of family affection, lies the brighter future for the children of America? The reader cannot shirk his share of responsibility for trying to find an answer to this question.

Nor can any of us hide behind the excuse that it is impossible now to be certain in every individual case. We hunger for certainty, but we must often act on probability.

The Quest for Certainty

In a third year class in high school, the writer once had a charming girl pupil to whom he had, in previous years, taught algebra and geometry. For six weeks or more this young girl had been studying civics. One night after school she came into the office with tears in her eyes and exclaimed, "Oh, isn't there some way that we can be as certain we are right in civics as we used to be in algebra and geometry?"

George Meredith (*Modern Love*, L) says, "Ah, what a dusty answer gets the soul when hot for certainties in this our life!" No, we can't yet be sure that the Department of Boarding Homes has done the best that could have been done for Steve and Anna and Nicholas in trying to keep them in touch with each other and with their father. Only one thing is as yet sure, and that is that the Department has tried hard to help, not only Steve, but the whole family. It has really tried to deal with "a total personality in a total situation."

So long as men are finite there can be no possibility that persons in charge of child welfare agencies and institutions can ever be wise enough to find out all of the real needs of every dependent and neglected child they seek to help—much less can they have such control of material, social, emotional, and spiritual resources as to be able to give every child all the help which they find he needs.

But there may be and should be a closer approach to these goals with each succeeding year, and also a constant thrill of adventure among child welfare workers who do their daily best at the job.

VI. The Need for Orchestration of Community Effort

So far in this chapter our illustrations, selected from ten different states, have dealt mostly with the efforts of individual agencies and institutions to take their own steps toward better care of dependent children. A few of them, like the New England Home for Little Wanderers, Coit House, The Children's Community Center of New Haven, and the Department of Public Welfare in Ohio, are rather definitely moving in the direction of what might be called an orchestration of community facilities for the better care of dependent, neglected and delinquent children. Such an orchestration is one of the long next steps that every community should be preparing to take. But before such orchestration or co-ordination can be taken in any community, there must be present all the different forms of care needed by all the dependent children of that community. For example (even though industrial justice and stability be achieved), there must be adequate facilities by outdoor relief, mothers' pensions or otherwise, for keeping in their own homes, on a supplemented home basis, all children who ought to be kept there. There must be foster family home care on a free basis, on a boarding basis, and on a wage basis for such children as respectively need these temporary or permanent substitutes for care in their own homes. Also, for the present at least, there must be institutional care for the children, few or many, that really need such care. There are those who will question this last statement. For the consideration of such persons two quotations from acknowledged champions of foster family home care are here inserted:

> It inevitably true that a small percentage of problem children, with habits of delinquency and personality characteristics so fixed that they refuse to recognize authority in a family or in a community, will have

to be cared for in institutions; and it is undeniable that a well-directed and constructive institutional policy can accomplish much.[42]

Occasionally there comes a time when group care is the only hope, because the child is entirely controlled by his impulses and proves unmanageable even in a good environment.[43]

In addition to all the foregoing facilities there must be available competent case-workers, doctors, psychologists and psychiatrists —in short, personnel who are competent to use all the persons and things and forces necessary to meet the whole range of needs of the dependent children of the community. And right here comes in the question of what proportions of our home care, institutional care, foster free home care, foster boarding home care, etc., do the dependent children of the community really need? Without an approximate answer to this question no adequate community planning or orchestration is possible. So far as the writer is aware, the question has nowhere been adequately answered.

A Jewish Survey as a Start toward Orchestration

The nearest approach that has yet been made to a deliberate, well founded judgment as to the relative numbers of dependent children who, for their own good, ought to be cared for in institutions and in foster homes, relates to the Jewish children of New York City. This judgment concerns the children of a single religious faith, and the present stage of development of institutions and agencies in a single city. It is based upon a count of dependent Jewish children in Greater New York on May 1, 1926. At that time there were:

In seven orphan asylums	2,623	children
In three placing-out agencies	940	"
Total	3,563	"

---

[42]Healy, Bronner, Baylor and Murphy, *Reconstructing Behavior in Youth*, New York and London, 1929, p. 4.
[43]*Ibid.*, p. 221.

The method of study of these children, in brief, was this:

First, all records with regard to the child, or his family, found in either the children's organizations, family welfare societies, hospitals or any other places, were read.

Second, the facts in these records were checked back with organizations, particularly the children's organizations.

Third, wherever indicated as desirable or valuable, the homes of parents or relatives were visited.

Fourth, with respect to children placed in foster homes, a given number of foster homes indicated later were visited and studied.

Many conferences were held with workers and executive directors of institutions.[44]

The Bureau of Jewish Social Research extended its studies to include the histories of dependent children in other cities, involving "more than one million pieces of information." On the strength of these researches, the survey reports that, in the opinion of those who made the study, the following allocation of children for care would more nearly meet their needs than the allocation that had actually been made:

Allocation	Number of children	Percent of total number of children
Institutional care (7 institutions)	1,067	30.0
Foster home care (3 agencies)	1,689	47.5
Special institutional care	207	5.8
To be discharged	549	15.3
Probable discharge	51	1.4
Total	3,563	100.0

As to the care of children in existing institutions (some congregate, some cottage), compared with care by placing-out agencies

[44] Child Care Section of an unpublished Jewish Communal Survey of Greater New York, by the Bureau of Jewish Social Research, 1928.

in foster family homes, the contrast of numbers between the actual and the recommended allocations is shown by these figures:

	Actual number	Actual percentage	Recommended number	Recommended percentage
In orphan asylums	2,623	73.62	1,067	30.0
In foster homes	940	26.38	1,689	47.5
Total	3,563	100.00	2,756	77.5

In other words, the survey found 1,556 more children in existing institutions than in their opinion ought to be there for the good of the children involved. And, for the same reason, that is, the good of the children involved, they recommended that 749 more children than were already so placed should be put in foster homes.

In addition, they found 207 children now being cared for, either in institutions or foster family homes, who, on account of mental defect or other special needs, ought to be receiving a more highly specialized care elsewhere; and, finally, they found 549 children who in their opinion without doubt ought to be discharged, and 51 more who probably ought to be discharged.

Furthermore, the survey reported not only that the above number of children ought to be discharged but also that in their opinion 778 children or 21.8 percent of the whole 3,563 children ought never to have been admitted either to institution or placing-out agency—"had subsidy been granted when helping the mother who was otherwise able to care for the children, the children would not have been committed."

It is in this group of 778 that the most fertile field for discharge was found. This on the whole, indicates the great necessity for much more careful case work prior to commitment.

Of the provision that should, at the time of the survey, be made for the discharged children, the report further says:

Of those who are to be discharged, it is likely that the pension afforded by the state can be made available for 161 children; that subsidy from family welfare societies will have to be granted on behalf of the families of 119 children; and that only 147 might be discharged forthwith without subsidy or pension.

The number of children to be discharged is considerably smaller proportionately than the number recommended in an earlier study made by the Bureau of Social Research, and would indicate the increasing effectiveness with respect to follow-up by the organizations themselves and the Clearing Bureau.

Two of the functions of the Clearing Bureau above mentioned had been to focus all available information on the problem of allocating each dependent child to the institution or placing agency best fitted to give the child the care individually needed, and also to stimulate the discharge of children from institutions and boarding foster homes as soon as home conditions and the welfare of the child would permit. Of some success in securing discharges, the survey itself bears witness as quoted above. Of at least an opportunity to allocate on the basis of each child's need, rather than on the basis of only one or two available places, the open doors in the Manhattan agencies and institutions at the time of the survey bear witness. Each of the two child-placing agencies was always able to receive children, and in the two largest institutions there were respectively 36 and 183 empty beds—the last number in a cottage institution of the highest grade.

Again, the survey states that out of 390 children within the institutions, who presented behavior problems of major importance at the time they were admitted, 286, or 73.3 percent after an average stay of 3.3 years still presented behavior problems of major importance. As to these children, the investigators were handicapped in their analysis of processes, and in their definition of problems, because of the insufficiency of data. The institutions, as a general thing, did not have for the entire period of the care of the child records that would indicate just what the problem was and what processes were being used to help in its solution.

Of the group of 235 children who were behavior problems at

the time they were admitted to the care of placing-out agencies, only 98 (41.7 percent) showed behavior problems of major importance after the three-year period. Summarizing the care of such children under either method, the report goes on to say:[45]

> As a whole it will be noted that the boarding bureaus show an appreciably better piece of work with respect to behavior problems and help in the solution of these problems than do the institutions. It will be recalled in our statement of principles we indicated that severe behavior problems should be boarded out. Of the institutions really at work on the situation there is notable work being done in both the Hebrew Orphan Asylum, and at Pleasantville (the Hebrew Sheltering Guardian Society—a high-grade cottage institution) through subjecting behavior problems in the institutions to psychiatric procedures. Whereas these experiments should be watched with considerable interest on the part of the community, it is doubtful whether it would not be very much better in the light of achievements already made through the boarding bureaus, in the light of the fact that the boarding bureaus proceed entirely on a case work basis which is the best in these problems, and in the light of similar experience in other communities and similar apparent results, to board out these children and not to make further investments in their institutional treatment.

VII. The Dependent Child's Challenge to the Reader

To the reader, the chief meaning of this brief summary of a few figures from the survey of Jewish Dependent Children in Greater New York lies, not in the figures themselves or in their actual percentage relationships. It lies rather in the effort being made by the whole Jewish group in the largest city of the United States to study the success already achieved in trying to suit the action to the need of "each dependent child," and to find a procedure for more successful future action in the same direction.

[45]The apparent, or possibly real, conflict between some of the foregoing statements and the opinions of Healy, Bronner, Baylor and Murphy, quoted on pp. 312-13 of this chapter, may be due to our present imperfect knowledge of the actual results, in terms of the after-lives of the children themselves, both of particular varieties of institutional care, and of varieties of foster family care.

In short, this survey comes right down to the very nub of the matter—that from the very beginning, we must learn how, with all the aid that medical, mental and social sciences can give us, to deal with "a total personality in a total situation" on the individual case work basis. And this involves, not only an initial analysis of what the child needs, but a record of every investigation and diagnosis, and of all the detailed processes of care, so that we can check the reactions of the child at every step. Only so can we ever learn, not merely that we succeed or fail in the care of dependent children, but why we succeed or fail. Into this realm of effort only a few have as yet even tried to enter.

Some day we shall also see that not only the dependent child and the child presenting what we call major behavior problems, but every child by virtue of being "a total personality in a total situation," also needs a similar individualized treatment. Toward such a stage in our processes of care for dependent children have we been slowly—how slowly—tending since the days of Queen Elizabeth. To speed up this process is everywhere today the one next great step. To this end, in ways that the institutions and agencies cited are already trying, and in new ways to be discovered by themselves, every institution and foster family agency in the land is challenged to do its bit.

And the task as a whole is much greater than that of providing care such as each child really needs who must have temporary or permanent substitutes for his own home. The job, as we have already implied, of giving care in substitute forms for the child's own home is inextricably enmeshed with the job of giving suitable care to children in homes where parental care must in some way be supplemented from the outside.

We cannot here discuss such supplementary help as is given by public health nurses, hospitals, visiting teachers, probation officers, and protective work based upon enforcement of laws against cruel treatment and neglect of children. But some attempt must be made at least to suggest the great number of children living, every day of the year, in that uncertain no man's land between the secure, self-supporting, and independent family home, and the definitely provided substitute foster home, or institution. On February 1, 1923, the official estimate of children in the United States under care away from their own homes, omitting delinquents but including those in day nurseries and almshouses, in round numbers, was 250,000.[46] On the same date, the estimate for children receiving public aid at home with their own mothers was 121,000. If to this number we add an estimate of the number of children in poor families receiving relief in their homes on any one day during 1923, namely, 220,000,[47] we get a total of 591,000. In other words, an army of approximately 600,000 children is on any one day, and every day, living either in homes that are in danger of breaking, or else in substitutes for home that have already broken. In all these cases, with the exception of the foundling and the "only child" who has lost both parents, to suit the action to the real needs of the child involves his family. In a literal sense "their whole families come with them." They must, and should, come with them. The community cannot keep its eyes shut to this fact.

From England, also, we have up-to-date testimony as to the much larger number of children who are dependent in their own supplement homes than of those who are cared for away in some substitute for their own homes. The implication is clear that in England the socially-minded public has centered its attention and constructive effort too exclusively upon the dependent child in isolation from his own family group.[48]

[46]United States census report, *Children under Institutional Care*, p. 14. The number cannot be accurately stated because of inclusion of dependents with adults and with delinquent children in the same institutions.

[47]See National Conference of Social Work, *Report* for 1926, "How Much Child Dependency Is There in the United States?", pp. 148-51. This article was prepared by Georgia G. Ralph and wrongly credited to the present writer who read it to the conference.

[48]Webb, Sidney and Beatrice, *English Local Government—English Poor Law History;* Part II, "The Last Hundred Years," London, 1927-1929, p. 246.

To any one who looks with fresh eyes at the problem of how best to treat the perpetually recruited pauper host, it is hard to explain the almost universal failure, decade after decade, to give any comprehensive consideration to what was, after all, numerically one of the largest sections of the host, and the one, as we now imagine, of greatest consequence for the future. At all times in England and Wales, in 1834 as in 1908, whether we take the number simultaneously relieved on any one day, or the number of separate individuals relieved in the course of a year, we have to face the melancholy fact that about one-third of the whole are children under sixteen years of age. In the course of the year 1907 there were found, by actual count, to be no fewer than 564,314 separate children under sixteen relieved as paupers at one time or another, out of a total of 1,709,436. . . .

Unfortunately practically all the writers have confined themselves to the fifty thousand or so of children maintained as indoor paupers, and mostly to such among these as are of school age. The case of infants in workhouses, and that of the hundreds of thousands of children on Outdoor Relief, were hardly ever mentioned in reports or books, and do not seem to have been comprehensively dealt with until the Poor Law Commission of 1905-09 (especially in minority report).

This undue emphasis upon the care of children away from the family group is still true in the United States. The disproportion between the care given to the individual child and the neglect of the home from which he springs, is noted in an eloquent comment found in an old report, and worth quoting here:[49]

It seems often *futile* to take from a man and a woman one set of children and in a few years' time to be called upon again to take from them another set of children which they have been allowed to bring into the same surroundings of squalor and crime. We must work through every known public and private agency and devise an intelligent and effective cooperation to attain our ends [italics by the present writer].

Futile, indeed, in 1906! Futile, indeed in 1930! For a characterization of this kind of futility, and for the enumeration of many in-

[49] *Annual Report* of the Massachusetts Society for Prevention of Cruelty to Children, 1906, pp. 5-6.

dustrial, civic, and social activities which should be active in every community to prevent dependency, neglect and delinquency of children, the incurably optimistic reader is referred to a critical address by the gentlest spoken, but at the same time the sternest prophet, among all the child welfare workers of this generation, J. Prentice Murphy.[50]

The biggest job yet ahead is to find ways by which to know the assets and to learn how best to make continued use of them; not alone of the assets within the child himself, but also those of his whole family situation. Merely to discount the liabilities in both is not enough. It will not do to go on assuming, as we have done too often hitherto, that all of these family and community situations out of which our dependent children come to us offer only liabilities for the real welfare and growth of the child and for the family as well.

So at the end of our story of *The Dependent Child,* we find the welfare of this child as truly conditioned by his membership in a particular family as it was conditioned by his feudal status at the beginning of the story. Historically we have seen the child, as a physical being, shaken loose from his family and from its manorial habitat. We have also seen many a child, as a physical person, shaken loose from his natural family and parental habitat in America. We have seen these children, as physical persons, dwelling in almshouses, indenture family homes, orphan asylums, free foster family homes, and boarding foster family homes. But we have not so clearly seen that they have always carried with them the characteristics of their physical and mental heredity, and the warp and woof of their emotional inheritance.

And now stand by the side of a father and a mother who together have passed on life to their children and who have been privileged to watch over them from infancy until they are about to leave the parental roof for what men call their own way in the

---

[50] "The Superficial Character of Child Caring Work," in *Proceedings of the National Conference of Social Work,* 1922, pp. 25-41.

world. Stand close by these parents, listen to what they have to say and, in your imagination, share with them their emotions:[51]

To sum up then, what a modern parent may desire for children. First of all the health which gives the vitality and beauty on which all their functions will be built; next an early training that will call out in them friendliness, courage in thought and action, sensitiveness to love, to beauty, and the happiness of others; and a life which, by providing few but right outlets for fear and its correlative rage, will lead to the easy abandonment of the baser passions. Finally that their minds be filled with the visions of scientific and artistic achievement, inspired and tuned to understanding of human life by literature and poetry. Once their character has taken shape, let them know all that man is capable of, not only his heroisms, but his crimes, hypocrisies, his pitiful follies. Let there be no Achilles' heel of ignorance and repression through which lust for wealth or power or cruelty may enter to poison and corrupt the personality. So equipped, so armed, so adorned, pennants flying, sails swelling, bows lifting in eager pride, they glide to the launching, they the ark of our deliverance, the argosy of our adventure. Breathless in heart and body with the effort of creation, trembling with hope for their achievement and fear of their disaster, we watch, till life and vision fail us, their gallant progress towards the uncharted seas.

What is the child, any child, that we should draw upon all the resources of modern philanthropy and science for his sake, fill voluminous records with his individual histories and spend millions of dollars on his behalf in undertakings that are still inadequate to his needs? Why are we striving to "suit the action to the individual needs of the child?" Why do we quote the latest phrases of the psychologists and psychiatrists in our effort to comprehend the single least-favored child in our midst? Of what concern is it to us that we should see him "as a total personality in a total situation?"

In answer to such questions as to the value of a child, as to what a child really is, of the contribution from heredity and from his parents as companions, of the attitude of welcome that should be

[51]Mrs. Bertrand Russell in *The Right To Be Happy,* New York, 1927, pp. 238-39.

his at birth, of the possible influence of the child upon the world, and of our part in shaping that influence for good or ill, let the Prophet and the poets speak:

The Prophet says:[52]

It is not the will of your Father which is in heaven, that one of these little ones should perish.

The poet says:[53]

There was a child went forth every day,
And the first object he looked upon, that object he became,
And that object became part of him for the day or a certain part of the day,
Or for many years or stretching cycles of years.
. . . .
His own parents, he that fathered him and she that had conceived him in her womb and birthed him,
They gave this child more of themselves than that,
They gave him afterward every day, they became part of him,
The mother at home quietly placing the dishes on the supper table,
The mother with mild words, clean her cap and gown, a wholesome odor falling off her person as she walks by,
The father, strong, self-sufficient, manly, mean, angered, unjust,
The blow, the quick loud word, the tight bargain, the crafty lure,
The family usages, the language, the company, the furniture, the yearning, swelling heart,
Affection that will not be gainsay'd, the sense of what is real, the thought if after all it should prove unreal,
The doubts of day-time and the doubts of night-time, the curious whether and how.
. . . .
These become part of that child who went forth every day, and who now goes, and will always go forth every day.

[52]Matthew 18:14.
[53]Walt Whitman, "There Was a Child Went Forth," in *Leaves of Grass*.

Another poet says, as he welcomes his own child at birth and tries to express in words the meaning of a new child in the world:[54]

> Out of the deep, my child, out of the deep
> . . . Thou comest . . . .
> This main miracle that thou art thou,
> With power on thine own act and on the world.

So to the reader we refer something of the future welfare of the dependent child, and of all children. For to each child are we daily referring matters of unknown importance in every community of this our world. And of all that we do or fail to do for this child with power on his own act and on the world will it always remain true:

> These become part of that child who went forth every day, and who now goes, and will always go forth every day.

[54] Tennyson, *De Profundis*—The Two Greetings.

BIBLIOGRAPHY

References in footnotes to letters, unpublished surveys and reports which are available to the reader only by private arrangement with the author, the agency or the person quoted, are not as a rule included.

ASCHROTT, PRESTON-THOMAS, AND HENRY SIDGWICK, *The English Poor Law System*, London, 1902.

BIRDSEYE, CUMMING AND GILBERT, *Consolidated Laws of New York*, 1909. Volume 4.

BOSTON CHILDREN'S AID SOCIETY, *Annual Reports*, 1864, 1865, 1866, 1867, 1868, 1873, 1879, 1884, 1885, 1886, 1887, 1888, 1890, 1892, 1893, 1896, 1900, 1901, 1903, 1905, 1911.

———*Boston Children's Aid Society, Its Origin and Objects*, Special leaflet.

———*Boston Female Orphan Asylum, Reminiscences of*, Boston, 1844. Anniversary Sermons.

BOSTON SOCIETY FOR THE CARE OF GIRLS, *One Hundred Years of Work in Boston*, Boston, 1919.

BRACE, CHARLES LORING, *The Dangerous Classes in New York*, New York, 1880.

BRACE, EMMA, *The Life of Charles Loring Brace*, New York, 1894.

BRECKINRIDGE, S. P., *Public Welfare Administration in the United States, Select Documents*, Chicago University Press, 1927.

BRUCE, PHILIP ALEXANDER, *Economic History of Virginia in the Seventeenth Century*, New York, 1896. (Quoted from the *Records of Henrico County 1677-1692*, p. 424, Virginia State Library.)

BUREAU OF JEWISH SOCIAL RESEARCH, Child Care Section of an Unpublished Jewish Community Survey of Greater New York, 1928.

BUTLER, AMOS W., *Indiana—A Century of Progress. A Study of the Development of Public Charities and Corrections 1790, 1915*, prepared for the Indiana Board of State Charities. Ed. 31. Indianapolis, 1916.

CANADIAN COUNCIL OF CHILD WELFARE, *Juvenile Immigration*, Reports numbers 1 and 2, Ottawa, 1925.

———*Several Years After*, Publication No. 39, Ottawa, 1928.

CANADA, *Social Science Council of Canada's Child Immigrants*, Ottawa, 1925.

NEW YORK STATE BOARD OF CHARITIES, *Charity Legislation in New York 1609-1900*. Vol. III. *Annual Report*, 1903.

CHILD WELFARE LEAGUE OF AMERICA, unpublished reports of surveys, New York.

COIT HOUSE, *Annual Report*, Concord, N. H., 1926.

COOPER, JOHN M., "Directions for Investigation of Catholic Institutions for Dependent Children," in *Annual Report, National Conference of Catholic Charities*, 1928.

ENDERS, GEORGE C., [Statement of Christian standard of Child Welfare work.] *Christianity and Social Adventuring*, The Century Co., New York, 1927.

ENGLAND, *Report of Ministry of Health. Persons in Receipt of Poor Relief* (England and Wales), London, 1923.

———*Report of Poor Law Commission*, 1834.

FLEISCHMAN, S. M., *The History of Jewish Foster Home and Orphan Asylum Society of Philadelphia, 1855–1905*, Philadelphia, 1919.

FOLKS, HOMER, *Care of Destitute, Neglected and Delinquent Children*, New York, Edition of 1911.

GREGG, REV. E. M., Article on the early purposes of Mr. Van Arsdale in care of dependent children, in *Annual Report of the National Conference of Charities and Correction*, 1892.

HART, HASTINGS H., Article in *Annual Report of National Conference of Charities and Corrections*, 1884.

HEALY, BRONNER, BAYLOR, AND MURPHY, *Reconstructing Behavior in Youth*, New York and London, 1929.

HEBREW SHELTERING GUARDIAN SOCIETY, *Home Finder*, New York, January and February, 1928.

HOPKIRK, H. W., Article in *Child Welfare League Bulletin*, December, 1928.

JAMISON, A. T., "Connie Maxwell," in *The Monthly Bulletin of the Connie Maxwell Orphanage*, Greenwood, S. C., April, 1929.

JOHNSON, ALEXANDER, *The Almshouse*, Russell Sage Foundation, New York, 1911.

KESLER, M. L., *Mother's Aid, Thomasville Baptist Orphanage*, Thomasville, N. C., 1927.

———"Description of changes in the Thomasville Baptist Orphanage, Thomasville, N. C." In *Annual Report*, 1923.

KELSO, ROBERT W., *History of Public Poor Relief in Massachusetts, 1620-1920*, Boston, 1922.

LANGER, SAMUEL, Article in *Annual Report of Homewood Terrace*, San Francisco, 1922.

LEONARD, *Early History of English Poor Relief*, Cambridge University Press, 1900.

BIBLIOGRAPHY 327

LETCHWORTH, WM. PRYOR, "Orphan Asylums and Other Institutions for the Care of Children," in *New York State Board of Charities Report*, Albany, 1876.

LEWISOHN, ADOLPH, Article in *Report of Child Welfare Conference of the Child Welfare Committee of America*, New York, 1925.

MASSACHUSETTS STATE BOARD OF CHARITIES, *Annual Reports*, 1865, 1867, 1868, 1885.

MASSACHUSETTS SOCIETY FOR THE PREVENTION OF CRUELTY TO CHILDREN. *Annual Report*, 1906; *Annual Report*, 1927.

MCCLAIN, ESTHER, *Child Placing in Ohio*. Division of Charities, Ohio Department of Public Welfare, Columbus, 1928.

MCDONNELL, CLARA J., *Adoption Practices in Allegheny and Twelve Other Counties of Pennsylvania*, Carnegie Institute of Technology, Pittsburgh, 1925.

MERRILL, G. A., "State Public Schools for Dependent and Neglected Children," in *Report of Committee on History of Child Saving*, 1893. (A special volume of the National Conference of Charities and Corrections.)

MULLAN, REV. JAMES M. AND H. W. HOPKIRK, "Study of the work for Dependent Children (Orphan Homes) under the Auspices of the Reformed Church in the United States," in *The Social Service Commission of the Reformed Church*, Philadelphia, 1929.

MURPHY, J. PRENTICE, Article in *Annual Report of the Boston Children's Aid Society*, 1912.

———"A Study of Results of Child Placing," in *Annual Report, National Conference of Charities and Corrections*, 1915.

———"The Superficial Character of Child Caring Work," in *Proceedings of the National Conference of Social Work*, 1922.

NEW HAVEN, CONN., *Annual Report of The Children's Community Center*, 1928.

NEW YORK CHILDREN'S AID SOCIETY, *Annual Reports*, 1854, 1856, 1859, 1863, 1864, 1870, 1898, 1919, 1923.

———Special Circular, 1854 [?].

NEW YORK ORPHAN ASYLUM SOCIETY IN THE CITY OF NEW YORK, *Origin and History*, New York, 1896.

NEW YORK STATE ASSEMBLY, *Journal*, February 9, 1824.

NEW YORK STATE BOARD OF CHARITIES, *Annual Reports*, 1868, 1875, 1900, 1903.

NEW YORK STATE CHARITIES AID ASSOCIATION, *News*, November, 1927.

NEW YORK STATE SENATE, *Document No. 8*, 1857.

New England Historical and Geneological Register, Vol. XXXIV., Boston, 1880.

NEW ENGLAND HOME FOR LITTLE WANDERERS, Unpublished Manuscripts by Rev. Edward C. Winslow, *How It Came To Be What It Is, and How They Did It*, Boston, 1929.

———*Advocate*, Boston, June, 1922 and September, 1929.

NICHOLL, R. G., *History of the English Poor Law*, New York, 1898.

NORTHERN HOME FOR FRIENDLESS CHILDREN, *Annual Report*, Philadelphia, 1839.

PARKER, IDA R., *Fit and Proper*, Church Home Society, Boston, 1927.

PENNSYLVANIA BUREAU OF CHILDREN, DEPARTMENT OF PUBLIC WELFARE, "Hello Central" in *Bulletin*, February 1926 and October 1927, Harrisburg, Pa.

PHILIPSON, *Letters of Rebecca Gratz*, Philadelphia, 1929.

Psychiatric Clinics for Children in the United States, Directory of. Second Edition, Commonwealth Fund Division of Publications, New York, 1928.

PUBLIC CHARITIES OF PENNSYLVANIA, *Almshouse Child*, Philadelphia, 1924.

RALPH, GEORGIA G., Manuscript Report of Study of Records of New York Children's Aid Society, 1853-1922.

———[Wrongly credited to Henry W. Thurston] "How Much Child Dependency Is There in the United States?" in *Annual Report, National Conference of Social Work*, 1928.

REEDER, R. R., Article in *Charities and Commissions*, 1903-1908. Vols. XI-XIX.

———*How Two Hundred Children Live and Learn*, New York.

———Article in *The Survey*, April and October, 1925, and January, 1929. New York.

RHODE ISLAND CHILDREN'S FRIEND SOCIETY, *Annual Report*, 1928.

RICHMOND, MARY E., *Social Diagnosis*, Russell Sage Foundation, New York, 1917.

———*What Is Social Case Work?* Russell Sage Foundation, New York, 1922.

ROBINSON, M. F., *Poor Law Enigma*, London, 1911.

RUSSELL, MRS. BERTRAND, *The Right To Be Happy*, New York, 1927.

SAVAGE, REV. E. P., Article in *Home Finder of Minnesota*, 1904. (Organ. of the Minnesota Home Finding Society.)

SMITH, VIRGINIA I., Article in *Report of the Committee on History of Child Saving*, 1893. (A special volume of the National Conference of Charities and Corrections.)

Social Service Review, "An Early Experiment in Child Placing." University of Chicago Press, June 1929.

BIBLIOGRAPHY

TOWLE, CHARLOTTE, Abstract of paper on "Evaluation of Homes for Child Placement," in *Annual Report of National Conference of Social Work*, 1927. In full in *Bulletin of the National Committee for Mental Hygiene*, 1929.

UNITED STATES CENSUS [report], *Children under Institutional Care*, 1923.

———*Paupers in Almshouses*, 1923.

UNITED STATES CHILDREN'S BUREAU, *Importation of Dependent Children*.

———Publication 150, *Children Indentured by the Wisconsin Public School*.

WEBB, SIDNEY AND BEATRICE, "English Local Government," *Poor Law History*, Part II, "The Last Hundred Years," New York and London, 1929.

WHITE HOUSE CONFERENCE, THE FIRST, "On the Care of Dependent Children," in *Proceedings*, Washington, D. C., 1909.

———THE SECOND, *On the Care of Dependent Children*, United States Children's Bureau, Publication No. 62, Washington, D. C., 1919.

———THE THIRD, *On Child Health and Protection*, November, 1930.

INDEX

Adler, Dr. Herman, 199
Adoptions, low standards of, in Massachusetts, 232 ff; in New York, 234; in Pennsylvania, 236
Aim diversifies work, 187 ff
Allocation of children in England in 1923, 251 f
Almshouse and indentured children in Massachusetts, 161 f
Almshouse for children in England, 27 f, 243 f
Almshouse for children in United States, 28 ff, 204 ff
Almshouse for dependent children recommended in New York, 1824, 19 ff
Almshouses, growth of, 89; persistence of, 89
American Educational Aid Society, Origin and purpose of, 146 f
American Legion, program of, viii
Apprentice, in 1601, in England, 7; of dependent child in Massachusetts, 1747, 15 f. *See also* Indenture
Aschrott, Preston Thomas, and Sidgwick, 7

Baker Foundation, *see* Judge Baker Foundation
Barnardo, Homes, 252 f
Battis, Roy James, 297
Baylor, Edith M. H., 198, 264, 313, 317
Begging in England, 5
Behavior Clinic of New England, Home for Little Wanderers, 275 f
Behavior Clinics, essential conditions of, 276 f
Birdseye, Cumming and Gilbert, 35 f
Birtwell, Charles W., 161-201; aim of, first stated, 185 f, 194 f; as seen by a Board member, 181 f; attitude of, toward use of kinship assets, 191 f; comes to Boston Children's Aid Society, 179 f; comparison of work of, with that of Brace and of Van Arsdale, 161, 259; early methods of, in investigation of foster homes, 188 ff; how Boston task looked to him at first, 183 ff; looks back upon work, 196 f; slogans by, 185 f, 196 f

Black death in England, 4 ff
Blind, segregation of, 36, 87
Boarding-out, beginnings of by Boston Children's Aid Society, 174 f, 178; lack of, in the United States (Charts), 236 f; in England, 248 f; in Massachusetts, beginnings of, 169 f
Boretz, Mary E., 301
Boston, child emigration from, 108 f
Boston Children's Aid Society, origin and object of, 170 ff; research by, 262 ff; self-criticism by, 261 ff
Boston Female Orphan Asylum, indenture from, 57 ff; origin of, 54 f; song for annual meeting of, 56 f; children in, 170 f
Boys, eight to ten, perplexing, 174
Brace, Charles Loring, Jr., fulfills father's work, 139; starts boarding-out by New York Children's Aid Society, 139 f; study of placed-out children by, 131; succeeded father, 131
Brace, Charles Loring, Sr., 92-160; choice of life work by, 95 f; comparison of work of, with that of Birtwell and Van Arsdale, 161, 243, 259; education of, 93 f; criticism of child placement by, 123 ff; first appeal by, 100 ff; instructions to visitors by, 113 ff; origin of methods of, 113; reaction to criticisms by, 128 ff; travels of, 94 f; vow of, 94
Brace, Emma, 92
Breaking up of families, 213, 224, 225, 229, 230
Bronner, Augusta, 198, 264, 313, 317
Bruce, Philip Alexander, 15
Bureau of Jewish Social Research in New York, 314 ff
Butler, Amos W., 63

Carstens, C. C., 226 ff
Case conferences, beginnings of, in Boston Children's Aid Society, 195
Case records for foster home children in Massachusetts, beginnings of, 163 f
Case work, ideal of, in the air in Boston in 1886, 186

INDEX

Case worker, essentials of, 285 ff; value of, 277 ff
Catholic Protectory of New York, 124 ff
Certified Homes and Schools in England, 248
Charity, 6
Charts showing distribution of dependent children away from their own homes, February 1, 1923, 236 f
Chicago Juvenile Court, clinic in, 273
Child dependency: how much in United States, 319; in England, 320
Child, dependent, challenge to the reader, by, 317 ff; meaning of the story of, 198 ff; under feudalism, 2 f; under slavery, 1 f. *See also* Indenture.
Child life, in mixed almshouses, 27 ff
Child-placement, pioneer, in southern Illinois, 151 ff
Child-placing, by State of Ohio, 292 ff
Child, use and development of assets in own family, 191 f
Child, what does he need?, 185 f, 196 f
Child Welfare League of America, 216, 218, 222, 223, 224, 226, 229, 230, 231, 232, 267, 271, 276, 281, 288
Children, born out of wedlock, 224 ff, 231 ff
Children in almshouses, 1880-1923, 37
Children, different needs of, recognized, 177 f
Children in an Orphan Asylum, Woman who was neighbor to, 82 ff
Children, in mixed almshouses of the United States, 28 ff
Children, levels of care for,
Children, reasons for placement of, in orphan asylums, 40, 86
Children under institutional care in 1923, United States Census report, 39 f, 87, 236 ff
Children, vagrant in New York in the fifties, 96 f
Children's Aid Society, responsibility of, to the community, 193
Children's Community Center of New Haven, 279 f
Cincinnati Orphan Asylum in 1835, song sung by the orphans in, 59
Cincinnati Orphan Asylum, 271
Clinics, psychiatric, 272
Cobb, Dorothy C., 274
Coit, Henry A., 278
Coit, House, transitions in, 278 f

Community effort, orchestration of, 312 ff
Community, responsibility of a children's aid society to, 192 f
Connecticut County Homes, origin of, 62 f
Cook, Rufus R, "Uncle Cook" of Boston, 172 ff, 175 ff
Cooper, Dr. John M., 265 f
Connie Maxwell Orphanage, 285 ff
County Children's Homes: in Connecticut, 62 f; in Ohio, 294 f
County Courts and Supervisors in Illinois, social investigations by, 225 ff
County Child Welfare Boards in Ohio, 294 f
Courage, Needed to answer questions, What does the child need?, 194
Deaf, segregation of, 36, 87
Dependency, child: how much in England, 320; in United States, 319

Dependent Child, Challenge to the reader by, 317 ff; meaning of the story of, 198 ff; nature of problem, 9
Dependent Children, segregation of, from Mixed Almshouses in England and United States, *see* children, dependent, 88
Dewey, John, 271
District Schools in England, 88, 245
Dusty answer, 311

Eaton, Benjamin, indenture of, in 1636, 15
Elizabeth, Queen, 4
Emigration of dependent children westward, 92-160
Enders, George C., 264
Evans, Mrs. Eva L., 146
England, adoption of infants in, 254 f; allocation of Children in 1923, 251 f; boarding out in, 248 f; certified homes and schools in, 248; district school in, 245 f; farm school in, 245 f; grouped cottages in, 246; indenture in, 250 f; "ins and outs" in, 251; persistence of work house care in, 249 f; scattered homes in, 246 ff; trends in, 255 ff; trends in, since 1834, 243 ff; work house school in, 244 f

Farming-out in 1601, 7, 24
Feeble-minded, segregation of, 36, 87

INDEX

Fernald, Dr. Walter, 36
Feudal care, first substitute for, 3 f
Feudal order passing of, in England, 4 ff
Feudalism, dependent child under, 2 f
Fleischman, S. M., 66
Folks, Homer, vii, 36 f, 40, 86, 88
Forty-third act of Elizabeth, 4 ff; summary of, 7
Foster home and institutional care of Jewish children in New York, 314 ff; finding in Boston, early, 176
Foster mother, standards of foster home care by, 300 ff
Foundling Hospital of London, 253 f
Free foster home, placement method in, limitations of, 134 ff

Gallub, Pauline, 66
Goddard, Henry H., 274
Gratz, Rebecca, as prototype of Scott's Rebecca in Ivanhoe, 66
Gregg, Rev. F. M., 149
Grouped Cottages in England, 246

Hamilton, Mrs. Alexander, 42
Harrisburg, Pa., self-criticism in institution of, 280 f
Hart, Dr. Hastings H., description of child emigrants in Ohio by, 107 f; study of placed-out children in Minnesota in 1884 by, 114 ff, 124, 132; superintendent of Illinois Children's Home and Aid Society, 152, 155 f, 226, 297
Hartley, Robert M., 98
Healy, Dr. William, 198, 264, 272 f, 313, 317
Hebrew Orphan Asylum of New York, 68
Hebrew Sheltering, Guardian Society, cost of, 266; origin of, 68 f
Hello Central, 207, 219
Henry VIII, 6
Henry, E. J., Autobiography of, 77 ff
Home level, permanent substitute for, Introduction, 8
Home Library, beginning of, by Boston Children's Aid Society, 177
Homewood Terrace, transitions in, 289 ff
Hopkirk, H. W., 267, 287
Hoover, George K., as superintendent of Illinois Society, 152

How can I start from where I now am?, 202
How Two Hundred Children Live and Learn, 53
Hoyt, Charles A., 30 ff
Hurd, Hon. Harvey B., 152

Illinois Children's Home and Aid Society, 140-60; innovations in, by Dr. Hart, 155 f; progress of, under Mr. Reynolds, 157; steps in development of, taken by the writer, 156; study of intake of, in 1921, 225 ff; transition in, recent, 297 ff
Indenture, as a step forward, 10 ff; abuses of, in Massachusetts, in 1844, 57 ff, in 1867-68, 163 ff; as stimulus to overwork a child, 210 f; by Boston Children's Aid Society, 171; contract of, used in Wisconsin in 1923, 209 f; experiences of children under in Wisconsin, 211 ff; for young children, 10 f; form and Spirit of, 92; in American Colonies, 12 ff; in 1844, as a Hudson River farmer saw it, 18; in England, 250 f; purposes of, 12; in Massachusetts, in 1636, 13, in 1747, 15 f; in Virginia, 1686, 14 f; origin and nature of, 10 ff; questions raised by practise of, in Wisconsin, 214; reasons for repealing indenture laws in Pennsylvania in 1927, 207 f; revolving fund for, in 1609-14, 10 f; tendency of effect of, on dependent child, 16 f
Independent home levels, xiii
Indiana, County Homes in, 63 f
Indianapolis Orphan Asylum, boarding foster home care by, 299 f
Infant adoption in England, 254 f
"Ins and Outs" in England, 251
Institution, conglomerate population in an, 222 f
Institutional and foster home care of Jewish children in New York City, 314 ff
Institutional Substitutes for the mixed Almshouse in the United States Summary, 86 ff
Institutions for children in 1800, 40
Investigation of foster homes, early method of, by Birtwell, 188 ff
Is it I?, 203
Ives, L. Silliman, 126 f

Jamison, Dr. A. T., 285
Jesus, 197, 323
Jewish Foster Home and Orphan Asylum in Philadelphia, motto of, 66; origin of, 66 ff
Jewish Survey in New York, 313 ff
Johnson, Alexander, 27
Johnson, William L., 138
Jones, Cheney C., 279
Judge Baker Foundation, 190
Justices of the peace in England, in 1601, 7

Kesler, M. L., 281 f
Kelso, Robert W., 13 f
Kids with fathers and mothers have the edge on us, 241 f
Kimbark Family, 304 ff
Klein, Philip, viii
Knight, Rev. Frederic, 273 f, 276, 278

Labaree, Mary S., 219
Laws, Elizabethan, 8
Lawton, Ruth, 263
Leonard, 14
Letchworth, William P., 32 f
Levels of care of children, xiii
Lewisohn, Adolph, 266
London, Foundling Hospital of, 253 f
Lord of the Manor, 2 f
Lowe, Moses, indentured as an infant, 15 f
Lynn, Dr. L. Ross, 288 f

Manor in England, 2 f
Massachusetts, low standards of adoption in, 232 ff
Massachusetts State Board of Charities, beginnings of case records of, 167 f; work of, for almshouse and indentured children, 161 ff; work of State Agent of, 163 ff
McClain, Esther, 64, 215, 238, 292, 296
McDonnell, Clara Josephine, 236
Medical Care in Thornwell Orphanage, 288 f
Merrill, G. A., 65
Meaning of the Story of the Dependent Child, 198 ff
Measuring rod, the, in Pennsylvania Institutions, 219 ff
Michigan, origin of state public school, 65 f; transitions in, 298 f
Mixed workhouse, 8
Monasteries, 6

Money Economy, 4 f
Murphy, J. Prentice, 198, 261, 263 f, 313, 317, 321

Nancy T——, 303, 310
National Children's Home and Welfare Association, 140 f; members of in 1923, 158; questions for, 159 f
National Conference of Charities and Corrections, *Special Report* of, 1893, 63
Negro Children, 1
New England Home for Little Wanderers, early placement and publicity methods of, 108 ff; transitions in, 273 ff
New occasions teach new duties, ix
New Orleans Jewish Orphans Home, 68
New York Children's Aid Society, p. nos., 92 ff; changes in attitude of, toward kinship ties, 303 ff; changes in methods of, as result of self-criticism, 137 ff; criticism of emigration work of, 123 ff; distribution of children in states by, 121 ff; forms of work started by, 99 f; magnitude of emigration work of, 121; stories of first placements of children by, 102 ff; stories by men placed by, as boys, in the West, 116 ff
New York Catholic Protectory, 124 ff
New York City, facilities for care of destitute children in 1853, 97 f; schools of, 1853, 97; vagrant children in, 96 f
New York Colored Orphan Asylum, origin and purposes of, 60 f
New York Juvenile Asylum, 98; story of boy placed in West by, 118, ff
New York, low standard of adoptions in, 234
New York Orphan Asylum Society of New York, Cottage Home at Hastings, 53; first building of, 42 ff; health problems in, 52 f; housekeeping of, 43 f; indenture from 45 f; intake and care of children by, 45 ff; life in, as told by a former inmate, 50 f; origin of, 41 f; religious teaching in, 47; second site and building of, 49 f; song sung by children at public meetings, 51 f; story by man placed by, as boy in the West, 116 ff

INDEX

New York State Senate, *Document No. 8,* 1857, 28 ff
Nicholls, R. G., 11, 27
Northern Home for Friendless Children in Philadelphia, origin of, 61 f
Northrup, Rev. Cyrus, 149

O'Boyle, Rev. Patrick A., 124
Ohio, County Child Welfare Boards of, 294; first County Children's Home in, 64 f; transitions in, 292 ff; trends and goals in, 296 f
One hundred years' work in Boston, 54
Orchestration of community effort, 312 ff
Orphan asylums, as a step forward in child care, 39-91; auspices of, 86 f; growth of, 90; of New Haven, 279 f; stimulus to build, 90
Orphan Asylum Children, woman who was neighbor to, 82 ff
Orphan Asylum Inmates, autobiographies by, 69 ff, 71 ff, 77 ff
Other side of the fence, 82 ff
Outdoor relief in 1601, 7
Overseers of Poor, Parish, 7

Paine, Robert Treat, 182
Palmer, Professor Herbert, 181
Parable of the Sower, 196 f
Parker, Colonel Francis W., 271 f
Parker, Ida R., 233
Paupers in Almshouses, United States Census report, 1923, 19, 37 f
Peabody, Professor Francis G., 181
Peasant upon the Manor, 2
Pennsylvania, low standards of adoption in, 236
Perkins Institution for the Blind, 36
Permanent substitute for Home Level, xiv-xv, 8
Personality, A total in a total situation, 199
Philipson, 66
Pine Farm of Boston Children's Aid Society, 171, 175, 180, 194
Placing children in almshouses, revolt against, 35 ff
Planlessness, 223
Poor, auction of, in New York in 1824, 21; classes of, in England in 1601, 7; classes of, in New York in 1824, 21; methods of care of, in New York in 1824, 21 f

Poor Houses in England, in 1601, 7; in other states than New York, in 1924, 23
Poor Law Commission, English, 1834, 27
Poor relief a public concern, 7
Probation in Boston in 1866, 173
Psychiatric clinics, 272
Public School state, in Michigan, 36
Purposes, three life; Brace, 93 f; Birtwell, 185 f; Van Arsdale, 142
Put yourself in the child's place, 237 ff

Queries for the reader, xvi-xvii, 159 f, 194, 260, 322 f
Quest for certainty, 311
Quinlan, Gertrude, 65

Ralph, Georgia G., viii, 121, 319; Study of records of New York Children's Aid Society by, 132 ff
Receiving Homes for Illinois child placement work, 148
Reader, Queries for, Introduction, 159 f, 194, 260, 322 f
Reeder, Dr. R. R., 53 f
Reformed Church Program of 266 ff
Research by Boston Children's Aid Society, 262 ff
Retrospect and Questions 258 ff
Reynolds, Wilfred S., 226, 229
Rhode Island, Children's Friend Society, 282 ff
Richmond, Mary E., 272
Robinson, M. F., 250
Rochester Orphan Asylum, 82 ff
Rogers, Annette P., 182
Roman Catholic Church, 6
Russell, Mrs. Bertrand, 322

Sadler, Lillian, 60
Savage, Rev. E. P., 144 f, 147
Scattered Homes in England, 246 ff
Schools of New York in 1853, 97
Selectmen in Massachusetts, 1747, 15
Self-criticism in Boston Children's Aid Society, 261 ff
Separate Schools in England, 88
Settlement, legal: defined, 13; difficulties over, in New York in 1824, 22 f; illustrations of, 13 f; laws concerning, 32
Shaw, M. Louisa, Legacy from, to Boston Children's Aid Society, 178
Sheffield Union, in England, 246 ff

Slavery, dependent child under, 1 f
Social service, inadequate, 222, 230, 232; needed at front door of institutions, 223
Society for the Relief of Widows with Small Children, 1797, 40 ff
Staigg, R. M., 182
Standards of foster home care by foster mothers, 300 ff
State Children's Home Societies, beginning and development of, 140 ff; extension and purposes of, 149 f
Steinhausen, Mrs. Theodore, 82
Stoneman, Albert H., 298
Stories by New York boys placed in the West, 116 ff
Substitutes for home levels, xiv-xv
Supervision, beginnings of personal, by Boston Children's Aid Society, 176 ff, 192; of placed-out children by correspondence not adequate, 129 f, 162, 180
Supplemented home level, 8
Survey, Jewish in New York, 313 ff
Survivals, (of Outworn attitudes and methods, 202-242); in a city in a West South Central State, 224; in a city in a Pacific State, 222 f; in a city of a West North Central State, 223; in a county of an East North Central State, 223 f; in a Mountain State, 229 f; in a Pacific State, 230; in a school for delinquent girls in a South Atlantic State, 216; in a South Atlantic State, 230 f; in a West North Central State, 232; in an institution in a North Central; in an institution in a South Central State, 217 f; in an institution of a South Atlantic State, 218 f; in an Ohio County Children's Home, 215; in Pennsylvania institutions in 1926, Recreation, etc.; of almshouse care in the United States, 204; of almshouse care in Pennsylvania, in 1921 and 1923, 204, 206, 207; of indenture until 1927 in Pennsylvania, 207 f; of indenture in Wisconsin in 1923, 208 ff; Recreation, 221; State Law and standards, 221; Social service and record keeping, 221; in institutions of Pennsylvania, sanitation, 220; health, 220; diet, 220; education, 220

Taylor, Ethel, viii, p. 110
Temporary substitutes for home level, 8
Thornwell Orphanage, 287 ff
Thurston, Charlotte S., viii
Towle, Charlotte, 277
Timpson, Margaret, 253
Transitions toward better attitudes and methods, Ch. X; in attitudes toward kinship ties, in New York Children's Aid Society, 303 ff; in Boston Children's Aid Society, 261 ff; in Catholic Studies, 265 f; in Coit House, 278 f; in Connie Maxwell Orphanage, 285 ff; in Illinois, 297 f; in Harrisburg, Pa., 280 f; in Homewood Terrace, 288 ff; in Indianapolis Orphan Asylum, 299 ff; in Michigan, 298 ff; in New England Home for Little Wanderers, 273 f; in New Haven, Orphan Asylum, 278 ff; in Ohio, 292 ff; in a Protestant denominational program, 264 ff; in Rhode Island, 282 ff; in Thomasville Baptist Orphanage, 281 f; in Thornwell Orphanage, 287 ff
Trends and goals in Ohio, 296 f
Trends in England, since 1834, 243-257; summary of, 255 ff

Union, poor law in England, 8
United States Census report, 1923, 237
United States Children's Bureau, 208, 209, 211 ff

Vagrant Children in New York in the Fifties, 96 f
Van Arsdale, Martin Van Buren, 140 ff, 243, 259, 297; and almshouse children, 142 f; and Mr. Birtwell, 161; and Mr. Brace, 161, 163; and American Educational Aid Association or Society, 146 ff; and National Children's Home Society, 147; first child taken by, 144 f; poverty of, in first years of child placement, 148; revelation of method to, 142 f; vow of, 142; work for Evanston Industrial School for Girls, 143
Villein upon the manor, 2
Vows, slogans and purposes, 93 f, 142, 187 f
Van Arsdale, Mrs. Martin Van Buren, information by, 141 ff

Wandering in England, 5
Washburn, Miss, Visitor for Boston Children's Aid Society, 180 ff
Webb, Sidney and Beatrice, 243 ff, 319
What is a child?, 322, 324
What is the present?, Preface, 258
White House Conference, First, 272; Second, 272; Third, viii
White list of institutions in Pennsylvania, 219 ff
Whitman, A. F., 264
Widow's Pension, 274
Wilcox, Mrs. A. M., story of pioneer child placement in Egypt, southern Illinois, 151 ff
Williams, C. V., 293, 297
Winslow, Rev. Edward C., 108 ff
Woman who was neighbor to children in an Orphan Asylum, 82 ff
Workhouse care of infants in England, persistence of, 249 f
Workhouse in Bristol, England, 1697, 8
Workhouse School in England, 244 f

Yates, Philosophy of, in 1824, 25
Yates, *Report*, 1824, in New York, quoted, 19 ff

Care of Handicapped Children. Introduction by Robert H. Bremner. 1974

[Chenery, William L. and Ella A. Merritt, editors]. **Standards of Child Welfare:** A Report of the Children's Bureau Conferences, May and June, 1919. 1919

The Child Labor Bulletin, 1912, 1913. 1974

Children In Confinement. Introduction by Robert M. Mennel. 1974

Children's Bureau Studies. Introduction by William M. Schmidt. 1974

Clopper, Edward N. **Child Labor in City Streets.** 1912

David, Paul T. **Barriers To Youth Employment.** 1942

Deutsch, Albert. **Our Rejected Children.** 1950

Drucker, Saul and Maurice Beck Hexter. **Children Astray.** 1923

Duffus, R[obert] L[uther] and L. Emmett Holt, Jr. **L. Emmett Holt:** Pioneer of a Children's Century. 1940

Fuller, Raymond G. **Child Labor and the Constitution.** 1923

Holland, Kenneth and Frank Ernest Hill. **Youth in the CCC.** 1942

Jacoby, George Paul. **Catholic Child Care in Nineteenth Century New York:** With a Correlated Summary of Public and Protestant Child Welfare. 1941

Johnson, Palmer O. and Oswald L. Harvey. **The National Youth Administration.** 1938

The Juvenile Court. Introduction by Robert M. Mennel. 1974

Klein, Earl E. **Work Accidents to Minors in Illinois.** 1938

Lane, Francis E. **American Charities and the Child of the Immigrant:** A Study of Typical Child Caring Institutions in New York and Massachusetts Between the Years 1845 and 1880. 1932

The Legal Rights of Children. Introduction by Sanford N. Katz. 1974

Letchworth, William P[ryor]. **Homes of Homeless Children:** A Report on Orphan Asylums and Other Institutions for the Care of Children. [1903]

Lorwin, Lewis. **Youth Work Programs:** Problems and Policies. 1941

Lundberg, Emma O[ctavia] and Katharine F. Lenroot. **Illegitimacy As A Child-Welfare Problem, Parts 1 and 2.** 1920/1921

New York State Commission on Relief for Widowed Mothers. **Report of the New York State Commission on Relief for Widowed Mothers.** 1914

Otey, Elizabeth Lewis. **The Beginnings of Child Labor Legislation in Certain States;** A Comparative Study. 1910

Phillips, Wilbur C. **Adventuring For Democracy.** 1940

Polier, Justine Wise. **Everyone's Children, Nobody's Child:** A Judge Looks At Underprivileged Children in the United States. 1941

Proceedings of the Annual Meeting of the National Child Labor Committee, 1905, 1906. 1974

Rainey, Homer P. **How Fare American Youth?** 1940

Reeder, Rudolph R. **How Two Hundred Children Live and Learn.** 1910

Security and Services For Children. 1974

Sinai, Nathan and Odin W. Anderson. **EMIC (Emergency Maternity and Infant Care):** A Study of Administrative Experience. 1948

Slingerland, W. H. **Child-Placing in Families:** A Manual For Students and Social Workers. 1919

[Solenberger], Edith Reeves. **Care and Education of Crippled Children in the United States.** 1914

Spencer, Anna Garlin and Charles Wesley Birtwell, editors. **The Care of Dependent, Neglected and Wayward Children:** Being a Report of the Second Section of the International Congress of Charities, Correction and Philanthropy, Chicago, June, 1893. 1894

Theis, Sophie Van Senden. **How Foster Children Turn Out.** 1924

Thurston, Henry W. **The Dependent Child:** A Story of Changing Aims and Methods in the Care of Dependent Children. 1930

U.S. Advisory Committee on Education. **Report of the Committee, February, 1938.** 1938

The United States Children's Bureau, 1912-1972. 1974

White House Conference on Child Health and Protection. **Dependent and Neglected Children:** Report of the Committee on Socially Handicapped — Dependency and Neglect. 1933

White House Conference on Child Health and Protection. **Organization for the Care of Handicapped Children, National, State, Local.** 1932

White House Conference on Children in a Democracy. **Final Report of the White House Conference on Children in A Democracy.** [1942]

Wilson, Otto. **Fifty Years' Work With Girls, 1883-1933:** A Story of the Florence Crittenton Homes. 1933

Wrenn, C. Gilbert and D. L. Harley. **Time On Their Hands:** A Report on Leisure, Recreation, and Young People. 1941